The American Jew, 1585–1990

The American Jew, 1585–1990: A History

Jacob Rader Marcus

CARLSON
Publishing Inc

BROOKLYN, NEW YORK, 1995

Library of Congress Cataloging-in-Publication Data

Marcus, Jacob Rader, 1896–
    The American Jew, 1585–1990 : a history / by Jacob Rader Marcus.
        p.   cm.
    Includes bibliographical references and index.
    ISBN 0-926019-89-9 (alk. paper)
    1. Jews—United States—History.   2. United States—Ethnic
relations.   I. Title.
E184.J5M199   1995
973'.04924—dc20   95-21034

Typographic design: C.J. Bartelt

Text typeface: Adobe Janson Text

Composition: Joseph E.L. Fortt

Case and jacket designs: Ann Harakawa

Index prepared by Scholars Editorial Services, Inc., Madison, Wisconsin.

Printed on acid-free, 250-year-life paper.

Manufactured in the United States of America.

First printing, October 1995.

Contents

CONTENTS

Acknowledgments

No book writes itself. It is a pleasant task to thank the many who have helped write *The American Jew*. Abraham Peck, the administrative director of the American Jewish Archives; Kevin Proffitt, the chief archivist there; and Eleanor Lawhorn, the archive's secretary, have been towers of strength. The University of Cincinnati library, the local libraries of Cincinnati and Hamilton County, and particularly Hebrew Union College's library all generously shared their treasures. My friends at the American Jewish Historical Society never hesitated to send me copies of their most precious possessions. Dr. Gottschalk, president of the Hebrew Union College–Jewish Institute of Religion, has always taken a personal interest in my work. Malcolm Stern, the late distinguished genealogist, never failed me. My good friend Leonard N. Simons of Detroit, philanthropist and bibliophile, clucks sympathetically when I run into trouble; I can always turn to him for a good word; thank you, Leonard. Mrs. Etheljane Callner, my secretary for more than forty years, has been my strong right arm; I am truly grateful to this magnificent human being and indispensable aide. Dr. Roger Daniels of the University of Cincinnati, the authority on immigration, was most gracious when I sought his advice. Judith Daniels, a university instructor, has checked everything that I have written, and I do not move without her. For a long generation my friend and colleague, Dr. Stanley Chyet, historian at the California branch of the Hebrew Union College, has helped me. Words cannot express my gratitude for his devotion and expertise. Many others have assisted and advised, but regrettably I leave them unnamed; I fear I may omit a good friend; I forbear lest I offend.

Part I
The Colonial Period:
1500–1776

1. Jews in the New World

JEWISH HISTORY THROUGH THE AGES, 1200 B.C.E.–1654 C.E.

Bands of bedouin came out of the desert and the fertile crescent about 1500 B.C.E. and gained a foothold in what is today Israel. They called themselves Hebrews. About the year 1000, there was a short-lived Davidic and Solomonic state, which was succeeded by two separate commonwealths, Israel and Judah. Israel, the northern half, fell to the Assyrian invaders in 722; Judah was conquered by other Mesopotamians in 586. Dozens of other city and regional polities were to rise and fall in the same years during the first pre-Christian millennium. What, then, is the significance of these two Israelitic states? These ancient Israelites and Judeans are American Jews' ancestors. They are the people whose literature is the Bible.

The true heroes of this age were the prophets, men who preached a universal message—the fatherhood of God and the brotherhood of all men, women, and children. They cried out inexorably for love, justice, compassion. The Bible was to become a book of world historical importance. Centuries later it helped give birth to Christianity. A standard edition of the King James version of Scripture contains 1,272 pages, 876 pages of which are a translation of the Hebrew Old Testament. The Christians are still nine-thirteenths "Jewish." In the seventh Christian century the nomads of Arabia brought forth a new religion, Islam. Their legendary ancestor was Ishmael, a son of Abraham, the first "Hebrew." Moslems were profoundly influenced by Hebraic teachings. Almost half the world today, well over three billion Christians and Moslems, has been moved by the social passion of the Hebrew prophets.

The ancient Israelites refused to die. Phoenix-like, in the sixth and fifth pre-Christian centuries a new religioethnic group rose in Jerusalem. These were the first Jews, and their religion was Judaism. When in 168 B.C.E. Palestine's Syrian overlords proscribed the Jewish religious way of life, the Jewish leaders Judah Maccabee and his brothers rose in revolt. All five brothers died of violence, but they won the right to worship God according to the dictates of their conscience. The Romans who assumed control of the Maccabean state in 63 B.C.E. permitted the Jews to practice their religion, but now political oppression impelled them to rebel. They held the Romans at bay for years, but Jerusalem finally fell and the reborn Jewish state came to an end (70 C.E.).

But Judaism did not end. The leaders fashioned a new religious, cultural, and spiritual Palestine. They built schools and compiled new codes, the Mishnah and the Palestinian Talmud. The Law, the Torah, the Teaching, was to become a new portable homeland. The ultimate domination of Christianity in the Roman Empire in the fourth century precluded a vigorous Jewish life in Palestine. The children of Israel were disabled politically, economically, socially, and religiously. As early as the year 200, however, Jews were already well aware that they had no future under the Romans. So they created a new center in Mesopotamia, one that was to exercise religious hegemony over world Jewry into the tenth and eleventh centuries. They produced a new body of learning, the Babylonian

Talmud, the foundation on which modern Judaism is built. Jewishly, this Talmud is more important than the Bible.

By the year 1100, Mesopotamia, the whole Near and Middle East, was in political turmoil. There was no future for Jewry in the basin of the Tigris and Euphrates rivers. Now, for the first time, Europe began to emerge as a world Jewish religious center; its leaders were Spanish and Franco-German rabbis. Spain's Jews were to experience a Golden Age under the Arabs in the Iberian Peninsula. Spain became a land of poets, rabbis, scholars, scientists, philosophers, diplomats, and merchants. Among the most notable of these early Spanish leaders was Samuel Ibn Nagrela (993–1056), an accomplished Arabist, a learned Hebraist, a grammarian, a poet, a Talmudist, a patron of learning, a commander of troops in the field, and the vizier ("prime minister") of the Moorish state of Granada. The medieval world's most distinguish Jewish scholar, Moses Maimonides (1135–1204), was a Spanish-born physician, philosopher, and author of an all-embracing code of Jewish law. (It is unfortunate that this Arabic-Jewish culture flourished in the days before printing. The contribution to world culture that might have been made never came into being.) Jewish life in Spain came to an end in 1492 with a decree expelling all Jews. The Christian state that supplanted the Muslims and dominated the Iberian Peninsula tolerated no Jews.

The medieval sciences so characteristic of Spanish Jewry were not cultivated by the Franco-Jewish rabbis, who were primarily Hebraists, Talmudists, and pietists. Despite frequent persecutions, disabilities, and expulsions, central European Jews managed to survive in many German cities and states. Because there was no overall German state, there could be no total expulsion as in England, France, and Spain. Jews held on in central Europe until the eighteenth century when conditions improved. Discrimination, however, persisted. In 1761, Jacob Alexandre, a feebleminded French-Jewish beggar, entered a church and ate a holy wafer. For Catholics this was the Body of Christ. For him it was a cracker; he was hungry. But he had committed a capital crime and was sentenced to prison for life. Twenty-eight years later, with the coming of the French Revolution, he would not even have been arrested for this "sacrilege."

By the sixteenth century, Poland, the largest state in Europe, sheltered a sizable Jewish community. It speedily became world Jewry's Talmudic study center and was to remain the heart of traditional learning until it was destroyed by the Germans in World War II. Jewish folk culture here was Yiddish. There was very little secular learning, virtually no arts, and no sciences. No Jewry can rise above the cultural level of the land in which it lives. Beginning in the year 1648, thousands of Jews lost their lives in the wars the Cossacks and Ukrainians waged against their Polish overlords. Shocked by this disaster, Polish Jewry listened when told that Shabbethai Zevi was God's promised Messiah (1665). In the next century, many Polish and Lithuanian Jews, embracing pietism, gave birth to a new Hassidic movement. They may have been influenced by the German Christian pietism that in the 1700s was to inspire thousands of Christians. Hassidism was a new cult if not a new faith, a religion of joy, ecstasy, humility, and morality. Devotion was more important than doctrine.

The 1640s and 1650s were sad decades in the Polish lands. A few Jews, sensing that there was scant hope for them among the Slavs, fled to Germany and Holland. There was a new day dawning in the West. Deism, a faith that rejected revealed religion, rose in the seventeenth and eighteenth centuries, attracting the intelligentsia. It undermined Christianity and as a humanistic philosophy paved the way for tolerance, even for Jews. Some writers suggest that history gave birth to deism to serve as a philosophical underpinning for the new commercial and industrial revolutions in process; others point to the exhaustion of both Catholic and Protestant after more than a century of bitter warfare designed to reunify all Christendom. In any case, money fortified the new national state. Not religiosity but productivity was imperative if the modern state was to grow strong. A medieval Jewish moneylender was despised; a modern Jewish banker was cultivated. The road was now open to Jewish businessmen. The children of Abraham were encouraged to settle in the new transatlantic territories.

THE FIRST JEWS IN THE NEW WORLD

Colonists were an integral part of mercantilistic empire building. The American colonial world was born in October 1492 with the first landfall of Christopher Columbus. This man was no Jew, as some writers intimate, but the first man over the ship's side may well have been Columbus's interpreter, Luis de Torres, a born Israelite. Many Marranos—Spanish Jews who had typically been compelled to accept Christianity—fled to the new Spanish-American colonies where they hoped to escape the Inquisition. It was a vain hope. These émigrés, who secretly practiced a form of Judaism, fell victim to the Inquisition that followed them and rooted them out. Luis de Carvajal y de la Cueva, a Portuguese of Jewish origin, was appointed the ruler of the frontier kingdom of Nuevo León in 1579. He was no secret Jew, yet he was to die in prison, and his sister and most of her children were burnt at the stake. In 1639, Francisco Maldonado de Silva was incinerated with several others at an auto-da-fé in the plaza of Lima, Peru. Although reared as a Christian, this descendant of conversos turned to Judaism after reading a Christian polemical work. He circumcised himself, studied the faith of his ancestors, and observed the dietary laws, but he was betrayed by his sister whom he sought to convert. When warned by a member of his family to abandon his newfound religion, he responded, "If I had a thousand lives I would gladly lose them in the service of the living God." The Spanish tolerated no Jewish colonists in their New World empire. Devotion to Catholicism was deemed more important than the need for colonists. The Spanish-American martyrs live in Jewish history as shining examples of heroism.

In 1654, the Dutch were expelled from Brazil where they had established a colony. Some of the Jews among them settled in French Martinique—despite a fourteenth-century decree expelling them from the mother country—and succeeded in building an impressive community on this prosperous island. Jean Baptiste Colbert, France's mercantilist secretary of state for naval affairs, encouraged the Jewish newcomers, but shortly after his death, Catholicism, as in Spain, triumphed over mercantilism, and the Jews were driven out. This was in the 1680s. A *Code Noire* (slave code) then published included an article proscribing Jews. It was republished in eighteenth-century French Louisiana but seems to have been honored only in the breach. It was also ignored when Spain took over the province in 1762. When a priest landed in New Orleans with the hope of establishing an office of the Inquisition, he was politely shipped back to his Spanish home.

Despite the expulsion from Martinique, Jews remained in the French islands, particularly Haiti, until the blacks rebelled in the 1790s and drove the whites out. Spanish and Portuguese Jews, both secret and open adherents of the faith, were already tolerated in eighteenth-century Bordeaux, France. By that time the West Indies administrators had opted for a mercantilistic acceptance of Jewish businessmen.

JEWS IN THE ENGLISH CARIBBEAN

Unhampered by the strong Catholic hierarchical controls that characterized the eighteenth-century French, the English Protestants found it easier to pursue mercantilistic goals. They were more tolerant of Jewish newcomers. Thus it was that Jews who settled in the English colonies in the West Indies were allowed to remain and lead openly Jewish lives. By the 1650s, Jews had settled in Barbados and Jamaica, and after a time they drifted into other West Indies islands controlled by the English. Barbados had a congregation in each of its two towns; by 1700, Jamaica had three sanctuaries. Though encouraged to settle in England's Caribbean colonies, Jews were never exempt from vexatious disabilities. Despite their acceptance in the islands, emancipation in Europe itself was a slow process. Europe had an anti-Jewish tradition that was pre-Christian.

The English Plantation Act of 1740 was primarily addressed to Jamaica. Parliament, wishing to encourage Jews to build foreign trade, made the naturalization process easier. By the eighteenth century, Jamaica's imports and exports were more important than those of all the British North American colonies. Despite the restrictions under which the Jews in the

English West Indies continued to labor, they did not hesitate to anglicize themselves. Thus we have Jews who bore the names Green, Brown, Barrows (Barrows may well be Baruch). It was ironic that when emancipation came in the nineteenth century, black freedmen—Christians—received the franchise before it was granted to their former Jewish masters. The achievements of Jews in England's American colonies may even have influenced the slow-moving English to speed up the enfranchisement of the Jews in the English homeland. The family ties that marked many of the Sephardim (Spanish-Portuguese Jews) in the islands are reflected in the will of Elias Valverde of Bridgetown, Barbados:

> Lastly, I give my tender embraces to my dear and loving wife, praying the Almighty to protect and bless her and my dear and well-beloved children, whom I earnestly charge to have continually before their eyes the fear of God and the respect of their mother, and to keep unanimously and lovingly together, regarding the eldership of one another like good brethren. And so taking my leave and farewell of all my relations and friends, like a penitent sinner I beg pardon of all the world, and sign this my last will and testament in the Island of Barbados aforesaid the third day of July, one thousand seven hundred and thirty nine.

JEWS IN THE DUTCH CARIBBEAN AND SOUTH AMERICAN COLONIES

The Dutch, like the English, had staked their claims to colonies in the Caribbean and West Indies. They ruled in the Brazilian bulge, in Surinam to the north, and in the island of Curaçao hard by the coast of Venezuela. The Portuguese had been in Brazil since the early 1500s, and among their settlers were crypto-Jews, so-called new Christians, often victims of forced conversion. In 1630, the Dutch, impelled by the desire to profit from the sugar industry and its ancillary slave trade, seized the western bulge of the huge Brazilian territory and built a large colony with its capital in Recife (Pernambuco). It was not long before there was a good-sized Jewry. When two congregations opened their doors, Recife became the first legally recognized Jewish community in the New World. Unfortunately, the colony was of short duration. When it was retaken by the Portuguese in 1654, Protestants and Jews were expelled. Some Brazilian refugees returned home to Holland; others sailed for the nearest havens, Surinam in Guiana, or the French, English, and Dutch possessions in the Caribbean.

The Brazilian émigrés who opted for the Guiana lands were not the first Jews there. Israelites had settled in that well-watered area in earlier decades. The English and Dutch competed for Jewish settlers, who were considered intelligent, innovative, hardworking—a useful element. The Dutch in 1667 finally limited their Guiana colonization to Surinam. The Jews established two communal centers, one in the interior, the other in the country's capital, Paramaribo. The up-country settlement was the Joden Savanne, an all-Jewish town with its own synagogue. Many of the countryside settlers were sugar planters, and the slaves who tilled the soil were often converted to Judaism and rested on the Sabbath. Paramaribo Jews included a very substantial number of Germans, Ashkenazim. The two groups had their separate synagogues, but even the Germans adhered to the Sephardic ritual. Surinam Jews were an autonomous, privileged group. Many of them were at home in the disciplines that characterized the elite of the Enlightenment, though here, too, their distinction as people of culture and political standing did not spare them from anti-Jewish prejudices.

Curaçao, another Dutch colony, was the largest of Holland's West Indies islands. The Jewish community, centered in the capital city Willemstad, was large and wealthy. The island was primarily an entrepôt exploiting its geographical position off the coast of Venezuela, carrying on trade with the Spanish South American lands and the other Caribbean islands. Jews had settled in Curaçao in the middle decades of the seventeenth century, about sixteen years after its conquest by the Dutch West India Company. A beautiful synagogue built in 1732 is still standing; the Curaçaons called their congregation Mickve Israel, the Hope of Israel—a Messianic name: God is the hope of Israel and will save [it] in time of trouble (Jeremiah 14:8). The French Revolution and the Napoleonic conquest of Europe's Netherlands brought freedom to the Jews of Holland in the 1790s. It was not long before all of the Netherlands colonists in the New World were also granted equality and the privileges of Dutch citizenship.

2. Building Jewish Communities in the New World

The English, French, and Dutch colonies in the Guianas and the Caribbean area were very important in the seventeenth and eighteenth centuries. Sugar was king. The West Indian trade was more profitable than that of the British North American colonies until the early nineteenth century. By the eighteenth century, relatively few Jews were sugar planters of consequence; most of them were shopkeepers, a modest middle class engaged in distribution of goods, fulfilling an important need in the pioneer communities. The Dutch and English colonies sheltered well-established congregations, comparable often to urban communities in Europe. The level of secular culture was often high, and the new Enlightenment could boast of many Jewish votaries. Even rabbinic culture had successfully made the transatlantic crossing. There were learned rabbis, scholars, some advanced Hebrew instruction, and a host of social welfare pious associations, almost twenty in Curaçao in the eighteenth century. These made provision for the poor, sent gifts to the Jews of Palestine, and washed and buried the dead. A female confraternity reverently prepared Jewish women for burial. Nevertheless there was always anti-Jewish prejudice.

Jews in the Dutch colonies looked to Amsterdam, those in the English colonies to London's Sephardic Bevis Marks, the Gate of Heaven, for religious guidance. Immigration of Jews to the Caribbean world was not significant numerically; the dawn of modernity—mercantilism and the Enlightenment—induced most Jews to remain in western and central Europe.

Peter Stuyvesant, the governor of Curaçao, was also the governor of New Amsterdam on the Hudson. In 1654 he was dismayed when twenty-three Brazilian Jewish refugees sought a haven in his Christian community. This tiny group constituted world Jewry's most remote western outpost.

THE DUTCH PERIOD IN NORTH AMERICAN JEWISH HISTORY

Though Europe's Jews were to exercise hegemony over world Jewry until 1914, as early as the 1650s there was already a tiny Jewish community on the Hudson, in Dutch New Amsterdam. In the last days of August 1654 or the first week of September, twenty-three refugees set out from Brazil after it was retaken by the Portuguese. There is no evidence that the goal of these twenty-three was the North American Dutch town of New Amsterdam. Their ship was taken by Spanish privateers, and the Spanish-Portuguese conversos on board were removed and shipped back to Spain to face the Inquisition. The unconverted Sephardim and Ashkenazim were released and took passage on another vessel, which took them to New Amsterdam. They arrived on the island of Manhattan a despoiled, impoverished, sorry lot. Three hundred years later, American Jewry, five million strong, was the largest, the most cultured, and the most affluent community in all Jewish history.

Were the twenty-three the first Jews in New Amsterdam? There were at least two other Jews in town. Solomon Franco, a Jewish businessman, had walked the streets of Boston in 1649 at a time when Myles Standish and John Alden were still alive. Franco, a poor man, was "warned out" of Boston and shipped back to Holland. In 1585—thirty-five years before the coming of the Pilgrim fathers—the mining technologist Joachim Gaunse (Ganz), a Prague Jew, landed on Roanoke Island. Sir Walter Raleigh and his associates had sent him over with others to report on the mineral potential of the new continent. The following year, Sir Francis Drake took him and the other colonists back to England, where in 1589 he was charged with blasphemy; he had denied the divinity of Jesus.

The twenty-three arrivals in Holland's American colony were not welcomed by the director general Peter Stuyvesant. An uncompromising Calvinist, he wanted no Jews. The Dutch West Indies Company also opposed the settlement of Jews in the New Netherland colony. The newcomers were at first restricted in trading, not permitted to purchase land, refused the right to worship their God publicly, and denied all honorary office and burgher status. It was even suggested that these refugees be invited to live off by themselves in this tiny town of about 120 houses and 1,000 inhabitants. Though Stuyvesant and his employers despised Jews—their correspondence is packed with anti-Jewish epithets—the Dutch West Indies Company was a stock company organized for profit. Since Amsterdam Jews were stockholders, the profit-conscious, mercantilist directors had no choice but to tolerate these new arrivals. They were also Dutch subjects. By 1657 Jewish businessmen were permitted to carry on trade relatively unhampered. They were merchants, importers and exporters, dealing in a variety of commodities but specializing in liquor, tobacco, and furs. They reached out northward to do business in Britain's New England provinces, although the English monopolists always tried to keep Dutch competitors out of their colonies. Turning southward, they traveled as far as Maryland.

The handful of Jews in New Amsterdam—refugees and newcomers from the Netherlands—enjoyed the security of an organized Jewish religious community only briefly. They had borrowed a Scroll of the Law from Amsterdam and even dreamt of praying in a synagogue of their own. The very thought aroused the ire of Stuyvesant. If he permitted the Jews to worship publicly, he would have to tolerate Lutherans! In the early 1660s the tiny Jewish community began to dwindle. Manhattan was no rich "sugar island," the Native Americans were an ever-present threat, and the government was autocratic. Conditions for Jews were far better, economically and politically, in the Guianas. Jews, never very numerous, stopped coming to North America, and most of those here left for fairer prospects. The Scroll of the Law was returned to its donors in Holland (1663), and religious services came to an end. The community had expired. A year later the English took possession of the town. New Amsterdam became New York.

ASSER LEVY, THE MAN WHO STAYED

Among the three or four Jews whom the British inherited in 1664 when they seized New Netherland was a man who called himself Asser Levy Van Swellem. He was one of the original Brazilian refugees, but his origins were actually East European. He was a "Litvak" whose family had come from Vilna. Like the others who landed in 1654, he had been despoiled. He was so poor that he could not afford to pay the military exemption tax imposed on Jews. He declared his willingness to stand guard on the walls with the trainband and won that right. He was stubborn, insisting that he was a burgher, and won that battle too. Levy was a typical self-made man; he nibbled at everything to feed his appetite. He became a merchant, a broker, a factor, a notary, a moneylender, an exporter and importer, a de facto attorney, a liquor dealer, and a butcher who built a slaughter-house on Wall Street—obviously a good location for an abattoir. In 1661 he bought a house and became the first Jew to own a home in this country. In 1671 under the English, he sat on a jury—a very rare privilege for a Jew. The defendant was the former director general of New Netherland, Peter Stuyvesant; *ha-galgal hozer*, the wheel revolves. When the estate of the affluent, respected "Mr. Assur Levy" was probated in 1682, his possessions included a Sabbath lamp, a wine goblet for the Friday night service, a spice box for the Saturday night ritual, a pistol, and a sword. He was a Jew, a frontiersman, a symbol of Jewish continuity on American soil.

THE ENGLISH PERIOD IN NORTH AMERICAN JEWISH HISTORY

WHERE THEY SETTLED

After the British forces drove the Hollanders out of North America, five new Jewish communities were established in the course of the next century. At the time New Amsterdam was taken by the English, there were probably fewer than twenty Jews in town, but by the 1690s a synagogue community was reconstituted in New York. Newport Jewry came into being in the 1740s after a false start in the 1670s–1680s. Philadelphia—a colony of Jewish New York—started holding services in the 1740s. Charleston (Charles Town) Jews had a religious quorum no later than the 1750s, though a group of French Jewish exiles had settled in town as early as the 1690s. (They may have been Huguenot Marranos who fled when the Protestants were exiled by Louis XIV.) Savannah Jewry began as a formal colony established by Sephardic philanthropists in 1733, just a few months after the first governor of the Georgia colony, James E. Oglethorpe, landed. Christian speculators and Anglo-Jewish philanthropists dreamt of large Jewish colonies in the American provinces. The Gentiles wanted to sell land; the Jews wanted a place to ship their poor. Montreal was the last of the six new Jewish towns. The French, who tolerated no Jews, had been driven out, and the English were glad to welcome Jews whose loyalties were to England rather than to the French ancien régime. In all of these six towns, congregations—so it would seem—rose, only to fade and rise again before permanent synagogues were established. In addition, individual Jews were found in numerous towns and hamlets from Canada south to the Gulf coast and west to Michilimackinac. There was a wandering Jew almost everywhere.

These six towns served as core market centers for Jewish village shopkeepers. Savannah was a subregional center looking to Charleston. Boston had no quorum of praying Jews; the Puritans lusted for Jewish souls, not for Jewish competitors. Virginia, the largest colony, was rich tobacco country. Capital-poor Jews stayed away until after the Revolution, although a European college-trained physician lived in the capital, Williamsburg: Dr. John de Sequeyra, who told the world that a man could live forever if he feasted on a diet of tomatoes. Hartford, Connecticut, sheltered a roving Jewish peddler as early as 1670 when he was arrested and fined heavily because he was "notorious in his lascivious dalience and wanton carriage and profers to severall women."

Who came in those days to the colonies? Affluent Jews—particularly the Iberians—remained home in London, Bordeaux, Amsterdam, and Hamburg. A few paupers were occasionally shipped across the Atlantic Ocean by thrifty European Jewish communities. The British government sent its criminals, "transports," to America to serve as indentured servants in the provinces. Among them was Feibel of London, a fifteen-year-old boy who had stolen a handkerchief and was sentenced to seven years' servitude. Very few Sephardic Jews came here; Europe offered them more. It was different for Ashkenazim. As late as the 1770s, the principality of Lippe-Detmold informed the world that "All foreign beggars, collectors, [German] Jewish peddlers, Polish Jews, jugglers, bear-trainers and tramps are forbidden access to this country under penalty of sentence to prison. All gypsies caught will be hanged and shot." Disabilities at home helped push Jews out of Europe. Opportunity—a vista of success—pulled ambitious young German, Polish, and Russian Jews to these distant shores.

Nineteen-year-old Michael Gratz, an adventurer who had just come back from India, sailed for America in the 1750s to join his brother Barnard. Michael was to sire a daughter, Rebecca, who would become America's most distinguished Jewish woman in the early nineteenth century.

How many came? By 1775 there were somewhere between two thousand and twenty-five hundred Jews on this continent. Most of them lived uneventful lives and left few records. A few had large families, anywhere from ten to twenty children.

Rights and Disabilities

The Jewish newcomers were able, finally, to build stable communities on this continent because the corpus of disabilities imposed on them proved endurable. The petty Puritan legislation to which everyone was subject was annoying. Sunday traveling and closing laws were an economic hardship:

> Henceforth let none on peril of their lives,
> Attempt a journey or embrace their wives.

In 1668 a Jew was arrested for traveling through a Massachusetts town on a Sunday. There is no evidence, however, that anyone was ever charged with

> Hanging his cat on a Monday
> For killing a mouse on a Sunday.

Synagogue property was not exempt from taxation; Jews were taxed to maintain the established church. Honorific offices were denied them, and in some places they were not permitted to vote. But there were no compulsory ghettos, no mass riots, no intimidation by the Christian religious leaders. Jews were left alone in the conduct of their worship services, though Catholics were severely disabled and dissenting Protestants were harassed, and two or three years before the adoption of the Declaration of Independence, Baptists in Virginia were jailed. But—and this is important—Jews had full civil rights. They were rarely denied denization. They could settle where they wished, and after the 1740 Act foreign-born Jews could be naturalized, which permitted them to trade openly in all of England's colonies (thought not to hold office). They were allowed to omit the test oath "upon the true faith of a Christian." England was tightening its control over its colonies. It wanted to integrate all its subjects, including its Jews. Wealthy Jews speedily became part of the power structure.

How They Made a Living

Most of the settlers in North America were tillers of the soil. Jews, however, were not typically farmers. A few, very few, were plantation owners. Francis Salvador was one of these exceptions. His family, English settlers from the Iberian peninsula, had lost its wealth except for a huge grant in South Carolina. Seeking to restore the family's fortunes, Francis operated a large indigo plantation in the western part of the province where thirty slaves tilled his acres. As a cultured Englishman he was welcomed by the local gentry and co-opted to serve in the provincial congress in pre-Revolutionary days. Down in Georgia and probably in some other parts of the country, some Jewish entrepreneurs ran cattle and horses in the backcountry. Branded, the animals ran free. Mordecai Sheftall, a Savannah merchant, was the owner of the 5S—he had five children when he registered his mark in the brand book. Abraham and Abigail Minis were the owners of the A.M. After Abraham's death, Abigail continued to run his little empire as a rancher and merchant. She was aggressive and able, a true "woman of valor."

In the primitive agricultural economy of colonial America, artisans were important. Jews were shoemakers, soapmakers, coppersmiths, tailors, saddlers, glaziers, tobacconists, chocolate makers, and distillers. Many of them, petty shopkeepers, sold the products they made. Myer Myers of New York was a skilled silversmith who hammered out beautiful ornaments for the Scrolls of the Law, a Hanukkah candelabrum, and also a baptismal bowl for a church. After the Revolution he was to become president of the Gold and Silver Smiths Society of the city. For the most part, Jews avoided the professions. They could not take a Christian oath to serve as lawyers, but they could act in a lay capacity. Physicians and surgeons who had trained as apprentices were not uncommon, but neither law nor medicine offered attractive rewards. The populace was inclined to believe that the lawyers destroyed the purse and the doctors destroyed lives.

During the series of Franco-British wars that wracked Europe, India, and America from 1689 to 1815, as England set out to undermine France as a world power, army supply was important. There were Jews who followed the army as peddlers and sutlers, but the greatest profits lay in high-level civilian army provisioning in an age when the quartermaster corps was not fully developed. The important figure in North America army supply was Jacob Franks, member of an Anglo-American consortium that included his relatives in London. They in turn co-opted Gentile partners who had influence in Parliament. The Gentiles secured the contracts; the Jews did the work and shared the profits. Army provisioning had been a Jewish business for centuries. Solomon de Medina around 1700 had an arrangement with the duke of Marlborough:

> A Jew and a general both joined a trade;
> The Jew was a baker, the general sold bread.

The Frankses in America apparently were not privateers preying on the commerce of the French and their allies. Other Jews, however, invested substantial sums arming vessels that set out with the hope of seizing lucrative prizes. Very few Jews ever succeeded in bringing a rich prize into port.

By the Treaty of Paris in 1763, France lost practically all of its vast American holdings. The Jewish merchants, particularly the Philadelphians, rushed in to exploit the newly conquered areas. They sold goods to garrisons, to the French habitants, to English settlers, and to the Native Americans. Frequently they accepted furs as a medium of payment and exchange. Goods were shipped as far west as the Mississippi. The chief outpost of the Pennsylvania outfitters was Fort Pitt, Pittsburgh, at the forks of the Monongahela and the Allegheny rivers. In New York the Gomezes had established a trading post about the year 1717 among the warlike Indians in the Devil's Dance Chamber. This was dangerous country:

> For none that visit the Indian's den
> Return again to the haunts of men.
> The knife is their doom, oh sad is their lot;
> Beware, beware of the blood-stained spot.

For the Canadian Jews, the fur trade was all-important. Though the New Yorkers and the Pennsylvanians were also heavily involved, fur exports to England were relatively insignificant. The big money was in tobacco, not a Jewish business.

It did not take the Jewish merchants long to realize that the vast acreage west of the Alleghenies could well become a haven for poor Europeans. Jews and Gentiles rushed into the land business. Large new colonies were organized. Jewish capital was invited, even though Jewish settlers would never have been given full political rights. In the 1770s, David Franks, the army purveyor, Joseph Simon of Lancaster, and Barnard and Michael Gratz of Philadelphia were partners in the Illinois and Wabash Land Company. The holdings of this consortium were estimated to cover sixty million acres, but when the new United States refused to recognize its Indian titles, the group ultimately lost its sizable investment. However, the supplies the investors shipped to the distant West served to open up the country to the men and women who crossed the mountains to seek new homes.

Basically the Frankses—colonial Jewry's most important business family—were merchant-shippers, the elite entrepreneurs of that age. They functioned as retailers, wholesalers, brokers, factors, maritime insurers, and even industrialists after a fashion. Their prime job was to export raw materials and import consumer wares. They exported timber, food, pig iron, furs, potash, naval stores, indigo, and whale oil to pay for the goods sent them by the English manufacturers. Aaron Lopez (1731–1782) of Newport was a classic merchant-shipper. This New Christian—secret Jew—fled from Portugal and settled in Newport where he reasserted his Jewishness. He began as a modest shopkeeper and coaster and, after a decade, emerged as a large-scale merchant who at one time owned or chartered about thirty vessels. His ships sailed to Europe and the Caribbean. The Newport men and women he subsidized under the put-out system manufactured shoes, garments, prefabricated houses, cheese, rum, potash, and soap. He was a whaler, a slave importer, and a member of the United Company of Spermaceti Candlers, a candle-manufacturing cartel. Lopez was involved in huge mercantile ventures, for he knew how to manipulate cred-it, but after his untimely death in a drowning accident, it was found that he had left an insolvent estate. He could not cope with the Revolution and its economic problems. Lopez was a cultured, generous man who was loved and respected by Jew and Gentile, a man of integrity. Ezra Stiles, the well-known Newport Christian minister, recorded his death in the following words:

> On the 28th of May died that amiable, benevolent, most hospitable and very respectable gentleman Mr. Aaron

Lopez. . . . He was a merchant of the first eminence; for honor & extent of commerce probably surpassed by no mrcht in America. He did business with the greatest ease & clearness, always carried about a sweetness of behaviour, a calm urbanity, an agreeable & unaffected politeness of manners. Without a single enemy & the most universally beloved by an extensive acquaintance of any man I ever knew. His beneficence to his fam'y connexions, to his nation [the Jews], and to the world is almost without a parallel.

British America's typical Jewish businessman was a city and village shopkeeper. He sold hard, soft, and wet goods, that is, hardware, tools, nails, yard goods, notions, and liquor: "We pour the spirits down to keep the spirits up." As was the case among Gentiles, Jewish female shopkeepers were not unusual. For the most part they carried small stocks. Survival was a struggle for all petty tradesmen with half-empty shelves and little capital. They were completely dependent on their Jewish regional suppliers, whom they could not pay if their customers, often carried on their books, were short of cash. Bankruptcies were not uncommon; for these unfortunates, America was no land of unlimited opportunity. The few successful dealers had well-appointed homes, good china, silverware, carpets and curtains, pictures on the walls, and even libraries of sorts.

With rare exceptions, the Jew in the colonies was a member of a broadly conceived middle class. Did he make a contribution to America's economy, this Jew who numbered but one in a thousand? He had not come here to make a contribution but to make a living and to be left alone. If he was a large-scale merchant, he carried on a national and international trade; if he was a shopkeeper, he offered his customers the goods they needed if they were to survive with a modicum of comfort. One cannot overemphasize the importance of the goods he stocked on his shelves. His store graced the Main Street of many an American town and city. He tied provinces together, he worked to dissolve parochialism, and, in a very modest fashion, he helped prepare the way for a united American people.

RELIGIOUS LIFE AND ORGANIZATION

Not all Jews who came to North America identified with their people. Some—we shall never know how many—came here and lived and died as Gentiles. Joseph Ottolenghe (d. 1775) was an Italian who began life in his native land as a modest Hebrew teacher. He moved on to London, was converted to Christianity, and was sent over to the colony of Georgia to teach Christianity to enslaved blacks. America gave him a chance to prove himself. He introduced silk culture, served in the Georgia House of Representatives, was appointed a justice of the peace, and died a large landholder. The more typical Jewish businessman was a religionist, often an individual of good stock, scion of a learned family. This Jew was very eager to establish a community with a synagogue, religious services, charities, and a Hebrew school for his youngsters. Community building was hampered by dissension, intergroup rivalry, and frustrations. Discipline was imperative and was not wanting; although Jewish villagers were frequently anything but observant, town dwellers were compelled to live a traditional life or suffer ostracism. When Hetty Hays bought some lamb that was not scrupulously kosher, she had to cleanse her kitchen utensils ritually.

The first Jewish institution to be established was the cemetery; New Amsterdam had one in 1655, Newport in 1678,

New York in the 1680s. There is evidence that some Sephardic Jews did not want to be buried in a cemetery with Ashkenazim, so they established their own cemeteries where the Ashkenazic dead were not welcomed. The cemetery was often followed by the organization of a synagogue. Structurally, no two synagogues were alike, but they all had a president and a board, a *mahamad*. New York's congregation had two classes of members. The first class had special rights, but no Jew was denied the opportunity to participate fully in the worship service. Support came from fees for seats and from freewill offerings. There were three salaried professionals: the beadle (shammash), the slaughterer (shohet), and the hazzan, the minister who chanted the services. The circumciser (mohel) was not a formal member of the paid staff. All three officiants received a salary, often meager, and grants of fuel and matzo for Passover. Most professionals hunted for extra income in order to eke out an existence.

Joseph Simson (1686–1787), a native of Frankfurt am Main, was appointed New York's beadle in 1738; less than a decade later he was president. The shammash was expected to keep the synagogue clean, polish the silver Torah ornaments, keep the eternal lamp lit, and be present at all circumcisions, marriages, and funerals. Simson, a good Hebraist, corresponded with Christian scholars. When he was one hundred years old, he was visited by Arthur Lee, the Virginia diplomat. Lee was somewhat taken back when he met the centenarian; the old Jew had blue eyes and a florid complexion—he did not look like a Jew! Jonas Phillips (1736–1803), another German, served as the shohet for several years after the end of the French and Indian War; he had been a sutler and merchant during the conflict. Bankrupted when peace was declared, he became New York's official slaughterer and almost lost his job on one occasion when he carelessly allowed his certifying pincers to fall into the hands of a Gentile butcher. (A kosher stamp could certify inferior uninspected meat as fit for Jews.) Later Phillips settled in Philadelphia where he prospered as a merchant. He married a sixteen-year-old girl who gave birth to at least seventeen children. Did she then give up the ghost? No, she lived to be eighty-five.

The country's outstanding hazzan (cantor)—actually, unofficial rabbi—was Gershom Seixas (ca. 1745–1816), the first native American to serve a congregation. On rare occasions he was called upon to preach an English sermon. Intelligent and cultured, he was well-read in deistic literature but always remained an observant traditional Jew. Respected and loved by his congregants, he was in no sense a servile hireling. During the British occupation of New York he continued to serve his congregants in Philadelphia. For many years he served as a trustee at Columbia College; this was his due as a clergyman.

From the vantage point of his high reading desk, Seixas was expected to keep an eye on the youngsters and suppress them with a monitory glance. Decorum was always a problem among these Jews; God is not an ogre. Protestant sepulchral silences were unknown in European synagogues, where worshipers wandered about and gossiped. Moses Lazarus, a collateral ancestor of Emma Lazarus, once referred to New York's Shearith Israel as a lunatic asylum.

WHAT DID THESE JEWS BELIEVE?

These new American Jews believed what their ancestors had believed since time immemorial. If asked about their credo, they could always cite the twelfth-century Maimonides who had put together the Thirteen Articles of Faith printed in the traditional prayer book though not recited in the worship service. This distinguished philosopher and scholar postulated an omniscient unitarian deity who gave his people a divine law that each Jew must observe unless willing to forfeit his share in the world to come. Jewry awaits the coming of the Messiah and the ultimate resurrection. When a Palestinian visitor, Rabbi Haim Isaac Carigal, preached in Newport in 1773, he told his audience that Jews were in exile because they had sinned, but if they repented—observed God's law, lived a moral life, and loved their neighbors—they would be restored. He spoke in an Iberian patois that at least 90 percent of his Jewish and Christian audience could not understand, but they certainly admired his Oriental garb—his fur hat, scarlet robe, green silk damask vest, chintz undervest, and Turkish girdle.

Daily prayer services were not always possible. However, the colonial Jews did keep kosher and intoned their Sephardic-rite prayers on the Sabbath. The seventh day was sacrosanct, in town at least; Lopez would dispatch no ship on the Sabbath. The life cycle ceremonies were not neglected: circumcision, bar mitzvah, marriage, funerals, and the recital of the kaddish, the Aramaic prayer for the dead. All these ceremonies, even funerals, were occasions for sociability. Jews never lost an opportunity to meet, drink a cup of tea, nibble cookies, give gifts, and offer home hospitality (some guests stayed for weeks). On Purim one might even enjoy a glass or two or three of porter, whiskey, brandy, gin, or sherry. There is reason to believe that Jews in America began slowly to neglect those religious customs and observances that did not appeal to them or were onerous. This policy of neglect—a form of adaptation—actually kept Orthodoxy alive; it was survival through evasion. There was to be no formal rejection of tradition until the 1820s, in Charleston, South Carolina, a cultural center.

Despite the personal frustrations and grudges that were played out on the synagogue floor, the concept of the universal brotherhood of Jewry prevailed. Every Jew in distress had to be helped, whether he was your neighbor or lived in another colony or in the West Indies, or in the Holy Land. Marranos, crypto-Jewish refugees from Spain or Portugal, were welcomed. The Gomezes, once outwardly Christian but always secret Jews, were leaders in New York's synagogue community. The religious faith that sustained a member of this notable clan is reflected in the following prayer:

> I pray to the great God of Israel to have mercy on my soul and enlighten me in His holy Law, forever to give me understanding, that I may not disobey His holy commandments and never forsake them. And that He may always direct me in the paths of life and refrain me from all evil, to advise and direct me to get my honest living. . . . And that I may always be charitable to the poor and needy.

CHARITY

The charities were inseparable from religion, and they were a substantial part of the synagogue budget. *Obras pias*, pious works, were important. This is documented by the colonial Hebrew term *sedaka*, meaning "righteousness," for the synagogue "treasury." You give because God will reward you and stave off death (Proverbs 10:2). Transients were a major problem. They never ceased coming, from all parts of Europe, Palestine, the West Indies, and Surinam. Foreign communities tried to ameliorate their pauper problem by shipping some of their impoverished to the colonies. The American congregations fed and housed these unfortunates and then dispatched them, with a sigh of relief, to the next Jewish community. However, in order to find a ship from one Caribbean island to another it might be necessary to send a welfare client first to North America—the longest way round was often enough the shortest way home. Visitors, "dignitaries" from the Holy Land, were accorded special courtesies, and they might well stay on for months. Petitionary circulars from Terra Sancta were respected. Ever since the 1760s, a special committee in New York had canvassed the colonies for funds to support the venerable Jewish community of Hebron. The Palestinians pray for us, they maintain Talmudic academies, and they are oppressed by the Turks; they must be helped.

The *sedaka* lent Michael Judah £5 to open a little shop in Norwalk, Connecticut. When he died in 1786 he left his pitifully small estate to support New York's synagogue and its impoverished widows. After making his fortune in Canada, Eleazar Levy retired to the large Jewish community of New York and invested his savings in a mortgage on land that is now the site of the West Point Military Academy. The inflation of the Revolution wiped him out; his debtors paid him off in worthless Continental currency. Shearith Israel rescued him by pensioning him off for the rest of his life. Funerals and burials were the obligations of the synagogues. There were no family plots; the deceased were buried serially. Those who had means paid a few pounds, and the poor were interred free. The all-inclusive social welfare activity of a congregation might well be summarized in the following laconic but eloquent quotation from the records of Shearith Israel: "To cash for lodging, boarding, doctering, and burying Solomon Solomons, £23,8,10."

Was there a concern for rehabilitation of wandering beggars and impoverished souls? No attempt was really made, but it was clear that the poor must not be punished. God has warned us: "The poor shall never cease out of the land" (Deuteronomy 15:11). Feed them. If a man wants to go into business, give him credit, a stock of goods.

JEWISH EDUCATION AND CULTURE

In Jewish tradition, education is primary. This is an ancient pre-Christian dictum. Learning, teaching—Torah—takes precedence over all other needs and values. When Newport Jews set out to build a synagogue in the 1750s, they announced that their house of worship would include a school. Still, teaching children, indoctrinating them, was deemed the obligation of the parent, not of the community. It follows, therefore, that parents would employ an instructor for their boys and girls. The man hired was called the rebbe, though often the hazzan would open a private school and undertake this task in order to augment his income. By 1731 a school to teach Hebrew was established in New York, the gift of a London Sephardi philanthropist. It was, we may be sure, a tuition school, but the children of the impoverished were taught gratis; the community was always obligated to provide for the education of the poor. By 1755 the Hebrew school had begun to teach secular subjects as well, reading, writing, arithmetic. The curriculum included Spanish, but there is evidence that this requirement was honored in the breach. Six hours were spent daily on Hebrew and the secular subjects in the summer, four hours in the winter (the community could not afford to supply candles when there was no daylight). By 1762 the language of instruction was English.

The ultimate educational goals of the eighteenth-century father were very modest. He was content if his son could learn the numerous basic Hebrew blessings, read Hebrew even if he could not translate it, and recite the required verses from the Bible when he was bar mitzvah, that is, when he became a "man" at the age of thirteen. It was hoped that the child would become observant and embrace the Jewish way of life because of his schooling, his participation in the life cycle ceremonies, and the instruction he received at home. Most youngsters who attended the Sabbath service could read Hebrew, and some were able to translate the text of the prayer book and the five books of Moses. When Gershom Seixas was appointed New York's religious leader in 1768, he was obviously familiar with the basic texts, for he had gone to the local Jewish day school. Indeed, when called upon he could write a simple Hebrew essay; it was he who wrote the Hebrew oration for Sampson Simson when the latter graduated from Columbia in 1800. There were one or two well-educated Jews in matters Hebraic in every town of size. They had been trained in Europe and usually possessed libraries that included the basic Hebrew classics and codes. The typical merchant or shopkeeper, however, had no desire to stand out as a Hebrew scholar. He hoped to become a successful businessman. Learned Hebraists and ordained rabbis stayed away from these remote British provinces; for them this was exile. Culturally by 1775, American Jewry had produced almost nothing of significance, only two thin volumes of translations of some of the standard Hebrew prayers.

REJECTION

It is obvious that Europeans who came to America brought their cultural baggage with them. The Gentiles were loaded down with anti-Jewish prejudices that they cherished. Englishmen who attended a London theater may well have been impressed by Marlowe's and Shakespeare's caricatures of a Jew. For most Christians, "Jew" was a word of contempt. There is no reason why a good Christian could not lustily sing the following verse of one of Isaac Watts's hymns:

> Lord, I ascribe it to thy grace,
> And not to chance as others do,
> That I was born of Christian race,
> And not a heathen or a Jew.

The Jews faced problems, not so serious, to be sure, but annoying enough. Increase Mather of Massachusetts denounced them for murdering the Lord of Heaven and announced that they were doomed to suffer till they embraced Christianity. They were vilified in the press and in the legislative halls; their cemeteries were often desecrated; practically every window in Newport's beautiful synagogue was once shattered. But there were never any mob attacks, nor did any provincial government lend its support to violence against Jews. The children of Israel learned to live with the denial of honorific offices. Restrictive Sunday laws applied to Christians as well as to Jews. In 1752 a warrant was issued in Stratford, Connecticut, for the arrest of a Christian couple accused of laughing on Sunday.

America Accepts the Jews

The Jews on the whole inspired little antagonism in the North American colonies. Did the provincials accept the Jews because they were the descendants of the Old Testament patriarchs? No. The Christians, after all, looked upon the Hebrew Bible as their own book and they themselves as the real heirs of God's promises. There were Christian Hebraists unsympathetic to the Jews. Ezra Stiles, the country's most erudite Orientalist, looked upon Jews as deicides. The Hebrew Bible served Christians as an authoritative code, and they turned to it when they sought divine sanction to execute witches or to revolt against the crown of England. When the Continental Congress prepared to adopt a seal for the new government, a committee of three, John Adams, Benjamin Franklin, and Thomas Jefferson, suggested that it depict the Pharaonic pursuers of the fleeing Israelites drowning in the waters of the Red Sea. The legend surrounding the seal would read: "Rebellion to Tyrants Is Obedience to God." In the end, the biblically inspired design was rejected in favor of a seal reflective of eighteenth-century mystagogy.

Jews were always a curiosity. Their very existence proved that the New Testament was authentic—who, having seen a Jew, could now assert that Jesus was a myth? They were needed, moreover, as shopkeepers, merchants, importers, exporters, and employers of labor. When the candle-manufacturing cartel met, it sought to avoid assembling on Saturday so the Jews might attend. The Jewish merchant in smaller towns was often a highly respected and influential member of the community. Gentile friends frequently became business partners, particularly in Philadelphia and among the Lancaster Jewish merchants. Two years before the skirmishes at Lexington and Concord, several editions of Josephus's *Antiquities* and *The Jewish Wars* and the story of the heroic Maccabeans were rushed into print. Americans, ready to revolt, turned to the ancient Judaeans for encouragement and inspiration. Freemasonry, which opened its doors to Jews, would mark a change in Jewish lives that was almost revolutionary. The Enlightenment reached out to embrace all men of good will. Entranced by this new philosophy of humanity, Jews rushed into the movement. Moses Michael Hays of Boston became the founder of a Masonic system that ultimately became part of the Scottish Rite. Wealthy, cultured families like the Levy-Franks clan of New York, Philadelphia, and Baltimore experienced no difficulty moving into the country's highest social circles. Ultimately this led to intermarriage and frequently to obliteration of Jewish identity. When Mrs. David Franks, a Gentile, recorded the birth of a daughter in the family Bible, her husband's Jewish identity was not entirely gone; she wrote, Rebecca was born "on Good Friday and Purim." Yet their children were all reared as Christians.

It would seem that no Jewish family in the Connecticut villages succeeded in surviving Jewishly. It has been estimated that the rate of intermarriage in the late eighteenth and early nineteenth centuries was about 16 percent. North America was a frontier continent in which anything could—and did—happen. Levi Solomon, a Freehold, New Jersey, peddler, married three times. He was buried between two of his wives, and the third was at his feet. He was well provided for in the Resurrection, although Jesus, the Jew, had warned that "in the Resurrection they neither marry nor are given in marriage" (Matthew 22:30). When Michael Judah's son, David, was born in Norwalk, Connecticut, of a Christian mother, the father brought in the circumciser from New York to "Judaize" his child. The circumcised David grew up to raise a Christian family. His son became an Episcopal clergyman, and two of this clergyman's grandchildren were notables: Theodore Dehone Judah planned the first railroad across the Sierra Nevadas; his brother, Henry Moses Judah, was a Union general in the Civil War.

Conversion of Jews to Christianity was rare. Apostasy brought few advantages except to those individuals eager to escape from Jewry and Judaism. A Portuguese New Christian, a secret Jew, fled to London and to the new colony of Georgia in order to practice his ancestral faith without hindrance. His children, free to live as they wished, preferred the Gentile way of life. There were, however, Gentile women who married Jews and embraced Judaism. When Judith Hart of Easton, Pennsylvania, married James Pettigrew, a Revolutionary War officer, they reportedly decided the boys would be reared as Christians and the girls as Jews. One of the sons became the mayor of Pittsburgh.

In essence, most Jews experienced no difficulty in becoming an integral part of the colonial world. The non-Jews accepted them. There was little if any objection in America to the colonial-oriented Naturalization Act of 1740. A similar law passed for England was speedily annulled (1753); the British refused to naturalize alien-born Jews in England.

THE JEWS ACCEPT AMERICA

Whether the motivation was expedience or principle, colonial Jews were tolerated if not fully accepted. In turn, the children of Abraham were only too happy to live in this country. Most of them came here with the capacity to read and write and they made sure that their children learned enough to carry on a business. Youngsters born in America received an elementary secular education in a private school or at the hands of tutors, and by the second half of the eighteenth century they could attend a Jewish all-day school in New York City. Higher education? Few felt any need for it or saw much purpose in it. The three Pinto boys went to Yale; a New York lad graduated from King's College, later Columbia. Moses Levy was the first Jew to matriculate at the University of Pennsylvania, and in later years he became a notable jurist. Richea Gratz, daughter of Michael Gratz, went to Lancaster's Franklin College in 1787. The school was then, probably, a modest academy. The children of affluent or wealthy families acquired a knowledge of foreign languages and were educated musically. Some Jews—not many—joined library societies, read newspapers and plays, and built libraries of their own, and it was not unusual for Jews of means to commission portraits. Higher education was no requisite for Jewish communal leadership where the successful merchants dominated.

Jews maintained their low profile, adapting their way of life to the contemporary culture. Feibush (Phoebus) became Phillips; Zvi ("deer") became Hart; Ribeiro became Rivers; Priscilla and Frances were the names given two daughters of Isaac Elizer. The Jewish historian Lee M. Friedman thought that the Sephardic Campanals of Ipswich had changed their name to Campbell, but the evidence is not convincing. Francis Salvador did not have to change his Marrano name (which translates as "savior"). Jewish men and women were garbed no differently from their Gentile neighbors, which seems to have puzzled and disappointed some non-Jewish observers. By 1745, Shearith Israel used no Portuguese in its records, and Seixas, the hazzan, had no knowledge of the language of his Iberian ancestors. The mother tongue of most early American immigrants was Yiddish or a related Judeo-German dialect, but these languages had no future here. The Gratzes wrote most of their letters in English; Rebecca, Michael's famous daughter, betrays no knowledge of the ancestral tongue in her voluminous correspondence. Those who clung to Yiddish interlarded it with English words. (The Pennsylvania Dutch, too, studded their German with weird English-like nouns and verbs.) More than one Jew wrote English but employed the Hebrew, not the Roman, alphabet.

Jews participated in the communal life of the general community of which they felt themselves an integral part. Participation is identification. Rhode Island Jewish merchants helped build streets and wharves, and they supported Rhode Island College and gave money to the Baptist church in Providence. A Stamford Jew was generous to a local Christian sanctuary. Philadelphia Jewry supported Benjamin Franklin's hospital, and Myer Hart of Easton helped build a local school. Simon Valentine, who spent some time in Charleston, South Carolina, was one of a committee charged with the important task of protecting the town from invaders. Newport Jews helped raise funds for an impoverished Gentile family in which the husband, wife, and all seven children were blind. In 1711, several of New York's Jewish merchants, including the acting hazzan, contributed funds to erect the steeple of Trinity Church. Savannah's Jews were members of the Union Society, the local social welfare organization, which embraced Protestants, Catholics, and Jews. When Boston's port was closed by the British in 1774, Jacob Rodrigues Rivera was put on Newport's committee to collect supplies for the beleaguered Massachusetts town.

America gave the Jews the opportunity to explore an attractive new world. Despite the threats of congregational presidents, individuals were less observant and social controls could not always be maintained. Enquiring souls visited churches and read the New Testament. Lopez, the quintessential Jew, did not hesitate to send his son to board with a Christian farmer who certainly kept no kosher table. There were some men so apathetic in matters Jewish that they found it possible to take the Christian test oath when it served their purpose. But let it be clear: There were not many who distanced themselves from their people. Jews enjoyed their customs and traditions; they cherished their differences yet always wanted to be typically American. When Charleston Jews buried their volunteer cantor, a shopkeeper, they exulted in the inscription inscribed on his tombstone: The R.[ight] R.[everend] Moses Cohen, D.D.

THE ANGLO-AMERICAN COLONIAL JEW: A RETROSPECT

Who was this colonial Jew? An individualist, an enterprising European, an observant Jew determined to carve out a place for himself in the remote transatlantic provinces. He was a courageous man; it took dogged determination to cross the Atlantic in a tiny schooner and begin life in a strange new world. He was a frontiersman endowed with the traits that made it possible for him to wrest a livelihood for himself and his brood in the towns and hamlets on the edge of the wilderness. Ezekiel Solomon trekked from Montreal to Michilimackinac. Barnard Gratz of Philadelphia once crossed the Blue Ridge and Alleghenies on horseback to Pittsburgh with a pistol and his prayer shawl in his saddlebags. He cleared no forest and ploughed no furrow, but he brought his neighbors the cloth, the notions, the tea, and the coffee that made life endurable for them. He taught his Christian neighbors to live with Jews; that, too, was an achievement. And what happened to the Jew in Three Rivers, in Norwalk, in Lancaster, in Augusta, Georgia? He learned to trust his Christian friends.

The Jews from Lithuania, Russia, Poland, Hungary, Prussia, Hesse, Bavaria, Holland, France, Portugal, and Spain were all poured into one melting pot to emerge a new American Jew. This newcomer hoped to strike a balance between his old European loyalties and his new emotional attachments, but the scale was never to balance. He was destined to become less of a Jew and more of an American. He would always remain loyal to his faith and to his people. He would venerate the Torah, the Law, erect synagogues, chant the service, feed the poor. He was a creator, a founder, for he built Jewish communities all the way from the St. Lawrence to the pine barrens along the Savannah River. He survived through adaptation. His Judaism was, after a fashion, a religion of salutary neglect. In this America that he had taken to his heart there was no wall of separation between him and the Gentile next door. Few, very few, ever went back to Europe. The Jew was no alien in this land; this was home.

On July 4, 1776, the Declaration of Independence was proclaimed, and a new country was born. What did the children build on the foundations their Jewish parents had laid? Most of the country's Jews then still lived in five towns: Newport, New York, and Philadelphia in the North; Charleston and Savannah in the South. But there is good reason to believe that there were individuals and families in many other towns, villages, and hamlets all the way from Maine to the Gulf of Mexico. All told, there may have been as many as two thousand or twenty-five hundred Jewish men, women, and children in this country out of a total population of fewer than three million.

The Americans revolted against the British crown because they wanted to be independent or autonomous on their own terms. Inasmuch as the Catholic French had been driven off the continent, the Protestant colonies no longer needed the protective English troops. Of course, not all Americans were ready to secede. Many were Loyalists (Tories); very many, too, were neutrals; only a hard core were rebels, Whigs, Continentals. Most of the country's Jews, however, were "patriots" for the simple reason that they had experienced disabilities under the English, and the recently published Declaration of Independence implicitly offered them equality. The privileges English rule had given Jews only whetted their appetites. They wanted their rights whole and undiminished.

The Jews who then aligned themselves with the Whigs aided the new republic as soldiers and businessmen. Although there were probably no more than five hundred Jewish householders in the states, a substantial number served both in the militia and in the line regiments; several became commissioned officers and two reached the rank of lieutenant colonel. (Under the British no Jew could become a commissioned officer unless he took the standard Christian test oath.) Francis Salvador, the South Carolina plantation owner, was serving as a gentleman volunteer when the troops he accompanied were ambushed. He was fatally wounded, probably the first Jewish combatant to die in battle during the Revolution (July 31–August 1, 1776). South Carolina did not forget him. The plaque dedicated to his memory in a Charleston park reads:

> Born an aristocrat, he became a democrat,
> An Englishman, he cast his lot with America;
> True to his ancient faith, he gave his life
> For new hopes of human liberty and understanding.

Under South Carolina's first constitution, adopted March 26, 1776, only Protestants could hold high office. Francis Salvador gave his life for a state and a cause that had already denied him equal rights as a citizen.

The Jews had high visibility on Front Street and King Street. They were merchant shippers, small-scale army purveyors, privateers, and outfitters for George Rogers Clark as he marched to drive the British out of the trans-Allegheny West. The tailor Lippman Schneider wrote Congress that he was ready to supervise the manufacture of uniforms for the army. Isaac Moses & Company, noted blockade runners, gave the new government $20,000 in hard currency and accepted Continental paper in exchange. This was an act of faith. The most notable Jew of this period was Haym Salomon (ca. 1740–85). This Polish immigrant left home as a teenager, wandered through many European lands, learned languages, and landed in the British colonies a year or two before the Revolution. The disabilities imposed on all Jews in Europe made him an ardent American patriot. When the British occupied New York City in 1776, his name was on a proscription list, and he was seized and imprisoned. It is highly probable that Hessian supplymen with the British—probably Jews—offered to secure his release if he would work for them. He assented but speedily began his role as an underground agent helping imprisoned American and French soldiers escape. Betrayed, he fled for his life to Whig Philadelphia where he became a shopkeeper, merchant, and bill broker. Robert Morris, superintendent of finance, called him in and ultimately appointed him his chief broker. Salomon was something of an alchemist. He turned paper—bills of exchange—into ready money and helped Morris secure the funds he needed to outfit the armies that forced Cornwallis to surrender at Yorktown. Even after the fall of the British forces,

Salomon continued to help Morris during the difficult days when the Americans were negotiating with the British for recognition. It was Salomon who lent money—at no interest—to the almost penniless James Madison, thus enabling the future champion of the Constitution to continue his congressional activity. When Salomon died in 1785 he was insolvent; he lies buried in an unmarked grave. There was no money even for a modest tombstone, yet no American Jew has a greater monument. In 1941 Chicago citizens erected a larger-than-life statue heralding the achievements of this Polish immigrant.

Part II
The Early National Period: 1776–1840

3. Jews Become Citizens

ACHIEVING POLITICAL RECOGNITION

In July 1776, Jonas Phillips, a Philadelphia merchant, wrote his Amsterdam supplier a Yiddish letter ordering some goods that he hoped would evade the British blockade. He enclosed a printed copy of the Declaration of Independence but made no comment on the declaration itself. Was he skeptical? A dozen years later, the Constitution of the new republic had been written and ratified by all the states (1787–90). Article VI was explicit: "No religious test shall ever be required as a qualification to any office or public trust under the United States." The First Amendment, adopted in 1791 to reassure apprehensive legislators, reinforced the above article: "Congress shall make no law respecting an establishment of religion, or prohibiting the free exercise thereof."

Religion, officially and formally, was to receive no federal tax support in the new nation. Apparently all American Jews were now federal citizens in every sense of the term. Some years earlier, the Northwest Ordinance (1787) had abolished religious deterrents to office in any new territory or new state: "No person, demeaning himself in a peaceable and orderly manner, shall ever be molested on account of his mode of worship or religious sentiments, in the said territory." Proud of their several legislative achievements, the American people determined to celebrate, and on July 4, 1788, they staged a federal parade in Philadelphia, the greatest spectacle the country had ever witnessed. The gaping multitudes saw a sight never before witnessed on this or any other continent: "The rabbi of the Jews, locked in the arms of two ministers of the gospel, was a most delightful sight." The Messiah was apparently just around the corner.

The powers of the federal Constitution were strictly delimited; the states were reluctant to surrender any of their traditional prerogatives. How did this federal legislation—the Constitution and Bill of Rights—affect the country's Jewry? Any native-born politically disabled Jew of the British colonies could now aspire to become president of the United States, but the thirteen autonomous states still retained most of their vested privileges. The Constitution had no authority to emancipate the Jews within the thirteen different states. New York's Whig patriots—exiled by the British occupiers of New York City—had met in Kingston in 1777 and adopted the state's first constitution. It gave Jews complete equality, though Catholics were not emancipated. It took more than a decade after the Declaration of Independence with its enticing "all men are created equal" before the Jews of Philadelphia, Richmond, Charleston, and Savannah were accepted as full fellow citizens by their Gentile neighbors. Most of the states wanted no Jews in high office; the ecumenical approach of the Constitution did not appeal to them. Jacob Henry (1776–1847), a state legislator in North Carolina, faced removal from office when it was discovered that, as a Jew, he had not taken the required Christian test oath. Fortunately, he was allowed to retain his seat because his fellow legislators, friends, declared that a Jew could hold a legislative but no civil office! The effort to confer full citizenship on Jews in Maryland dragged on for twenty-nine years. Not until 1826 did liberal Christian leaders of the struggle emerge victorious: "The stain upon the constitution of Maryland is blotted out forever, for in the march of the human mind it is impossible to recede." This was the exultant cry of Benjamin C. Howard, a Christian, later a United States congressman. That very same year, Jacob I. Cohen Jr. (1789–1869), was elected to the Baltimore City Council, ultimately to become its president.

In the states where Jewish communities were established, the younger native-born eagerly took advantage of their privileges as citizens. They were elected or appointed to municipal, county, and state offices. Dr. Levy Myers was a member of the South Carolina state legislature as early as 1796. Federal offices, of course, were always open to them. In 1813 Mordecai Manuel Noah (1785–1851) was appointed by President James Madison as consul to Tunis. Jews had served in the U.S. Army since the Revolution. A Lieutenant Colonel Bush hoped that George Washington would appoint him postmaster general. Simon Magruder Levy, a professional soldier and veteran of the Ohio Indian wars, was half of the first graduating class (of two students) at West Point. About two decades later, young Alfred Mordecai, a cadet at the Point, was appointed acting assistant professor of mathematics while still a student (in later years he became one of the country's most distinguished ordnance experts). During the War of 1812, Bernard Hart of New York City served as the quartermaster of the state's militia division (Bret Harte, the writer, was his grandson). Another Jew who made a career for himself in this second conflict with England was Mordecai Myers, a captain in the thirteenth U.S. Infantry. His exploits, truly impressive, are recorded modestly in an autobiography that his family published. Writing to a dear friend, the Jewish owner and editor of the *National Advocate*,

Captain Myers said that "sum must spill there blud and others there ink." This ardent patriot—his family had been Loyalists, Tories, during the Revolution!—was later elected a member of the New York State Assembly and was twice mayor of Schenectady. He had no patience with Christian religionists who wanted to breach the wall between church and state.

Chapman Levy and Philip Phillips, both South Carolinians, were colonels in militia regiments. Another son of Loyalists who made a career as an officeholder was John Jacob Hays, of the Westchester County, New York, family. After leaving Canada, where his father had fled, young Hays finally settled among the French in Cahokia in the Illinois country. Out on this frontier he supported his family as a fur trader and farmer, postmaster, sheriff of St. Clair County, collector of revenue for the Illinois territory, and Indian agent at Fort Wayne. His children were reared as Christians.

In the 1830s, when Texas asserted its independence from Mexico, a number of young Americans rushed to defend the new republic. Among them was Leon Dyer of Baltimore, who became a major, and Dr. Moses Albert Levy, surgeon in chief of the Volunteer Army of Texas. Uriah P. Levy (1792–1862), a fifth-generation American, started his naval career as a ten-year-old cabin boy, became captain of a ship before he was twenty, was commissioned a lieutenant in the U.S. Navy, and shortly before the Civil War erupted served as "commodore" of the Mediterranean Fleet. He was one of America's highest-ranking naval officers.

Plagued by disabilities, all European Jewries, except those of France and Holland, turned to the United States as the exemplar of egalitarianism. In turn, Jews here looked upon America's emancipatory legislation as a commodity for export.

After the Constitution was adopted in 1788, Richmond Jewry met in a banquet where the following toast was offered: "May the Israelites throughout the world enjoy the same religious rights and political advantages as their American brethren."

4. Jewish Communities in the New Nation

AMERICANIZING AN OLD FAITH

When the Bill of Rights was adopted by Congress in 1791, there were six Jewish communities in the country: Newport, New York, Philadelphia, Charleston, Savannah, and Richmond, a new grouping. Savannah was slow to get off the ground, and Newport would be a Jewish ghost town by 1800. New York, with its fine port, was assured a great future. But Charleston was then the largest and most cultured Jewish community in America. It would reign supreme till the 1820s and then decline when the old Southwest—Alabama, Mississippi, Louisiana, east Texas—blossomed. A great change was in the making. The older Jewish communities were Sephardic dominated, ritually and socially; the new emergent communities would be populated by Ashkenazim, central and east Europeans, and a sprinkling of English. These recent arrivals had their own "Hebrew" ritual, and the native-born looked down upon them. The old-timers spoke English and knew the amenities, whereas most of the new arrivals spoke German and only an imperfect English. Social differences and traditions also tended to keep the two groups apart. Influenced by the new American libertarianism, New York's Jewish community—Shearith Israel—employed grandiloquent Enlightenment phraseology as the leaders fiddled with new constitutions. This euphoric aberration, however, soon evanesced. Apathy was mounting; discipline was imperative; indeed, all Sephardic congregations were determined to maintain autocratic control.

In the long run, the effort to maintain one monopolistic congregation would fail. American democracy could not be denied as multiple synagogue communities arose in the larger cities. With synagogues competing for members, more ritual latitude was tolerated. By 1840 there were about twenty Jewish communities in the United States, and at least fourteen of them employed "non-Sephardic" Hebrew prayer books. All these new congregations except St. Louis were east of the Mississippi.

To get a sense of the daily life of any Jewry, one will do well to pay less attention to the synagogueal constitutions than to the bylaws and the minutes: Little children must be kept at home lest they disrupt the services; don't outsing the cantor; leave your outer garments, umbrellas, and canes in the empty pews; don't spit on the floor if you chew tobacco; don't mount the reading desk if you have muddy boots; bordello owners and prostitutes may become members if they turn over a new leaf and lead a virtuous life; blacks are not welcomed as members even if they live a Jewish life. Mr. Marks of Philadelphia had a black domestic servant who was a meticulous observer of Jewish tradition. When the congregation refused to bury her, Mr. Marks and his friends smuggled her into the cemetery and performed the traditional rites.

The Southerners were less observant than the Northerners. In New Orleans, for example, Jewish law was neglected and flouted and concessions were common. Intermarriage was tolerated. Christian wives and uncircumcised children were given a resting place in consecrated soil. When Manis Jacobs, president and acting rabbi of a New Orleans congregation, was buried, his Catholic spouse attempted to slip a crucifix into his coffin.

Rebecca Gratz of Philadelphia, however, observed the dietary laws even when she visited a fashionable spa, and New York's Shearith Israel subjected its minister to an inquisition when it was reported that he had eaten oysters. Despite the prevailing neglect of ceremony and ritual, America's Jews remained a religious people even though not all Jews were religious. Churchgoing Christians rallied around Jesus; Jews rallied around one another in their houses of worship. There was no town without at least one Jew determined meticulously to maintain the faith. Cashier Moses Seixas would not report for work on Saturday in Newport's bank. He employed a Christian lad to bring his keys to a Gentile clerk. The boy was rewarded with matzo on Passover and goodies on Purim. Pious Jews enjoined their children to live the good life. When young Aaron Levy came to the United States in 1795, his "baggage" contained spiritual food for the road; it reads as follows:

> Open your doors to the poor . . .
> Observe the Sabbath . . .
> Practice love and truth throughout your life . . .
> Give money to the poor . . .
> Turn aside from evil and do good . . .

In this early national period the two outstanding Jewish ministers were Gershom Seixas and Isaac Leeser. The native-born Seixas served Shearith Israel in New York from 1768 to 1816. Even though he was unordained, people respected and admired him, and he was looked upon as an exemplary rabbi. Isaac Leeser (1806–68), who also ministered to a Sephardic congregation, was a native of Germany. After he came to this country as a teenager he went to work for an uncle in Richmond. Four years later (1828) he wrote a long article in the local press defending his people from an anti-Jewish attack in the London *Quarterly Review*, one of the most prestigious periodicals in the English literary world. Impressed by his brilliance and his devotion to Judaism, Congregation Mikveh Israel of Philadelphia appointed him its minister in the autumn of 1829. He was an author, an apologete, a theologian, a translator, an educator, and the country's first "rabbi" (he too was unordained) to preach regularly. By 1839, at the age of thirty-three, he had already published two catechisms, a theological defense of Judaism, six volumes of the Spanish-Portuguese Jewish prayers in Hebrew and in English, two volumes of sermons, and an elementary Hebrew textbook for Rebecca Gratz's Sunday school. During the next twenty-nine years, by virtue of his writings and his all-embracing vision, he became the country's most distinguished defender of the faith. He was the founder of America's modern Jewish Orthodoxy, and though an uncompromising traditionalist, he was thoroughly and utterly American in all of his activities.

SOCIAL WELFARE IN THE JEWISH COMMUNITY

THE NEWCOMERS INSURE THEMSELVES

Charity—"pious works"—was always important in the colonial period. There were times when one-fourth of New York's total budget went for relief to the local poor or to the itinerants who were always arriving. Dispensing charity was the job of the synagogue community and, to some extent, remained a congregational obligation well into the nineteenth century. The end of the Revolutionary War brought an important change, however. Semiautonomous and autonomous societies devoted to social welfare now made their appearance. Soon there was no major town without at least one such organization, and in some cases social welfare associations even predated organized prayer groups. Some societies dedicated themselves to immigrant aid; others set out to help orphans or indigent parents; most were sick care and burial associations. The seal of Charleston's 1784 Hebrew Benevolent Society is monitory. It depicts a skeleton with a scythe in one bony hand and an hourglass in the other. The Hebrew legend inscribed is mordantly elegant: Charity saves from death. America's first permanent non-Sephardic congregation, Philadelphia's Rodeph Shalom, began in 1802 as a burial fraternity.

By 1813 the burial societies had changed significantly by introducing a mutual aid dimension—unemployment and death insurance as well as grants to sick members and their widows. In 1819 Rebecca Gratz and her friends at Philadelphia's Mikveh Israel organized the Female Hebrew Benevolent Society and then set out thriftily in those sad days of financial depression to help only those of good moral character; they subsidized but two petitioners and kept a substantial balance in the bank. By 1822 a Philadelphia beneficent society had largely emancipated itself from synagogueal sponsorship and had effectively become an autonomous institution, open to all Jews in town. In a way this marked the faint beginnings of a secularized Jewish social welfare system. Originally the Hebrew Benevolent Society was limited to sick care and burials. In the course of time, as its members became more affluent, it tended to become an all-purpose communal charity agency. The community was beginning to expand and extend its reach.

JUDAH TOURO, AMERICAN JEWRY'S MOST FAMOUS PHILANTHROPIST

Judah Touro (1775–1854), the son of a Newport cantor-rabbi, was reared by an uncle after his father died. In 1801 he left home for the Franco-Spanish town of New Orleans where he carried on business as a merchant, broker, and real estate investor. He grew with the city, and as it prospered he became very wealthy. Touro, a bachelor, was thrifty, withdrawn, crotchety, a loner. His best friend—and testamentary legatee—was a non-Jew, Rezin Davis Shepherd, who had rescued the wounded Touro from the battlefield when Andrew Jackson defeated the English in the War of 1812.

Touro made few friends among the local Jews, neither the wealthy and assimilated elite nor the more humble newcomers who had established a congregation in 1828. Though no convert, he owned a pew in a Christian meetinghouse and bought two churches that he let his friend, the Reverend Theodore Clapp, use rent free. He invested heavily in a bond issue for the local Catholic cathedral. In 1839 he gave a matching grant of $10,000 to complete the building of the Bunker Hill monument in Boston. The cornerstone had been laid in 1825, but there was not enough money—or patriotism—in New England to finish the project. There is some evidence that Touro sought no recognition for his generosity. It was the poet William Cowper who wrote: "God works in a mysterious way his wonders to perform." By 1847 Touro had purchased a building, renovated it as a synagogue, and started attending services. Back in the fold as a practicing Jew, he may have had intimations of mortality; he died in 1854. Before he passed away, his Jewish friends beseeched him to do something for Jewry. It was a long, hard struggle, but when his will was probated it was found that he was as generous to Jews as he was to Christians. He gave New Orleans Jewry his synagogue, a hospice-hospital, and funds for a Hebrew school. All told, about three dozen American Jewish institutions were left substantial sums. The needy Jews of Palestine received $60,000—a handsome legacy. But non-traditional Jewish congregations were given nothing; Touro was a staunch Sephardi. His grave in Newport bears the following inscription:

> The last of his name; he inscribed it in the
> book of philanthropy to be remembered forever.

Touro sought no immortality; apparently he had no vanity. His gifts gave new life to dozens of important Jewish institutions in large centers. After a fashion this meant resurrection for them and for him, too.

MAKING A LIVING

MERCHANDISING

Before there can be philanthropy there must be money, a job, surplus cash. Here in early America the Jews who made a living—who survived—ran the gamut from the indentured servant to the wealthy merchant shipper, industrialist, and investor. Economically, Jews nibbled at almost everything. At the bottom of the economic ladder was the bond servant, a "white slave." When two such men who had sold their services to pay for the Atlantic crossing landed in Philadelphia on the afternoon before the Day of Atonement, they were speedily redeemed by some of the city's Jews. At the top of the social and economic heap in the South was the planter, a social arbiter and political power. Pitifully few Jews belonged to this category, and even they were not welcomed by the Gentiles. There were

59

also Jews who believed in the conquest of the soil. Mordecai Noah and Moses Elias Levy wanted to colonize European Jews in the American states. Noah fantasized; Levy ran a large plantation. Jews of lesser means owned small farms, a respectable occupation. At times, however, even farming was the last resort of the unemployed.

Jews had peddled in America ever since the seventeenth century, and they were still peddling in the early decades of the twentieth century. The pack peddler plodding on the country roads carried cheap jewelry, notions, clothing, and, on occasion, a music box that played "Yankee-Doodle." The farmer's wife was glad to buy his needles and thread. In turn, what did America do for the immigrant peddler? It became a forcing house. German-born Louis Stix, later a wealthy merchant, started out as a peddler. He invited a farmer's daughter to a dance, then left her stranded when he was tired. The next day Stix's Americanization was speeded up when the young woman's father drove him off the place with a pitchfork. Some central European states compelled the youngsters to learn a trade, here in America there was an astonishing assortment of immigrant Jewish craftsmen and artisan shopkeepers: furriers, makers of trunks, saddles, hats, watches, combs, distillers, carvers, gilders, seal engravers, chandlers, umbrella makers, brewers.

At least 50 percent of the Jews in Americas's towns were merchandisers, most of them living east of the Mississippi. Jacob Franks, a fur trader in Green Bay, Wisconsin, since the 1790s, built the first gristmill, sawmill, and blacksmith shop in that part of the old Northwest. Lewis Polock sold saddles and clothing in 1839 in Yerba Buena, California (in 1847 his village changed its name to San Francisco). As in colonial days, shopkeepers handled hard, soft (dry), and wet goods. Country storekeepers often engaged in barter, accepting produce, staves, hides, and furs. Brokers had a wide reach. They were agents, intermediators who bought and sold on commission, lent money, handled bills of exchange, dealt in real estate, and issued insurance policies. Auctioneers were primarily job lot dealers, ready to store goods in a warehouse until a customer was found. The Jew who was no trader might well work for the government in the customs house, run a livery stable, serve as a police officer, or own a tavern or a boardinghouse. Some able men took their time till they found themselves. Raphael Moses lived in South Carolina, Pennsylvania, Florida, and Georgia. He was an auctioneer, a bookkeeper, a peddler of watches, the owner of a "cheap cash store," a dry goods merchant, a speculator in stocks, a railroad official, a banker, a politician, an officer in the Confederate Army, and a distinguished lawyer and orator. One New York old-timer had an art studio. A St. Louis pioneer sold Old Master paintings. Others made their living selling wallpaper, music, stationery, fruit, clothing, drugs, and lottery tickets. A large-scale Philadelphia merchant owned a dry goods emporium that was patronized by the family of a United States president. This bazaar owner catered to the carriage trade and advertised that he carried the latest Parisian styles.

THE MERCHANT SHIPPERS AND LAND SPECULATORS

If a city or village shopkeeper was at the bottom of the mercantile hierarchy in the days of Jefferson and Madison, the merchant shipper was still at the top. This capitalist, who was prepared to buy or sell almost anything, was primarily an exporter of American products in exchange for consumer goods. Americans exported cotton, tobacco, lumber, naval stores, indigo, rice, pig iron, furs, and provisions; they imported cloth, sugar, coffee,

61

and a large variety of finished products. Jewish businessmen not only imported goods from the most distant lands but also made personal visits. Isaac Levy went to Calcutta, his trip there and back lasting well over a year. The Ettings of Baltimore were heavily involved in the China trade. Ben Etting made seven trips to Canton. On one trip, he reached home in ninety-eight days with a cargo of shawls, satins, and firecrackers. Sol Etting, his uncle, was one of Baltimore's important shippers and venturesome businessmen. He established a water company, served as a councilman, and chaired a committee in one of the city's hospitals. Private patients paid $4 a week; the dead could be interred for $3.

Moses Myers of Norfolk, Virginia, a Revolutionary War blockade runner, was still in business in the first two decades of the new century. Four years after emerging bankrupt from the post-Revolution panic, he had recouped his fortunes and built a beautiful mansion in the city (it is still standing). In his new career he became a coastal shipper, a commission agent, a trader shipping wares to Europe and the Caribbean, as well as a broker for the Dutch, French, and other European governments. He exported and imported products and wares on a large scale. He chaired a branch of the city council and served as an officer of the local regiment of militia. He, too, was ruined by the seven-year depression that began in 1815. Then President John Quincy Adams appointed him Norfolk's customs collector, the agent for the Marine Hospital, and the superintendent of lights. Myers received the office only after a struggle. Incumbent politicians opposed him because he was not amenable to bribery. His life was a tragic one: several of his children died before him, and when a local citizen, Richard Bowen, clubbed him brutally, Moses Myers's son, Samuel, picked up his gun and killed the offender. It was imperative that a southern gentleman defend the honor of his family.

SPECULATION IN LAND

In 1763, after the French and Indian War, there was a rush to organize companies to buy and sell lands in the trans-Ohio regions, but all these efforts profited no one except, in the short run, the Indians who were given expensive gifts to alienate their hunting grounds (the federal government, however, later ignored these grants). After 1776, when titles were good, there was a stampede to this new Klondike. The Gratzes were partners in companies that owned hundreds of thousands of acres in western Virginia and the upper Ohio Basin. Cohen & Isaacs, of Richmond, acquired thousands of acres in what would be Kentucky by barter from Revolutionary War veterans who had been paid in land scrip by a grateful Virginia. The surveyor who billed the firm for his work in 1784 was Daniel Boone. Two years later, Aaron Levy of Pennsylvania laid out the town of Aaronsburg in Centre County. In order to attract settlers he donated lots for schools, Christian churches, and cemeteries. One of the largest Jewish land speculators in the South was Charleston's Michael Lazarus, whose grandfather was one of the founders of the Charleston Jewish community and whose father, Mark, was a Revolutionary War veteran with a heroic record. No later than 1820, Michael, still in his early thirties, purchased more than 156,000 acres in the neighborhood of present-day Miami; he paid $1 an acre—a good price in those days. Lazarus sent his steamboats up the Savannah River in order to open up the western South Carolina and eastern Georgia lands.

THE NEW ECONOMY

The new economy of the early nineteenth century left many American Jews untouched and unchanged. Whether Northerners or Southerners, they remained modest shopkeepers. As purveyors to the masses they rendered an important service. Most of them belonged to the lower middle class, although there were wealthy individuals in every town. Slowey Hays of Richmond died the richest woman in Virginia. (This was Papa's money, Moses Michael Hays of Boston.) In 1788 practically every Richmond Jew had a black domestic servant. Recent central European newcomers to Baltimore had no domestic help in 1820; ten years later, ten out of twenty-four had blacks—freedman—to serve them. It was not easy to make a living, and at least twenty of the years between 1776 and 1840 were very bad. A substantial number of Jews in this country were always poor, yet they did not become petty offenders since they could always turn for help to the Jewish charities.

A New York magistrate testified that only rarely was a Jew arraigned in his court, but he probably had never met Mr. William Jones. This Englishman made no contribution to American Jewry, though he had an international reputation and was well educated. Back in England he had been a fence. Here in New York he forged banknotes, sold worthless stocks, and induced his victims to purchase fraudulent debentures. His original name was Isaac Solomon (and some think he was the original of Fagin in Dickens's *Oliver Twist*). Solomon ended his life in Australia, a criminal and a transport, but a member of the Hobart synagogue.

As the market and industrial economy evolved in the United States, the new central and east European immigrants made few contributions; they had few skills and less capital. There were, however, exceptions. Enterprising Jews speculated in the buying and selling of huge tracts of land. Banking and industry opened new vistas. Brokers on the stock exchange were no longer petty traders. Able Jewish entrepreneurs became insurance executives, built railroads, and extended their reach to India and China. Well-educated natives now turned to the professions. Jonas Phillips, who came here from Germany in the 1750s, had been a clerk, a humble synagogue hireling, and finally a merchant. One of his sons was a physician, another owned a newspaper, a third was an actor, still another was an influential lawyer whose son served in Congress.

Jewish brokers had dealt in government paper since the Revolution. When stock exchanges—formal or informal—were first organized, Jews were founding members. Long before the establishment of railroads, Jewish businessmen were patrons of good roads, turnpikes, and canals. In Baltimore, Solomon Etting and Jacob I. Cohen Jr. were among the city fathers who founded the Baltimore and Ohio Railroad; the resources of the new West had to be tapped if Baltimore was to compete with New York and Philadelphia. Michael Prager, a member of a family of London and Amsterdam entrepreneurs, was a founder in 1792 of the Insurance Company of North America. Jewish businessmen pioneered in maritime, life, and fire insurance. The Wolfes of Virginia and New York built a huge liquor company that sold its products in both America and Europe. Jews directed banks all the way from Newport to New Orleans, and there were at least five banks in South Carolina that were owned or serviced by Jewish personnel. Publishing appealed to the "people of the book." Benjamin Levy of New Orleans—a businessman's publisher—put his name on 130 imprints. Aaron Hart of Philadelphia was the brains of the firm of Carey & Hart, publishers of national repute and scope and a rival of Harper & Brothers. Hendricks family members were American Jewry's most notable industrialists. Harmon Hendricks specialized in processing copper, and it was copper from his mill that went into the boiler room of the *Savannah*, the first sailing ship with an auxiliary engine to make the Atlantic crossing. (Even so, the trip took almost a month.) One of the owners of the *Savannah* was Isaac Minis, whose family had come to Georgia only a few months after Oglethorpe landed. And the clothing industry? There was as yet no large ready-to-wear garment industry, for no good sewing machine would be available until 1851. Jews seem to have dominated the trade in secondhand renovated garments. A Christian is reputed to have said: "We Gentiles take our religion of the Jew, why not our clothes?"

The new economy, the business culture, required a host of professionals. Jews, alert to opportunity, were found in every nook and cranny of the national economy and polity. Before 1840 they appeared as apothecaries, engineers, teachers, interpreters, accountants, metallurgists, administrators, notaries, portrait and miniature painters, economists, educators, building contractors, journalists, physicians, and lawyers. Dr. Isaac Hays of Philadelphia was a medical practitioner of note who helped found the American Medical Association and wrote its code of ethics. Four of the country's distinguished counselors-at-law were southern Jews: Solomon Heydenfeldt, Philip Phillips, Gustavus Adolphus Myers, and Judah P. Benjamin. Moving westward, Heydenfeldt became the first elected justice of the California Supreme Court. He was a very competent practitioner. When a man named Gallagher murdered Lewis Polock in a brothel, Heydenfeldt got him off with a fine and a few weeks in jail. Philip Phillips tried hundreds of cases before the United States Supreme Court. Gustavus Adolphus Myers was one of a committee of two who met with President Lincoln on April 5, 1865, and helped negotiate the terms of the Confederate surrender four days before Grant met with Lee at Appomattox Courthouse. Judah P. Benjamin was the attorney general, the secretary of war, and secretary of state of the Confederate States of America. Myers, Phillips, and Heydenfeldt, although marginal Jews, were ready to help their fellow Jews when called upon; Benjamin, interested only in his career, never played any part in Jewish life.

JEWISH EDUCATION AND CULTURE

Jewish literary and folk culture are inextricably tied up with religion. There are numerous Jewish benedictions: One thanks God on meeting a scholarly person, a learned Jew, on seeing a rainbow, on glimpsing a blossoming tree, on smelling a flower, on eating a piece of fruit, and on escaping from pirates or other great dangers. The annual liturgy of the synagogue still includes the reading of the entire Pentateuch and chapters of later biblical books. The Hebrew schools during this period were under synagogue control, to a greater or lesser degree. The sermon was integrated into the worship service as an intellectual exercise. The school was a religious, not a lay, institution; all apologetic and polemical works were responses to attacks on Jews as nonconformist religionists.

The rebbe, the private Hebrew teacher, may well have been the most important agent in transmitting Jewish culture, for it is not improbable that the number of privately taught students outnumbered those who attended classes. There was no well-established Jewish religious school system in any town. Many towns had no Jewish all-day schools, and very few of these educational establishments enjoyed continuity. All required tuition, with the local congregation, as in colonial times, subsidizing the poor. The textbooks used would seem to have been the prayer book and the Hebrew Scriptures. Other texts were available, but there is no evidence that they were required reading. There were some—not many—moderately successful Hebrew and all-day schools. New York stumbled along even with an occasional government subsidy. We deserve help, argued the New Yorkers. We teach religion, which the free public schools do not, and we train better citizens! Actually, synagogues were not notably concerned with education. Synagogue constitutions make little or no mention of schooling; the congregant was satisfied if his son could read—even if he could not understand—the text. Adult education, though attempted, whether in classes or lectures was of little consequence. There was no Jewish college until 1855, two hundred years after the first émigré came to New Amsterdam. The Puritans had a college—of sorts—sixteen years after they landed in New England.

Jewish Literature

On festive occasions Hebraists wrote poetry and original prayers. When German mobs in 1819 attacked Jews, Penina Moïse invited the victims to sail for these shores:

> If thou art one of that oppressed race,
> whose pilgrimage from Palestine we trace.
> Brave the Atlantic—Hope's broad anchor weigh;
> A Western sun will gild your future days.

Dr. Jonas Horwitz, refuting the geologists, set out to defend the biblical story of creation. Journalist Isaac Harby criticized Shakespeare's depiction of Shylock. Grammars were published by Jews—and by Gentiles, too—primarily for the use of Bible-loving Gentiles. Dr. Isaac Nordheimer, the first scholar of scientific caliber, was the author of a Hebrew grammar and a chrestomathy. Moses Lopez printed a Jewish holiday calendar, a boon to scattered Jews in distant villages. Editions of the Passover ritual and the Sephardic Hebrew prayers had been produced in this country by 1837.

During this early national period, Jews were constantly goaded by missionaries and evangelical believers determined to save Jews from going to hell. Conversion threatened the very existence of the Jew; if Christianity were the only true faith, then Jewish martyrs had died in vain. Apologies for Judaism and polemics against Christianity were imported from London or reprinted here. Two English apologias—written in London and Jamaica—staunchly defended traditional Judaism but with equal Enlightenment fervor declared that all religions pursue the same ethical goals. Deists and freethinkers like Thomas Paine were attacked because they had no respect for the Bible. General works defending Judaism were not uncommon. Isaac Leeser wrote *Jews and the Mosaic Law* (1834). Abraham Collins, a belligerent polemicist, insisted that Jesus had been a good, observant Jew. Solomon Henry Jackson—plagued with a sense of guilt for having married out—published the first American Jewish periodical, *The Jew* (1823–25), which limited itself almost exclusively to antimissionary tract material. The Jew, said Jackson, will not convert; on the contrary, the Christians—all of them circumcised—will yet stream into Jerusalem and worship the God of Israel.

The Sunday School

Somewhat belatedly, Rebecca Gratz and her friends opened the first Jewish Sunday school in 1838. The pattern was totally Christian, and acculturated Jews loved it and adapted it for use in their East Coast synagogues. It met only on Sunday for a brief two hours. Isaac Watts's (Christian) hymns were sung; the Bible was read; "religion" as a discipline was emphasized; and Christian catechisms, properly sanitized, were used. Later, Jews wrote their own catechistic works. A textbook by Simha Cohen Peixotto had a run of at least thirteen editions. Her sister, Mrs. Pyke, published a rhymed catechism:

> Q. What would your wish be when you die?
> A. That God may take me when I die to live with him
> above the sky.

The teachers were gentle and affectionate women. The annual examination gave the youngsters a chance to show what they knew, and they left happy, bearing gifts and awards. Being Jewish was a pleasant experience for these boys and girls. The poor among them—it was something of a mission school—were given clothing. The fifteen newly established central European Ashkenazic conventicles opened no Sunday schools during this period.

A Cultural Revolution: Secularizing the Medieval Jew

For most Americans, the 1775 Revolution was primarily political; for the Jew it was both political and cultural. The accomplishments of American Jewry from 1585 to 1775 were insignificant, but during the next sixty-four years, 1776–1840, there was no area of cultural advancement in which Jews did not participate. America's Jewish notables during these decades were, with certain exceptions, of native stock. Leeser, the community's leading religious leader, and the Leo-Wolf clan of college-trained physicians were central Europeans. Lorenzo Da Ponte (Conegliano), a convert to Catholicism in Europe and the man who was responsible for bringing Italian opera and culture to America, was a native of Ceneda, Italy. Henry Russell (né Levy), an Englishman, was the country's most popular ballad singer. Julius R. Friedlander, another convert, established one of the first schools for the blind. One of his blind students, whom he had taught to "read," wrote the following epitaph on a drunkard:

> Here lies entom'd within this marble vault,
> One who 'twas said had but a single fault . . .
> His name was Sandy:—be it known to all,
> A faithful follow'r of Prince Alcohol—
> Who for his great devotion to the bowl
> Lost first his body, and at last—his soul.

For Jews there was to be a veritable explosion in the arts, sciences, and literature. A St. Louis family of Jews taught foreign languages and music, and in their roles as merchants sold Old Masters; a Titian, a Rubens, a Leonardo could be bought for less than $100. Jewish lawyers wrote legal manuals and compiled digests of state laws. A New Yorker published an anthology of prose and verse. Competent men began to make their appearance as journalists, belletrists, and poets. There was even an authority on gems. A son of Gershom Seixas established a school for the deaf. There was a geologist, a librarian, a dentist. Several Jews, men and women, had studied medicine in the Philadelphia medical schools. Louisa B. Hart, Rachael Mordecai, and Rebecca Gratz were women of high intelligence and some literary ability.

71

Secular Schools

Both in the North and in the South, Jews in modest numbers started going to secondary schools and colleges. In 1787 one of the Gratz girls, Richea, matriculated at Franklin College in Pennsylvania, and twelve men earned a law degree at the University of Pennsylvania. Jacob Mordecai, a devoted religionist, ran an academy for girls in Warrenton, North Carolina. Dr. Elias Marks of Columbia and Barhamville, South Carolina, opened a more advanced and prestigious academic institution; the course lasted five years. Marks, a student of the classics, had translated the aphorisms of Hippocrates. This distinguished educator informed his pupils that literary pursuits were compatible with good housekeeping. Attendance at religious services was compulsory. He had opted for Christianity, whereas his brother Alexander, a committed Jew, once went to court to affirm his constitutional right to keep his place of business open on the first day of the week, Sunday. The Jewish Marks, a merchant, had a fine library. Cultured Jews—autodidacts for the most part—were proud of their book collections. Many of them, from Newport south to Savannah, supported the subscription libraries, the local historical society, and the literary associations that met at least annually to listen to the declamations of their favorite orator.

EMINENT AMERICAN JEWS

THE SOUTH

Mordecai M. Noah once wrote that the weight of Jewish talent was in the South, and he was not altogether wrong. Charleston, though small by later standards, sheltered the most cultured Jewish community in the United States for the first two decades of the nineteenth century. A substantial number of natives in the community knew foreign and classical languages (but not Hebrew!). They could write and speak well, and some even wrote poetry. These educated professionals of all sorts owed their success to the need for their services. Professionally trained whites were at a premium in the South in 1810, where a very substantial minority of the population were enslaved blacks. In the drive toward the new Southwest as the Atlantic coastal cotton lands became less productive, a number of Charlestonian Jews, most of them marginal Jews, moved to Alabama, Mississippi, and Louisiana. Several who settled in New Orleans became leaders.

The Charlestonians were very talented. Philip Phillips made a career in South Carolina, Alabama, and Washington, D.C., as one of America's most distinguished lawyers. He married a daughter of the scholarly Jacob C. Levy, who wrote for the *Southern Quarterly Review* and left unpublished a learned defense of his people, "Vindiciae Judaeorum." Phillips's brother-in-law, Samuel Yates Levy, a poet, was reading Virgil at the age of seven. Two of the Levy daughters were brilliant. One, Phoebe Levy Pember, wrote a charming autobiography. Her sister, Eugenia, Phillips's wife, who described herself as a "frail" woman, married at sixteen, bore nine children, was twice imprisoned by the Union authorities during the Civil War as a rebel, and lived to be eighty-one.

Like Levy, Jacob Newton (né Nunez?) Cardozo (1786–1873) was a Jew who identified strongly with his people. He was also an enthusiastic cultural nationalist who believed that America was destined for great things because of its devotion to liberty, learning, and the arts. An autodidact, he succeeded in becoming a highly respected journalist, editor, and laissez-faire economist who studied the writings of Adam Smith, David Ricardo, and Thomas R. Malthus. Cardozo, a Democrat, was a free trader and an antitariff man. He defended slavery and was convinced that the black's lot as a slave was justifiable. The South, he pointed out, would do well to turn to the textile industry and process the cotton it raised. Rumor had it that he was the father of the black branch of the Cardozos, one of whom, Francis Louis Cardozo, would make his mark in the Reconstruction period.

THE NORTH

Mordecai Manuel Noah was one of the best-known Jewish laymen—North or South—in antebellum days and certainly the most interesting one. He was consul to Tunis, editor of several New York City newspapers, an accomplished belletrist, a Democratic politician, a lawyer (who probably never wrote a brief), a judge, a surveyor of the port of New York, and a sheriff of New York County. According to a contemporary story, a Gentile is reported to have said, "It would be a pity to have a Jew hang a Christian." The retort was, "Fine Christian who has to be hanged." Noah, author of several plays, was a dramatist of some distinction (one of his plays had a "breeches" part for a woman; the plump blonde heroine wore trousers). His heroic melodramas ardently championed freedom and the suppression of tyranny. Noah was an orator of note. The Gentiles rushed to hear him as he always titillated their religious sensibilities. He was the city's outstanding Jewish apologete, often called upon to speak for the Jews. He defended them when they were attacked and edified them when they met as Jews on festive occasions.

Noah's fellow Jews honored him with the presidency of the prestigious Hebrew Benevolent Society. The anti-Jewish prejudice Noah had experienced in public life guaranteed his devotion to the Jewish people. Unusual was his strong and constant commitment to the restoration of a Jewish state—as God had promised. Noah was a political Zionist prepared, at least so he claimed, to build a new state even if it took an army of Jewish volunteers. He wanted a Palestine Jewish common-wealth that would reflect the high ideals of America's Founding Fathers. In this aspiration he was a spiritual ancestor of the twentieth-century Zionist leader Louis D. Brandeis.

"Major" Mordecai Manuel Noah's home was certainly a kosher one. Shearith Israel, his congregation—which never elected him president!—would have denounced him otherwise; observance of kashrut was almost a prerequisite for member-ship. Yet his seven children hung up their stockings on Christmas. The rebirth of the Third Jewish Commonwealth, the State of Israel, nearly a century after his death guarantees that Noah, the Zionist or proto-Zionist, will live on in Jewish history.

Dr. Isaac Hays (1796–1879) of Philadelphia will always occupy a niche in general American history—an honor not accorded Noah. Hays was American Jewry's first physician of scientific caliber. Dr. Daniel Levy Maduro Peixotto (1800–43), who wanted college-trained physicians to be equally at home in the sciences and the fine arts, was a founder of the New York Academy of Medicine. He was certainly not comparable to Hays, since Peixotto was no scientist but a Jewish communal activist. Hays, though no marginal Jew, had other goals and devoted his life to the advancement of the sciences. A pioneer eye and ear surgeon, he edited works on ornithology, botany, physics, and medical terms and projected a large-scale encyclopedia on medicine. His most significant work, which makes his place in American medical history secure, was editing the major medical journals of his day. Hays was asked by his colleagues to write the code of ethics for the American Medical Association that he helped bring to birth. This scientist had come a long way since the time of his Yiddish-speaking immigrant grandfather, Michael Gratz.

5. Jews as Americans

REJECTION: THE DIFFICULTY OF BEING A JEWISH AMERICAN

Between the years 1820 and 1840, more than 750,000 immigrants came to these shores from Europe. In the lands whence they hailed—with the exception of France, Holland, and Belgium—the Jew was deemed inferior. Their Christian upbringing typically predisposed Gentiles to look askance at Jews. They really had no choice: In belles lettres and in the theater the Jew was depicted or portrayed as a saint or a sinner. In Scott's *Ivanhoe*, Rebecca of York was a heroine worth emulating, but a study of the works of fiction in the American Antiquarian Society shows that the Jew was most frequently presented in an unfavorable light. The audience was generally given what it wanted: the Jew as an unsavory character. In 1800, in a Federalist-Jeffersonian political war of words, Solomon Simson, an eminent New Yorker, was depicted as a Shylock. Benjamin Nones, attacked as a bankrupt, a Democrat, and a Jew, retorted that though his family was poor, its members had not been taught to revile Christianity because it was not as ancient as Judaism: I fought in the Revolution to make the United States a liberal democratic republic. I am a Jew, and so were Jesus and his disciples! God, said a New York Christian, had inflicted the plague on the city because Sheriff Noah was a Jew. In 1794 President Washington went to the theater and saw *The Young*

Quaker, in which Shadrach Boaz, the Jew, was a consummate scoundrel. At one time or another some of America's most distinguished citizens—Washington Irving, James Fenimore Cooper, Alexander Hamilton, John Lothrop Motley, and Henry Clay among them—have disparaged or defamed Jews. Many Americans believed that this was a Christian state and that the Jew was not entitled to all the rights and immunities of American citizenship.

The Jews were generally not plagued with too many problems during the Revolution, but in Pennsylvania conservatives and religious leaders made sure that the new state constitution denied the Jews equality. In Georgia, the British governors denounced the Jews as leaders of the local revolutionists, and when the Jews sent their wives and children out of the war zone to neighboring South Carolina, a Charlestonian denounced the Georgians as wartime slackers. In 1813 Noah was appointed consul to Tunis, charged with the special task of redeeming American citizens enslaved by Barbary tyrants. In 1815 he was summarily deprived of his office and left at the mercy of the local authorities. The United States government insisted that he had rescued the wrong men, that his accounts were not in order, and that his religion was an obstacle to the exercise of his consular functions. Noah managed to escape from Tunis and fought for vindication, writing two works in which he reproached the Washington authorities. Using a phrase that George Washington had once employed, Noah accused the state department of having given a "sanction to bigotry." Noah insisted that he had been recalled only because he was a Jew. Noah's Jewish friends—some of them very influential—rallied around him, and Madison and Monroe, embarrassed, hastened to vindicate the hapless consul. Madison was no Jew-hater; Noah was probably the victim of a Washington intrigue. The result of it all was to make Noah a more intense Jew.

Another cause célèbre was the attempt of officers in the United States Navy to drive a Jew out of the service. The man was Uriah Phillips Levy, a cousin of Noah. Levy left home at the age of ten to work as a cabin boy, and before he was twenty was the part owner and captain of a merchant vessel. After playing a heroic role in the War of 1812, he entered the navy as a warrant officer and by 1817 had become a lieutenant. To quote Levy: "to be a Jew as the world now stands is an act of faith that no Christian martyrdom can exceed." He was court-martialed six times, was subject to two courts of inquiry, and survived to become a "commodore," the ranking captain in the navy. Admiring the Jew for his courage, Dom Pedro, the emperor of Brazil, once offered Lieutenant Levy command of a sixty-gun frigate. Levy answered that he "would rather serve as a cabin boy in his own service than as a captain in any other service in the world." As a naval officer, Levy fought to abolish flogging of seamen as a punishment for dereliction of duty, and he was convinced that he was primarily responsible for this reform.

Jews had an impact on the communities where they were firmly ensconced. By the 1790s, just a few years after the adoption of the Constitution, Jews enjoyed equality in every state where they were present in numbers. By 1840 the only states that refused to allow them to hold high office were New Hampshire, Rhode Island, Connecticut, New Jersey, and North Carolina, all of which sheltered few Jews. New Hampshire in that generation probably had fewer than a dozen Jewish souls. Its 1784 constitution had mandated that "No subject shall be hurt, molested, or restrained in his person, liberty, or estate

. . . for his religious profession" and then proceeded with almost typical cant to limit the rights of Catholics and Jews; full privileges were reserved for Protestants. Christians often enough looked at Jews through the spectacles of a hostile tradition. The excesses of the French Revolution frightened many; liberalism was deemed dangerous; the Second Great Awakening and revivalism were proving influential; many Christians were convinced that the best citizen was a white Anglo-Saxon Protestant. The adoption of the Constitution was very nearly the first step in the political emancipation of Jews, Catholics, and other nonconformists.

A Thanksgiving Day had been celebrated by the Pilgrim fathers after the first harvest. Later presidents, governors, and municipal authorities often asked the people to assemble in their churches and thank God for the past year's blessings. Not infrequently, governors addressed themselves to the Christian citizenry only, forgetting that there were also Jews in the state. When reproached, the governors nearly always excused themselves graciously. Governor James H. Hammond of South Carolina was a notable exception. When Jews objected to his invitation to assemble and worship God and His son Jesus Christ, the Redeemer of the World, he replied that this was a Christian country and that the ancestors of the Jews had persecuted Jesus.

From the fourth century on in Europe, wherever there was a Christian community, there were laws governing the Lord's Day, Sunday. Some of these laws had the effect of disabling Jews economically. Dutch and English Christian immigrants to North America carried their Sunday laws along with them when they packed their impedimenta. In 1655

Abraham de Lucena of New Amsterdam was threatened with a huge fine because he had kept his business open during the sermon. For Christians the Sunday law was quite simple—if illogical: God said in the Ten Commandments, "Remember the Sabbath day to keep it holy" (Exodus 20:8). For Jews, of course, the Sabbath was Saturday. The Christians arbitrarily decreed that the Sabbath was not Saturday but the Lord's (Jesus') Day, despite the fact that the Lord Jesus—a Jew—had rested on Saturday. Pious Christians in the early nineteenth century favored Sunday laws to force everyone to keep shops closed and to induce the masses to go to church. Many among them demanded that no mail be forwarded on the Lord's Day, and by 1850 some forty railroad companies controlling four thousand miles of roads had agreed not to move their mail cars on that day. Southern Christians were annoyed when Jews kept their shops open on the first day of the week, Sunday, so that the slaves—then on their free time—could go to the "Jew store" for their modest purchases. If they had no money, they could—would?—steal something from their masters, argued some of the slaveholders. The children of Abraham were to have trouble with the restrictive Sunday laws well into the late twentieth century.

Christianity, an evangelical faith, offered "salvation" and "eternal life" to all who believed in the saving power and grace of Jesus Christ who had instructed his disciples: "Go ye into all the world and preach the gospel to every creature" (Mark 16:15). It was imperative that Jews, "the cousins of our Lord," accept Christianity. Thus far they had refused to recognize Jesus, but once they had been converted, no one could maintain that the origins of Christianity were shrouded in myth; the converted Jew vouched for its historicity. In 1820, with the aid of Joseph Samuel Frederick Frey (né Levi), a learned autodidact and a Jewish convert to Christianity, the American Society for Ameliorating the Condition of the Jews was founded. It grew rapidly. Dozens of cells were established in cities, villages, and hamlets, bringing a glow of pride to the devout, convinced that they were speeding the coming of the millennium. The records indicate that American Christians of Jewish birth were not all of one piece. Some were scholars who thought Christian credentials would be helpful to their careers; others were sincerely devoted to their new faith; still others were persons of dubious character and conduct. Individual missionaries of Jewish origin attacked Judaism and questioned its spiritual quality. Loyal Jews were indignant: Had their martyrs, many thousands of them over the centuries, all died in vain? Jewish polemicists and apologetes were kept busy answering the missionaries. The drive to make the United States a juridically Christian country frightened the Jews, for if the church became established, Jews would become second-class citizens. Actually, these Christian propagandists did not wish to destroy Jews. They yearned to embrace them, to convert them, to hug them to death. If Jews would all become proselytes, a great problem for Christianity would be solved: There would be no Jews and no Judaism.

Rejection? The 1830s and 1840s saw Christians turning against Christians—burning a convent school in Boston, destroying churches in Philadelphia, murdering dozens of fellow Christians, driving the Mormons into the desert, denigrating the Freemasons, and dragging the abolitionist preacher William Lloyd Garrison through the streets with a rope around his neck. Rejection? Nothing like this happened to Jews in America—and they knew it.

ACCEPTANCE: ACCULTURATION AND ASSIMILATION

Jews accepted America wholeheartedly. This was their home, God's country. Many were third- and fourth-generation Americans. In the larger towns where they had built synagogues, they enjoyed all rights and immunities. Jews here were happy and grateful. When the British ravaged northwestern New York during the War of 1812 and appeals were made for funds, New York City's Jewry—maybe one-half of 1 percent of all the townspeople—contributed 9 percent of all the money raised. America was good to its Jews. Moses Michael Hays of Boston was to become grand master of the Masonic grand lodge of Massachusetts (Paul Revere was his deputy). When in 1788 Philadelphia's synagogue could not pay its mortgage, it appealed to the town's notable Gentile leaders, certain that "enlightened citizens . . . will subscribe generously towards the preservation of a religious house of worship." Samuel Delucena Ingham, Andrew Jackson's secretary of the treasury, was named after a Jew. In 1816 a Christian writer saw no reason why a Jew could not someday be elected president of the United States.

Jews were perfervid regionalists. In the 1830s, when the Southerners furiously fought tariff protectionism and some threatened to secede, two of the four Jewish state legislators in South Carolina sided with the states' rights element; the other two were Unionists. Jews also were eager to conform, and no matter the area of settlement or the intensity of their Americanism, they evinced a taste for American names. Here are a few samples from Charleston: Lewis, Morris, Pool, Simpson, Waterman.

Acculturation, the desire of Jews to be one with their fellow citizens, offered a dangerous challenge. The line between acculturation and assimilation is often invisible. (Assimilation, as interpreted by Zionists, is defection.) Acculturation was often accompanied by dejudaization and apathy. The big outside world seemed more appealing than the particularistic small Jewish one. There were times in the 1820s when Shearith Israel of New York City—often spoken of as the "mother synagogue" of America—could not muster a quorum of ten for a religious service. Some Jewish rationalists, deists or atheists, refused to affiliate with a synagogue. Parents on occasion refused to circumcise their sons, believing like a contemporary European rabbi that it was "a bloody barbaric rite." Because there were not enough cultured American Jewish women to go around and because proselytization was frowned upon, individual upper-class men were confronted with a dilemma: remain single, maintain a liaison with a Gentile woman, or marry out of the faith. Five sons and daughters of the devout Jacob Mordecai, the North Carolina educator, married Christians, most of them during his lifetime. Michael Gratz had five sons, and all remained single or intermarried. Ben Gratz of Lexington, Kentucky, married out twice and reared a Christian family, though he himself remained Jewish and even, to a degree, observant. When he died, the family imported a rabbi from Cincinnati for the burial service. There were only two Jews at the funeral, the corpse and the rabbi.

And then there is the complete defector. Alexander Bryan Johnson (1786/87–1867) was a child of rabbinic stock who hid his Jewish origin. This able man became a banker, married the granddaughter of John Adams, attended church, and wrote authoritative works on finance and the philosophy of language.

THE REFORMED SOCIETY OF ISRAELITES, 1824–40: AN AMERICAN FORM OF JUDAISM?

Ferment in matters religious was characteristic of the early United States. Moses Hart, a Canadian who frequently visited the United States, published a substantial brochure advocating a world religion for Jews, Christians, and Moslems. His church was a hodgepodge of rituals influenced in part by cultic innovations associated with the French Revolution. Calling his new system General Universal Religion (1815), he elected to remain Jewish. From 1818 on, several cultured American Jewish notables came forward with radical religious proposals, though their impact was negligible. During the long High Holy Day services in Wilmington, North Carolina, in 1821, women were co-opted to help read prayers, probably in English. Charleston Jewry, the country's most cultured Jewish community, was exposed to forces that were to influence it religiously: deism, the French Enlightenment, Unitarianism, the Jewish Reform movement in Germany. Sectarianism in American Protestantism was a paradigm for Jews seeking religious changes. Repelled as dissidents by the traditionalist synagogue, a group of young intellectuals in Charleston created the Reformed Society of Israelites for Promoting True Principles of Judaism. The established congregation was too cautious at the time to make concessions to modernity: "Touch not a cobweb in St. Paul's lest you shake the dome." The new "Reformed" organization was in effect a *kultusverein*, a socioreligious conventicle, a youth group in the guise of a congregation. This was a reformation in the Lutheran mode, a break with nearly two thousand years of traditional religion, what its leaders were pleased to call "bigotry" and "priestcraft." What was its rationale? Its champions wanted to cope with apathy by meeting the challenge of American culture. Had not Jefferson written that Jews must keep pace with the advance of time? The Charleston conventicle was an attempt to synthesize Americanism and Judaism. The society was to offer a new faith, not only for Jews here but also for those in distant lands. But what in their eyes was wrong with traditional Judaism? The worship service was exotic, alien, noneducational, unintelligible, and long; there was too little English and too much Hebrew. There must be no swaying of the body during prayer, no hawking of synagogue honors in Judeo-Spanish. What will the Gentiles think of us!

The society's outstanding leaders were Isaac Harby (1788–1828) and Abraham Moïse (1799–1869). Harby may have been chosen the leader since he was one of the older members (individuals could join at the age of seventeen). Harby, a wunderkind, was an educator, journalist, dramatist, critic, and litterateur of pronounced ability. Moïse would become a politician, a magistrate; he was highly competent and, it seems, led the organization after Harby's early death. No one in the group was knowledgeable enough Jewishly to create a new Jewish movement, and the society's rational approach reflects adolescence in judgment, if not in years. The members were ready to reject two thousand years of rabbinical teaching, remove their hats, and opt for art music, a short service, less Hebrew, more English, and a sermon. Finally, after much discussion, they published an English prayer book.

The society met annually to listen to an inspirational address, but it is difficult to determine how often it met for worship services. The members hoped to build a "temple" but lacked the means. Like the Protestants, they turned to the Bible—not the Talmud—as the prime source of their faith.

They rejected the traditional hope of return to Palestine; the United States was their Promised Land. They emphasized ethics and morals, the oneness of all humanity. This was full-blown classical Reform without benefit of evolution. The Reformed Society was welcomed by many but soon proved a failure. Its leaders, who gave it but a lick and a promise, had not filled their bellies with Jewish learning. They shaped no rich ceremonial, no pageantry, no warmth. Their new Judaism could not survive without a full-time officiant.

Still, their viewpoint was to make itself felt in Charleston. There were liberals in the traditional congregation, and some changes in worship practice could not be impeded. In 1836 Beth Elohim congregation appointed Gustavus Poznanski its new minister. He was not averse to certain reforms: The auctioning of honors in the synagogue was abandoned, there was no longer any objection to a sermon in English, and the congregation voted to install an organ in the new synagogue under construction. This last was a radical move to the left, but former stalwarts in the defunct Reformed Society of Israelites were now active members of the old congregation. At the dedication of the synagogue in 1841, Reverend Poznanski, in a moment of magniloquent euphoria, declared: "This synagogue is our *temple*; this city our *Jerusalem*; this happy land our *Palestine*." His religiopatriotic outburst was a genuflection in the direction of the Christian guests. (Poznanski was no flaming religious liberal.) The congregation was now definitely reformist, with a choir, an English sermon, and even an occasional prayer in the vernacular. The traditional prayer book was retained, however, since ideologically Beth Elohim had inched only a millimeter to the left. A few years later Reform congregations were founded in Baltimore and New York City. Did the Charleston "reforms"

87

solve the problem of religious apathy? In no sense. The Jew's prime loyalty, after all, was to America's attractive culture. That was what commanded his undeviating devotion.

Even so, Isaac Leeser, initiating something of an Orthodox counterreformation, began preaching his brand of modern Orthodoxy in 1830. Noah in New York told Shearith Israel—the bulwark of Conservatism—that modern music, an English address, and minor changes were necessary. A measure of acculturation was inevitably the norm even in the most traditionalist circles.

KLAL YISRAEL: KINSHIP AT HOME AND ABROAD

Despite the rejection of rabbinic teachings by the Reformed Society of Israelites, the Charleston radicals never divorced themselves empathetically from their fellow Jews. They, like Jews in general, retained an all-encompassing sense of kinship, what in Hebrew is known as *klal Yisrael*, the oneness of Jewry. When Solomon Simson reached out to India and China, he was not interested merely in making an extra dollar; the Indian and Chinese Jews were his own flesh and blood. This concept of *klal Yisrael* is shot through with ambivalence: Jews in the United States knew they were one, knew that they were a national community. They responded when called upon by other Jews, but they refused to establish an overall national body. There was too much likelihood of such a body becoming an authoritarian organization, and they were determined never to submit to any form of regimentation. When George Washington was inaugurated in 1789, two of the six Jewish synagogue communities wrote individual letters of congratulation to him, refusing to join the other four synagogues that had cooperated to write as one in wishing Washington well. American Jewry balked at any form of all-inclusive organization, although actually they were always a national community by consensus. When, in the 1830s, European Jews asked their coreligionists here to raise money for impoverished Palestine, the Americans readily agreed, but the new multicity Society for the Offerings of the Sanctuary, Hebrah Terumat ha-Kodesh, died after two decades. The concept of *klal Yisrael* operated best then as it does now—in moments of crisis.

In 1840 a Franciscan monk disappeared in Egyptian-ruled Damascus, and a Jew-hating American consul said that he had been killed by the Jews who wanted to use his blood for the Passover. Ritual murder accusations had caused the death of many innocent Jews throughout the ages. A number of Damascus Jews were arrested, and one was tortured to death. The civilized world, shocked, raised its voice in protest. The British, for political and humanitarian reasons, intervened to save the imprisoned. The Americans, shaken by this recrudescence of medievalism, followed the British lead. Pressured by the European powers, the Egyptians finally released the unfortunate Damascenes. Working together nationally, American Jewry—if somewhat belatedly—organized protest meetings in most large cities, but Shearith Israel, the oldest and most prestigious congregation in the country, refused officially to take any action. It would not allow New York Jewry to stage its meetings in the synagogue, insisting that, "No benefits can rise from such a course." By this act of refusal, the Sephardic Jewish leaders symbolically abdicated their moral leadership. They had run their course in this country, and the Ashkenazim, a majority group ever since the 1720s, were now to exercise spiritual hegemony over American Jewry.

From 1655 to 1801—146 years—there were only seven synagogue communities in all of North America. From 1801 to 1840—39 years—sixteen new synagogues opened their doors. All were, or soon became, Ashkenazic. These central and east Europeans newcomers were determined to be on their own ritually and socially, too.

Part III
The Dominance of the German Jews: 1840–1924

Introduction

By the late 1830s, somewhere between ten and fifteen thousand Jews lived in the United States. The vast majority were Ashkenazim, "Germans" and "east Europeans." Emigration from the German lands picked up about the year 1837, and by 1881 possibly more than one hundred thousand German Jews had emigrated for political and, primarily, economic reasons. Anti-Jewish prejudice was never absent in German-speaking territories. An obscure German Gentile pamphleteer, Hartwig Hundt, wrote that killing a Jew should be deemed a misdemeanor, not a crime. Jews suffered disabilities in many central European lands. There were widespread anti-Jewish riots in 1819. The Austrian authorities made Giacomo Meyerbeer, the Jewish composer, a "cavalier" when they invited him to conduct opera in Vienna. They knew that if they taxed him as a "Jew" when he entered Vienna he would not come.

A handful of the newcomers debarked at New Orleans and went up the Mississippi as far as Natchez. Some landed at Baltimore and went west on the National Pike. Many landed in Philadelphia, crossed the mountains to the Ohio River, and then moved on into the American heartland by water. Most Jewish immigrants, however, chose New York as their port of entry; the Erie Canal opened all of America to them. Many were artisans, though a few—like Dr. Abraham Jacobi, an 1848 revolutionary and the father of modern pediatric medicine—were professionals. Ultimately most of these western argonauts turned to trade: They were peddlers, apparel shopkeepers, jobbers, and wholesalers. By the 1850s, with the invention of a good sewing machine, some had become garment manufacturers.

6. The Creation of a New Community, 1840–1865

RELIGION AND EDUCATION

Practically all the newcomers were Orthodox religionists, in theory if not in practice. Laxity was the rule here in America where social controls were weak, but there was always a core devoted to Judaism. Hardly a town existed where Jews did not organize a prayer conventicle, since all they needed was ten male coreligionists over thirteen years of age. When they had a little money they hired an all-purpose factotum who served as rabbi, preacher, circumciser, Torah reader, shofar (ram's horn) blower, and dues collector. They were often an uncouth lot: "I do not want to have anything to do with Jews," said the discouraged rabbi Abraham Rice of Baltimore. Most of those who functioned as rabbis were freelances who knew a little Hebrew and took a job as a minister. Albert J. ("Roley") Marks, New Orleans's spiritual leader, is a classic example. When reproached on the High Holy Days for his unrabbinical behavior, he expostulated: "By Jesus Christ! I have a right to pray." In the 1850s and 1860s, however, learned competent rabbis could be found in the larger metropolitan centers: Isaac M. Wise, David Einhorn, Samuel Adler, Samuel Hirsch, Benjamin Szold, and Marcus Jastrow.

A town's rabbinical freelance was often its rebbe, its Hebrew teacher, instructing students privately or in a classroom.

There were also four other types of schools: afternoon, all-day (parochial), private, and Sunday schools. Occasionally the private school—such as the one conducted by Dr. Max Lilienthal in New York City—was a superior institution. Miss Palache of New York opened an academy primarily for girls. At a public examination in 1843 a four-year-old recited the Ten Commandments by heart in Hebrew! Rabbi Julius Eckman of San Francisco was the principal of a private school for youngsters. It was child-centered with its own junior congregation that included three- to five-year-olds. Except for the Sunday schools, which were well patronized by the youngsters, Jewish elementary educational institutions met with indifferent success.

ISAAC LEESER

The outstanding Jewish religious leader in the country was Sephardic Mikveh Israel's Isaac Leeser (1806–68) of Philadelphia. This modern Orthodox minister was determined to embrace America and at the same time to hew to the Orthodox line. To tie all Jews together he published theological apologies, attacks on Christian missionaries to the Jews, a Hebrew reader, English and Hebrew editions of the Sephardic and Ashkenazic prayer books, Hebrew and English Bibles, and ten volumes of sermons. He organized the first Jewish Publication Society and edited the first permanent Jewish magazine, the *Occident* (founded in 1843). Leeser was not always successful in what he set out to accomplish, but it was his schema for American Jews that was finally adopted. This pockmarked, unhappy bachelor, "whom celibacy had worn to the bone," was American Jewry's most important and insightful religious activist in the first half of the century.

SELF-HELP

Originally, in the colonial period, the congregation was the prime if not the sole source of communal aid and support. By the 1840s practically all philanthropies and social service organizations were carried on by separate agencies, and by the late 1850s local philanthropies in Chicago and New York had begun to federate. At first the mutual aid society was the most important. A member who joined and paid dues was guaranteed sick and death benefits, a necessity for newcomers, strangers in a strange land. The outstanding Jewish national insurance agency was the Independent Order of B'nai B'rith (Children of the Covenant), a fraternal order established in 1843. Almost immediately it reached out in many directions to raise the cultural and spiritual niveau of the immigrants. By the beginning of the twentieth century, it had established or supported a semipublic library, orphan asylums, a home for the aged, and a hospital and had begun publishing a national magazine of good quality. It hoped to further a farm movement and found a college. These Children of the Covenant set out deliberately to exercise leadership over the growing American Jewish community, and the fraternity even crossed the Atlantic and set up branch lodges in Europe. The B'nai B'rith avoided the pitfalls of dissension by forbidding religious and political discussion. Once Jews had provided for themselves through mutual aid congeries, they organized benevolent societies to make provision for those who had no means to help themselves. Almost every town in the country sheltered an organization of this type. Hospitals usually were costly to maintain, but they were founded after 1850 in the large cities. For a long decade they served often as hospices, shelters for unmarried sick peddlers, widows and children, itinerants, and the aged. The food was kosher, and there were no missionaries harrying the inmates to become Christian. Gradually, the hospitals introduced antiseptics and installed telephones. The first year's budget (1850s) of Jews' Hospital of New York was $5,500; by the 1990s, as Mount Sinai, its annual expenses ran into the many millions.

Support for all agencies was from dues, fees, and an annual fund-raising ball. People gathered together, danced through the night, gorged themselves with food and strong drink, and then listened to an eloquent plea for funds. By that time they were slightly inebriated and the extractive process was relatively easy. Christian notables often addressed them. When Benjamin H. Brewster, later an attorney general of the United States, spoke to the crowd at a Philadelphia Jewish ball, he told his listeners: "We are mingled together as one brotherhood in a sacred common cause. . . . I am a *Goy*, believe me, gentlemen, still I am cosher." The Jews loved it. In addition to the annual dances, there were concerts, theatrical affairs, strawberry festivals, raffles, and bazaars, all for the sake of charity.

SOCIABILITY, JEWISH CULTURE, AND RECREATION

By the 1850s the social club began to make its appearance in the towns and cities of the country. A newly founded society in a small town might well limit itself to a few potables, a box of cigars, and some card tables. By the late nineteenth century, clubs like the Phoenix in Cincinnati had a multistoried edifice with a huge kitchen, a large dancing hall, and a small theater where plays and musicals could be staged. (The Phoenix Club building still stands; it could not be built today for less than many millions.) Early in the twentieth century the Jewish country clubs, with their tennis courts, swimming pools, and golf links, appeared. When Cincinnati's Jewish country club first surfaced at an abandoned racetrack in the neighboring village of Norwood, a member made the longest drive in golf history. His ball landed in the gondola of a passing freight train, which carried it all the way to New York City!

Jewish literary societies were founded in the 1840s, primarily for young men. Women, at first, were not welcomed except as occasional guests. Later the ladies established their own groups. By the 1850s American Jewish youth had begun employing the name Young Men's Hebrew Association. Obviously this usage was influenced by the Christian YMCAs, but the organizations were dissimilar. The core of the YMCA was religious, Christian, whereas the young Jews who forgathered in the YMHA were interested in sociability and cultural improvement rather than religion. Cards were taboo. The men engaged in debates and the presentation of papers on current topics and problems, and very often the subjects discussed were of general rather than specifically Jewish interest. Plays were staged. By 1913 the hundreds of YMHAs and the few YWHAs had founded an association of their own, the National Council of Young Men's Hebrew and Kindred Associations. They prospered under the umbrella of their patron organization, the Jewish Welfare Board. The YMHAs were in no true sense a youth movement. Though young people wanted to go off by themselves, they treasured the same economic and social goals as their parents who met in the luxury clubs, the Phoenix, the Harmonie, the Concordia, the Standard, and the Mercantile. The largest clubs had library rooms, but they probably weren't as heavily patronized as their card rooms.

The pursuit of Jewish culture was not a major goal of the antebellum Jew. The apologias that were published were directed against Christian missionaries, hated because the conversion of one individual tended to disrupt a family. The German catechisms issued here were often on an adult level; it is hard to conceive that children could have begun to understand them. The prayer books that appeared with facing English or German translations were important: The intelligent enquiring reader would learn what the Hebrew meant. America lacked a single writer of Jewish fiction—in English or in German—who was nationally recognized. Some stories and books had originally been written as newspaper fillers, and the pirating of such material from the general press was common. Leeser's American Jewish Publication Society (1845–51) died because the approximately three thousand families in the United States belonged for the most part to the lower middle class and could not—or would not—pay $1 for an annual subscription to his book club. A second Jewish publication society died aborning in the early 1870s during a long economic depression, but it did produce an English translation of Heinrich Graetz's *History of the Jews*, an instructive volume on the Talmudic period in Jewish history. Leeser's *Occident* reached the remotest villages, where it was often thought a godsend by the one Jew in town. Other Jews were indignant when a copy of his paper was sent them—they did not want to be identified as Jews. Today the *Occident* may be deemed the best available source for antebellum American Jewish life. By 1860 Jewish weeklies and monthlies had begun appearing in a few metropolitan centers. The editors often leaned heavily on the best German Jewish newspapers, and translations from the rabbinical classics were not uncommon. True, there was very little sound Jewish scholarship in the United States before the

1850s, but the editors of all the papers were intelligent and knowledgeable, and these papers supplied much good, sound content. A man or woman who read the *Occident* or the *Asmonean* or the *Israelite* or the *Jewish Messenger* or the German-language *Sinai* was bound to become well-informed. The press was probably the most important instrument tying Jews together and heightening their sense of Jewish identity.

The old-line native-born and the incoming German immigrants had many opportunities to relax in the preradio and pretelevision days. Any Jewish assembly or gathering at a rite of passage served as an occasion for sociability. Whatever the goal or purpose of a communal organization—YMHA, a lodge with a secret handshake and password, ladies' aid, literary society—it also offered companionship and recreation. The masked Purim balls attracted hundreds if not thousands.

There were Jewish social clubs even in the small towns, where the clerks and the petty shopkeepers gathered in a modest rented room. If they could raise enough money they bought a billiard table. Three years after Sherman captured Savannah, the Harmonie Club—Jewish, of course—staged ten balls in one winter. In the big cities, say, in Cincinnati's Phoenix Club, the peddler who had become a wealthy garment manufacturer no longer needed to dream that he "dwelt in marble halls." By the early 1900s, the Jewish country club supplemented the city luncheon and dining clubs. The line between the rich and the less affluent Jews was sharply drawn, but wealth alone was not a guarantee of admittance. Russian Jews, even affluent ones, were not welcomed. "How shameful it is," said the Baltimore Reform rabbi Morris Lazaron, "for descendants of German Jewish peddlers to look down upon the descendants of Russian Jewish tailors."

In the 1920s, federal immigration acts were passed excluding Jewish newcomers. As the entrance of European Jews was cut off, the disparate ethnic elements of American Jews began to fuse. They all met together socially in the Jewish community center, the child and grandchild of the settlement house and the YMHA. The community center was to become the clubhouse of the middle- and lower-middle-class elements in the city and suburb. It was not a "class" or an ethnic preserve but a communal institution where all Jews were welcome.

ACCEPTANCE

As far as we know, all the Jews in the days before the Civil War had faith in the United States. They had it good here, and they knew it. Isaac M. Wise may have despised the whiskey-swilling gun-toting midwestern yokels, but he loved this country. The Jew accepted America, and America accepted the Jew. "The Hebrew persecuted and downtrodden in other regions," said President John Tyler, "takes up his abode among us with no one to make him afraid." In 1841 James Joseph Sylvester, one of Europe's most distinguished mathematicians, became a professor at the University of Virginia. His alma mater, Cambridge University in England, had denied him a post because he was a Jew (later Oxford University removed its restrictions and called him back to England to teach). Considerate Christians often referred to their Jewish friends as Hebrews or Israelites. For the Gentiles, the word "Jew" was nearly always a term of mild denigration. Jews were appointed consuls and diplomats; some went to the House and to the Senate. But in no place did they owe their election to Jewish votes. The Jews were too few in number until the early 1900s, when the New Yorkers began sending fellow Jews to Washington. In 1841, David Levy (Yulee) went to the House of Representatives as a delegate from the territory of Florida; in 1845 he sat in the Senate. (John Quincy Adams refers to him as an alien Jew with a dash of African blood.) Levy was born in the Caribbean Islands, as was Judah Philip Benjamin, whom Louisiana sent to the Senate in 1852. Neither Levy nor Benjamin had any interest in Judaism; Levy, baptized or not, was a believing Christian.

REJECTION

After the thirteen colonies became the thirteen United States of America, Jews were accepted, but acceptance had its limits. Readings from the New Testament were an intrinsic part of the public school curriculum. (The Jew, be it remembered, is the villain in the gospel narratives, where the Jewish priests are depicted as eager to see Jesus condemned and as urging the murder of a good man.) Sunday closing laws were imposed on Jews and Sabbatarians in many states. As late as 1840, three New England states plus New Jersey and North Carolina limited the local political rights of Jews. The Jews of North Carolina were finally emancipated in 1868 during Reconstruction, when freedmen, black and Christian, probably voted to grant Jews full rights. When Jews were finally accorded equality in an 1876–77 New Hampshire constitution, thousands of citizens still voted against permitting the 150 Jews in the state to hold office. This was one hundred years after the Declaration of Independence. In 1855, after some legislative jockeying in which the rights of American Jewish citizens were blatantly ignored, the United States Senate signed a commercial treaty with Switzerland that—however covertly—allowed American Jewish citizens to be denied immunities in some Swiss cantons. The United States was determined to sell its products to Switzerland even if the privileges of some Americans were bypassed. The Jews protested to President Buchanan and held a "national" protest meeting, but it was not till the late 1870s that American Jews were granted full rights in dealing with the Swiss.

American liberties are this country's most important export. American Jews here have always wanted Jews overseas to enjoy the privileges that distinguish this country. Thus it was that the Jews of the United States rose in wrath in the late 1850s when Pope Pius IX accepted the improper but canonically valid baptism of a Jewish child, Edgardo Mortara, of Bologna in the Papal States. Mortara's nurse had secretly baptized him when he was seriously ill to rescue his immortal soul (ca. 1854). In 1858 the pope learned of the baptism and insisted that the six-year-old child be taken from the arms of his parents and reared as a Catholic. The whole world—including some Catholics—protested, but to no avail. Jewish communities in the United States held protest meetings as far west as San Francisco. Again President Buchanan would do nothing; there were only 150,000 Jews in this country as against millions of Catholics who supported their spiritual overlord. Anti-Catholic Protestants joined with the Jews in their protests, but Jews continued to be apprehensive. There were authentic reports of Jewish orphan children in the United States who were taken in to be reared by well-meaning Catholics. With a gleam in his eyes, the popular preacher Raphael J. De Cordova asked his audience whether if his Holiness the Pope were to be carried off violently and circumcised, that would make him a Jew.

The Damascus blood libel accusation and the Swiss and Mortara affairs convinced America's Jews that if they were united into a well-organized national community and spoke as one, they would do more for themselves and world Jewry. Two religious leaders, Leeser of Philadelphia and Samuel Myer Isaacs (1804–78) of New York, pushed for a national Jewish assembly. As early as 1841 Leeser and another local official, Louis Salomon, had asked American Jewry to establish a federal union of congregations with a national board, an ecclesiastical tribunal, and a college to train congregational personnel, and to make a concerted effort to found Jewish schools in every town of size. Even though no congregation was to suffer any impairment of its autonomy, this hierarchical plan had been rejected. (A similar appeal for a national structure in 1848–49 by Isaac M. Wise as leader of the Albany, New York, congregation also found few supporters.) Only in 1859 was the new Board of Delegates of American Israelites (BDAI) able to win the approval of a substantial number of eastern congregations. This national federation had an all-embracing program: It collected statistics on American Jewry, fought efforts of Christians to baptize the American Constitution, maintained relations with Europe's Jewish defense organizations, encouraged Jewish education, opposed efforts to abridge the civil rights and liberties of Jews, and sent relief to communities in Palestine, North Africa and Eastern Europe. The BDAI was constantly hampered by lack of staff and finances. The fees for membership were small, but some congregations neglected to pay them. Leeser went along with the BDAI since it was nominally Orthodox, while Samuel Myer Isaacs was a tower of strength. This native of Holland functioned as New York City's Ashkenazic rabbi. He preached regularly in English, edited the *Jewish Messenger*, helped further a communal charity system, and favored the establishment of an all-day school and Jews' Hospital (Mount

Sinai). His descendants were notable communal and cultural leaders in the city.

SLAVERY AND THE CIVIL WAR

Isaacs was no friend of slavery, though like practically all Jewish officiants he dared not come out publicly as an abolitionist even in the North. Relatively few Americans were outspoken opponents of slavery, and the Jews—still less than 1 percent of the population—were afraid to express themselves. In May 1861, after Fort Sumter had fallen, Rabbi David Einhorn of Baltimore had to leave the city because of his antislavery views. There were a half dozen Jewish men and women who dared attack this peculiar institution of the South. Outstanding among them was the social reformer Ernestine L. S. P. Rose (1810–92), a native of Poland. She was a brilliant speaker, an egalitarian, and a feminist who was listened to with respect when she addressed state legislatures. On January 4, 1861, Rabbi Morris J. Raphall of New York City, a Bible scholar, was asked to speak on "The Bible View of Slavery." It was a national fast day, for the South was about to secede. Slavery was ostensibly the divisive issue, though actually the agrarian South was ready to dissolve the Union because it felt overshadowed by the industrializing North. Raphall was nationally known because of his lectures and an earlier appearance before Congress—the first Jewish clergyman to address that body. In 1860 when he appeared in Congress with skullcap and praying shawl, he was given a reverent hearing; but those journalists who catered to the mob had a field day: "going to pray for ten percent a month [usury]"; next thing you know we'll have "a pawnshop in the basement" of the House. In his 1861 address on slavery, Raphall said that the

Bible sanctioned that institution. Einhorn, Michael Heilprin, and some other Jews attacked him for admitting this, but, objectively speaking, Raphall was right.

Both in the North and the South, Jews flocked to the colors. It has been estimated that in a Jewish population of fewer than two hundred thousand there were about seven thousand in the armies of the North and the South. Many became officers, and several in the Union forces were brevetted as brigadier generals. At first only Christians were permitted to serve as chaplains, but by 1862 any "regularly ordained minister" could serve the troops. The North had two Jewish chaplains; the South had no Jewish chaplain as such but enjoyed the services of Chaplain Charles Goldberg, a convert to Christianity. After the war Goldberg settled in Texarkana, where he ministered to a church and, on occasion, even conducted services for the local Jewish community!

In November 1862 General U. S. Grant issued various orders forbidding Jews to trade in the areas controlled by his troops stationed on the lower Mississippi. On December 17 he issued General Orders No. 11 expelling all Jews from the area under his command. A delegation of Paducah, Kentucky, Jews, "exiles," appealed in person to Lincoln: "And so the Children of Israel were driven from the happy land of Canaan?" "Yes, and that is why we have come to Father Abraham's bosom seeking protection." And this protection they shall have at once, said Lincoln, instructing his General in Chief Henry W. Halleck to revoke G.O. No. 11.

All orders issued from November 1862 to January 1863 by Grant and the Washington War Office betray anti-Jewish prejudice. Why did Grant issue G.O. No. 11? A swarm of speculators, Gentiles and Jews, were buying cotton for the northern mills. Fortunes could be made. Jesse Grant, the general's father, and his Jewish partners were in this trade, though General Grant himself was not involved. It is still a mystery why the Jews were singled out. Someone in authority was looking for a scapegoat or was eager to eliminate Jewish competition in the purchase of cotton. In later years Grant saw fit not to exculpate himself. This Union general was no Jew hater but had Jewish friends and as president evinced concern for the persecuted Israelites in Rumania. He sent a $25 check to a Jew in Jerusalem who was seeking a dowry for his daughter and in 1870 appointed General Edward S. Salomon (Solomon) as governor of Washington Territory. In the very year and month that Grant issued G.O. No. 11, the Seligman brothers, whom he knew well, were selling millions of dollars of American bonds in Europe to help finance the North's war effort.

Individual Jews in the South stood out. In a region where there were about three million slaves, a competent, highly educated Jew could often make a career. David Camden De Leon was the first surgeon general of the armies of the Confederate States of America. Col. Abraham Charles Myers Jr. was the quartermaster general. Mrs. Solomon Cohen of Savannah, the matriarch of the Myers family, could brag that thirty-two of her descendants were fighting for the South. The most brilliant of the southern Jews was Judah P. Benjamin. His friend President Jefferson Davis appointed him attorney general, then secretary of war, and later secretary of state. There were those in the North who referred to him as a Jew with Egyptian principles; there were others, more objective, who thought that he was the brains of the Confederacy. When the war was over, knowing full well that he would be imprisoned, Benjamin fled to England where he became one of the country's most distinguished legal practitioners. Though no official convert to Christianity, he evidently had no interest in Jewry or Judaism. He was less an American Jew than an American of Jewish descent.

In December 1864 and January–February 1865, Mayer Lehman of Montgomery, Alabama, was designated an agent of the state of Alabama to negotiate with General U. S. Grant for permission to send $500,000 worth of cotton through the Union lines to provide for suffering Alabama soldiers in northern stockades. Lehman failed; Grant would not allow the cotton passage through the lines. When a few months later Lee surrendered at Appomattox Courthouse, Lehman knew it would be a generation before the South would rise again. He went on to New York and became a founder of a firm of commodity brokers. Although Mayer Lehman had failed in an attempt to help a few Alabama prisoners, his son, Herbert H. Lehman, as director general of the United States Relief and Rehabilitation Administration in World War II, successfully fed millions of men, women, and children all over the face of war-devastated Europe. When Mayer Lehman settled in New York he was one of many southern Jews who moved North, knowing that their fellow Jews would accept them. The Old South of Charleston, Savannah, and New Orleans thus died as its cultivated Jews were scattered.

During the first two years of the war, immigration to the United States fell off radically, but by 1863 the Europeans again turned to this New World and its beckoning vistas. That year the English-born Samuel Gompers, a lad of thirteen, landed in New York. He was a cigar maker. Years later he helped found the American Federation of Labor, which he presided over for almost forty years. In 1865 Jacob Henry Schiff, a young Orthodox Jew, age eighteen or nineteen, landed. He would after two decades become president of Kuhn, Loeb & Co., the country's largest Jewish banking house. The year before, in 1864, Sigmund Shlesinger had arrived from Hungary, a youngster of sixteen. After a year he went west. Failing to succeed in everything he attempted he volunteered as a scout in a company organized to protect the Kansas-Colorado border. On September 17, 1868, his company was ambushed by hundreds of Cheyenne, Arapaho, and Sioux. The scouts dug in on an island on the Arickaree Fork of the Republican River and held on there for nine days until relieved. Five scouts were killed, and eighteen were injured. During this battle on Beecher's Island, Shlesinger made entries in his diary: "scalpt 3 Indians . . . killt a coyote & ate him all up."

> When the foe charged on the breastworks
> With madness and despair,
> And the bravest souls were tested
> The little Jew was there.

7. Isaac Mayer Wise and the Germans

THE EARLY YEARS OF A SUCCESSFUL REFORMER, 1846–69

The year after the Battle of Beecher's Island, the first transcontinental railroad was finally completed. Two locomotives, one from the East, the other from the West, met face to face on May 10, 1869, at Promontory Point in the territory of Utah. Space and time were in a sense annihilated, and a country cemented together by four years of blood was now reinforced with bands of steel. Isaac Mayer Wise (1819–1900), now a rabbi in Cincinnati, hoped that the time had come to realize his dreams of a united American Jewry. The one-time small-town Bohemian religious factotum had come to this country in 1846. Europe, with its anti-Jewish disabilities, and America, with its economic and political lure, induced him to emigrate. He was very ambitious. When Albany's Orthodox synagogue employed him, he put on a black frock coat and emerged as the Reverend Isaac Mayer Wise (Weiss), D.D. No hireling, he broke with his congregational board in 1850 and created a new synagogue of his own. The liturgical reforms he instituted were not significant, though he no longer believed in the coming of the Messiah or in resurrection; any changes he contemplated would be well within the ambit of traditionalism, he insisted. This devotee of the French Enlightenment, this rather naive rationalist, was no religious radical despite his being fully aware of the teachings of Germany's Jewish reformers. He wanted a union of all of America's Jews, a common Hebrew prayer book, better-prepared rabbis, good schools, and a rabbinical seminary. Above all he was determined to be American Jewry's religious leader. The new "gospel" that would come forth from the American Zion would even have an impact on European Jewry and on Christendom, he hoped. It would be the highest triumph of humanity. No innovative religious reformer, he was an educator, an organizer, a teacher, a leader. Testamentary legatee of the unhappy Leeser, Wise reached some of the goals he had set for himself, founding the Union of American Hebrew Congregations and the Hebrew Union College and the Central Conference of American Rabbis. Wise may be deemed to have succeeded because he was a relentless fighter, a politician who never hesitated to beat a retreat. He was also a loyal friend, a charismatic personality, and a survivor.

In 1854, with his election as rabbi of Cincinnati's Bene Yeshurun, Wise became a national figure. Less than two years later he established English-language and German-language newspapers, the *Israelite* and *Die Deborah*, both designed to win friends and harass enemies. New York and Philadelphia Jews in the 1840s and 1850s talked of building a Jewish college. Wise went ahead and built Zion College (1855) as a secular institution that contemplated adding a Jewish theological faculty (it died after a year and a half for lack of support). The aging Leeser, in the last year of his life (1867), founded Maimonides College in Philadelphia. This rabbinical school also died within a few years for lack of money and a following.

Harvard College had been established in 1636 by a paltry few thousand souls bent on providing themselves with a learned ministry, but nineteenth-century American Jewry, a much larger group than the Puritan New Englanders of 1636, was less devoted. Indifference to Judaism characterized too many Jews in America throughout the century. The very year that Zion College was established, the ever-restless Wise called a national conference of rabbis and laymen to meet in Cleveland and create an overall religious union. The effort proved a dismal failure. United States Jewry could not—even today cannot—be united religiously. Wise at Cleveland stooped to conquer by embracing Orthodoxy but succeeded only in firming up traditionalism and radicalism. He himself was in the middle, a Conservative Jew, more or less.

The Civil War interrupted the religious and cultural development of American Jewry. Wise, a Democrat, was unhappy about the conflict. Cincinnati was a border town that faced the South (Kentucky) and the West (Indiana). The rabbi was an antiabolitionist. He knew that slavery had been abolished in most other lands of the Western Hemisphere and assumed it was only a matter of time before it would disappear in the United States as well. He was opposed to the war, but even he could never have imagined that the total casualties would approximate 780,000. "Silence is our policy" was the title of his antiwar editorial.

When in 1869 the German university-trained rabbis in America called a conference in Philadelphia, Wise joined them reluctantly. They had stolen a march on him; *he* had intended to call such a meeting. These radicals broke with Orthodoxy in explicitly rejecting the return to Palestine. Israel's mission was to win the entire world for prophetic ideals, and worship had to be in a language that people understood: Stress the vernacular! The Reformers were eager to improve the religious status of women as well, but these intellectuals did not succeed in fashioning a rounded-out program for a liberal Judaism. Why not? These pundits—brilliant, learned, and aggressively liberal as they were—were talkers, not doers.

The Union of American Hebrew Congregations (UAHC), for which Wise had campaigned over the course of a generation, came to birth in 1873. Its emergence at that time was the work primarily of dedicated Cincinnati laymen. Wise had made many enemies. His laymen were conservative, closer to tradition, and now they took over. Wise was never to control the new union; its lay leaders never forgot that their rabbi was their employee. The union was not at first an overtly Reform institution and included a number of Orthodox congregations. It set out to further elementary religious schools and to establish a seminary. Each congregation was to remain fully autonomous. Success was immediate. The UAHC began with twenty-eight synagogues in 1873; by 1900 about one hundred had become members.

Wise was more successful in controlling the destinies of the Hebrew Union College (HUC) when it opened its doors on October 4, 1875. HUC might have been called the Jewish Union College, but for many in the 1870s "Jew" was still a dirty word. Hebrew was biblical and more *raffiné*. The school's initial class numbered thirteen youngsters who were expected to study for eight years. Before the month ended, Julia Ettlinger, too, was admitted. She was eleven years old and was in the seventh grade of the public school. The students first met in the vestry rooms, that is, the cellar, of the Mound Street Temple. Because this was a college, it needed a library (the books were locked up every night in a small wooden box to protect them from the mice that ventured forth from the panels). By the 1990s HUC and its affiliates had ordained well over a thousand men and women who ministered to congregants on every continent; the sun never sets on a graduate of the Hebrew Union College! The college would ultimately become the heart of the largest liberal religious movement in the world. It was an American school that set out to foster an American type of religion, yet its founders insisted that it was rooted in rabbinic and biblical tradition. Reform, they believed, was an inevitable historical development of their ancestral faith.

THE GOLDEN AGE OF REFORM, THE 1870s

The new movement had reached its height, its zenith, if you will, by the year 1880. In 1878 the Board of Delegates of American Israelites and the Union of American Hebrew Congregations coalesced. By this act many eastern synagogues joined the UAHC and became an integral part of the expanding religious organization. Why did the Easterners join the Midwest-headquartered union? One can only guess. It may well be that the Easterners, mainly central European in origin, saw the East Europeans debarking in substantial numbers and suspected—correctly—that they themselves would be ultimately overwhelmed. The East Coast traditionalists felt they had little in common with the Polish and Russian Jews and much more in common ethnically and socially with the men and women of the union. The old Board of Delegates of American Israelites now became the new Board of Delegates on Civil and Religious Rights (BDCRR), the defense arm of the union seeking to carry on the work that, prior to the merger, had characterized it since its founding two decades earlier. Before very long, the BDCRR had become a one-man Washington lobby headed by Simon

Wolf (1836–1923). Early in the twentieth century some of New York's Jewish elitists tended to sneer at Wolf's efforts, but he was a devoted Jew and a Republican stalwart who had an entree in government circles. *Shetadlan* (mediator, go-between) Wolf was highly respected and often successful. He represented the union and the Independent Order of B'nai B'rith, American Jewry's two great nineteenth-century organizations. The Gentile politicians counted votes! Though the augmented UAHC of 1878 included eastern as well as southern and western synagogues, it never dominated United States Jewish religionists. Of the 278 established congregations in the country in the late 1870s, only 118 were members of the union (there were also dozens of East European conventicles that were never even counted).

The Reformers, confronting a Jewish tradition that was two thousand years old, struggled to find themselves in modern America. They tried to unite all Reformers. Wise pushed his *Minhag America* (the American synagogue ritual), but other notables wrote their own prayer books. Wise hewed to the standard moderate Reform line: In his book he rejected the concepts of a personal Messiah, resurrection, the restoration of the Palestinian state, the temple cult, and the sacrificial system. His patchwork prayer book, almost all in Hebrew, emphasizing immortality and universalism, managed to win many friends. Reform congregations were of two types: evolving Reform and immediate Reform. The Saturday service could not be saved—the Jewish community was in the main a business community, and Saturday was the big business day of the week—but Friday night took its place. It was a pragmatic change. Some congregations attempted to introduce Sunday services, but they were never popular. However there were some successful Sunday lectures in the big cities, and hundreds, among them many liberal-minded Christians, turned out to listen and to be influenced by what they heard. Congregations introduced the organ and hired choir singers—many of them Gentiles—while women came down from the gallery to sit with their husbands and sons in family pews. The once centrally located reading desk became repositioned and associated with the altar. Confirmation was introduced as a substitute for the medieval bar mitzvah ceremony. Hats were removed to approximate a Christian style of reverence. The Protestant church influence is obvious. Decades passed before all these changes were complete. Meanwhile, unhappy members left and joined or created Orthodox and Conservative congregations. The Conservatives, after all, had begun building a religious world of their own long before the Jewish Theological Seminary opened its doors in New York in 1887.

The census initiated in the late 1870s by the Board of Delegates of American Israelites, before it was merged with the Union of American Hebrew Congregations, was published in 1880 and presumably included all of American Jewry. It found two homes for the aged, four large fraternal orders with female auxiliaries, five hospice-hospitals, at least six orphan asylums, seventeen periodicals (one was German and one was Yiddish), and at least twenty-five literary societies and YMHAs. Apparently no effort was made to count East European immigrant prayer groups.

American Jewry was still predominantly Orthodox and Conservative. Though in the minority, the Reformers were convinced—because of their impressive national organizations— that they ruled the roost. On July 11, 1883, they met in Cincinnati for a threefold celebration: The first class of the Hebrew

117

Union College was graduating; the national Rabbinical Literary Association was meeting; and the union was now ten years old. A great banquet was staged in the Highland House on Mt. Adams. The men were completely at ease in this American Zion, and the women glowed. Gus Lindeman, a Jewish caterer, did himself proud. There were seven different alcoholic potables and three varieties of unkosher shellfish, to say nothing of (equally unkosher) frogs' legs. (Since this was a Jewish banquet there were, of course, no pork products!) When the forbidden shellfish and frogs legs were served at this Terefah (unclean) Banquet, as it would come to be called, only two rabbis walked out; others simply pushed the "unclean" tidbits aside. But the eastern traditionalists were angry. The union—a neutral religious organization—had ignored their sensitivities. The details of this banquet were published by a young woman, a stringer for New York's Conservative *Jewish Messenger*, who signed herself Sulamith. Her name was Henrietta Szold.

THE PITTSBURGH PLATFORM, 1885

As the 1883 banquet demonstrated, the Reformers were very sure of themselves. Apparently conditions changed radically two years later. When Dr. Alexander Kohut, a Hungarian rabbi, settled in New York—no American Jewish minister was more scholarly, more respected—one of his first official acts was to fire a broadside at the Reformers. Kaufmann Kohler (1843–1926) fired back: We are moving forward, not backward. But Kohler hastened to invite his colleagues to meet him in Pittsburgh. He sniffed a new wind. The East Europeans pouring into the country would inevitably push all of American Jews to the right religiously. The radical Pittsburgh Platform, now promulgated, showed that the Reform leaders were on the defensive and were consolidating their gains. Did they also want to tell the world that they were a different breed? That they were not to be identified with the East European immigrants?

In brief, the radicals assembled in Pittsburgh told the world, Jews and Gentiles alike: Christianity and Islam are sister religions that merit our respect; Judaism and science are congruent; moral law is more important than canon law; rituals must be retained only if they have ethical value; we Jews are not a nation and do not look forward to a Messiah to bring us back to a reborn state in Palestine; our mission is not to return to our ancient homeland but to teach the world to accept our ethical truths; we reject the (unscientific) concept of resurrection; we believe in the (equally unscientific) immortality of the soul; we will not surrender the Sabbath but have no objection to a Sunday service; it is time that we, too, confronted the evils of modern society by working for social justice. In essence, these radical Jewish evangelists urged both Jews and Gentiles to accept their liberal gospel.

The Pittsburgh program met with a mixed reception. Some southern rabbis ignored it. The Union of American Hebrew Congregations said that the rabbis who had met in Pittsburgh did not speak for its members. Wise, who had initially hailed the platform as a "Declaration of Independence," hurriedly issued a somewhat equivocal statement. Thus the Reform body politic did not embrace this new Torah, and the liberal rabbis did not meet again as planned in 1886. A few leaders among the non-Reform majority decided that the time had come to organize an anti-Reform movement and Conservative Judaism thus came to birth in a formal way, although as I have indicated, Conservative roots go back to 1841, when

Leeser and his friends called for a nationally structured American Jewry both traditional and modernistic. Most established Orthodox congregations were already inching to the left; America's cultural impact would not be denied. Embryonic Conservatives, a growing body, were receptive to the appeal of modern American culture but equally determined to hold on to the traditions and practices that had been sanctified by time. Philadelphia and New York Jews had been pushing for a rabbinical academy or college for decade (Maimonides College had closed by 1873). The Reform tendencies of the Union of American Hebrew Congregations and its Cincinnati seminary and the radicalism of the clergy who met in Pittsburgh in 1885 induced many to believe that it was time to establish a college that would train rabbis committed to time-honored Jewish beliefs and practices.

A year after the adoption of the Pittsburgh Platform, the first Conservative institution came into being, the Jewish Theological Seminary Association of America. The name stems from the Jewish seminary in Breslau, itself a fusion of venerable traditions and the new science of Judaism. The American leaders of the New York school were Rabbi Sabato Morais (1823–97) of Philadelphia and a group of sympathetic New York clergy and laymen. The seminary opened its doors in New York City in January 1887 in the vestry rooms of Shearith Israel. The seminary was clearly entrenched in Orthodoxy. Morais, the new head of its faculty, commuted from Philadelphia, where he remained the hazzan of Mikveh Israel, once Leeser's congregation. But the new college did not have a union of congregations to finance it and was moribund by 1902.

THE CENTRAL CONFERENCE OF AMERICAN RABBIS, THE BREAK WITH TRADITION, AND ANTI-ZIONISM, 1889–1900

When the Jewish Theological Seminary opened its doors, Wise realized that his hopes for an American Jewry cemented by a common approach to Judaism were unrealistic. Two years later, in 1889, he organized the Central Conference of American Rabbis (CCAR). The name was intended as a geographical reference, since the South had a rabbinical body that met occasionally in New Orleans and New York City had a metropolitan rabbinical association. Wise was able to establish a national rabbinical association of his own because he had a loyal core in the graduates of his seminary. He imposed no credo, even though the new body was implicitly revisionist, if not liberal. The CCAR was immediately successful. Every member could maintain his religious autonomy. Consensus was secured through the passage of resolutions. The adoption in 1892–93 of the two-volume *Union Prayer Book*—more reflective of a radical Reform stance than Wise's *Minhag America* had ever been— served as a bond to tie together practically all Reform Jews. The use of this new prayer book stopped the constant move to the left, and in a very few years this Reform "Book of Common Prayer" was introduced in about 150 synagogues. The leftists in the CCAR pushed the association to distance itself from halakah, tradition, canon law. In 1895 the members declared unequivocally that no past rabbinical work or code is the Word of God, that the body of rabbinic legislation had no absolute or binding authority. And the Bible? The Reform rabbis of the CCAR were prepared to reject it, too, as a divine work, though they stood mute. The O.M. (Old Man) was still alive, and Wise *knew* that God Himself had handed the Ten Commandments to Moses.

In 1896 the Viennese journalist Theodor Herzl published a pamphlet, *Der Judenstaat* (A State for Jews), in which he called on world Jewry to build a new homeland. The Western world, he believed, was not ready to accept Jews as equal citizens. Herzl's proposal caught on like wildfire, and political Zionism was born. The very next year, when the Reform rabbis met in conference at Montreal, Isaac M. Wise, the CCAR president, vigorously attacked the new Zionist movement. Why? Wise and the majority of the members—immigrants—had come from lands where Jews suffered abuse. America had welcomed them and offered them equality. Since America was open to all Jews, to work for the establishment overseas of a new haven for Jews was, they convinced themselves, almost treason to this country. The Gentiles would look upon us with suspicion! Wise, almost frantic, said that Zionism was "a prostitution of Israel's holy cause . . . a mad man's dance." The conference concurred.

8. The German Jewish Community Comes of Age, 1865–1924

POLITICS, OFFICES, AND WORLD WAR I

The central Europeans who started arriving in the late 1830s spent their energy becoming rooted and making a living. Later, after they and their sons were established, some turned to politics. They were solid citizens, responsible and trustworthy. There was hardly a state where they did not serve in the town councils as mayors and legislators. By 1924 America's Jews numbered about 3,500,000. They were city folk; they voted; they had influence. They went to Congress or became governors. By 1906 Oscar S. Straus was sitting in Theodore Roosevelt's cabinet as secretary of commerce and labor. In 1916 Louis D. Brandeis donned the robe of an associate justice of the United States Supreme Court. Ever since the Civil War many Jews had voted the Republican ticket, but after Woodrow Wilson was elected in 1913, most seem to have turned to the Democrats and remained loyal to this more liberal party throughout the twentieth century.

Simon Sterne (1839–1901), a lawyer, was typical of those individuals who were concerned with good government. In 1870 he was secretary of New York's Committee of Seventy, which succeeded in unseating Boss Tweed. In 1887 Sterne helped write the Interstate Commerce Act in an effort to limit the evils of unfair railroad practices. A generation later, in the 1920s, Belle L. I. Moskowitz (1877–1933) served as an aide to Governor Alfred E. Smith of New York, advising him in matters touching on housing, labor, and public relations; the well-being of the people was her concern. Whether Republicans, Democrats, or Socialists, practically all Jews were opposed to the restrictive literacy and immigration bills proposed in Congress in the early twentieth century. They fought a delaying action, keeping the portals open to hundreds of thousands of Jewish émigrés who otherwise would have been doomed to discrimination or worse in the post–World War I succession states as well as in Russia and Rumania.

Anticipating entry into World War I, the United States government appointed a Council of National Defense in 1916 to prepare the country for war. The seven civilians of its Advisory Commission were the wheelhorses who did the actual work of utilizing the country's resources to their fullest. Three of the seven were Jews: Samuel Gompers was a labor leader; Julius Rosenwald provided mercantile goods of every description; Bernard M. Baruch (1870–1965) performed yeoman service supplying raw materials. When it was imperative that all the resources of the country be mobilized, Baruch was appointed chairman of the War Industries Board in 1918 with almost dictatorial powers. He did a good job but made enemies—some powerful industrialists had to be whipped into line if the war was to be won.

In World War I some thirty-five hundred Jews were killed in action. Among them was Sergeant William Sawelson, posthumously awarded the Congressional Medal of Honor. Here is the official citation:

William Sawelson

Rank and organization: Sergeant, Company M. 312th Infantry, 78th Division. *Place and date:* At Grand-Pre, France, 26 October 1918. *Entered service at:* Harrison, N.J. *Birth:* Newark, N.J. G.O. No.: 16, W.D., 1919. *Citation:* Hearing a wounded man in a shell hole some distance away calling for water, Sergeant Sawelson, upon his own initiative, left shelter and crawled through heavy machine-gun fire to where the man lay, giving him what water he had in his canteen. He then went back to his own shell hole, obtained more water, and was returning to the wounded man when he was killed by a machine-gun bullet.

It is estimated that two hundred thousand Jews served in the armed forces. More than eight thousand were commissioned officers, and many were colonels. Strange to say, not one who saw battlefield service in Europe reached the rank of general during the actual conflict. Charles Henry Lauchheimer (1859–1920) of the Marine Corps, an administrator, was appointed a brigadier general in 1916. Joseph Strauss (1861–1948) was commissioned a rear admiral in 1918. The Jews had come a long way since colonial days when commissions in the armed forces were reserved for Christians only.

JEWISH EDUCATION AND CULTURE

The Emergence of America as a Jewish Cultural Center

The line between Jewish education and Jewish culture is an invisible one. Educational activities were reinforced by a host of cultural agencies, among them the home, synagogue, brotherhoods and sisterhoods, schools, teacher training congeries, colleges, yeshivot where Talmud was taught, libraries, rabbinical associations, a bureau for demographic research, a social workers' organization—which published the *Jewish Social Service Quarterly*—a farm school, fraternal orders, a national Hebrew-speaking group, the intercollegiate Menorah Association (1913), and the Hillel Foundations (1923). The Menorah movement came to birth in 1906 at Harvard to further Hebraic culture and ideals among Jews on the campus. Its later rival, the Hillel Foundations, was devoted to Judaism, culture, and the social needs of the undergraduates. In 1915 Henry Hurwitz, the Menorah chancellor, began to publish the *Menorah Journal*, which soon became the country's finest Jewish cultural periodical, for it opened new worlds of art and literature to campus youth. There were many American Jewish artists and musicians, but very few painters and sculptors employed Jewish themes. The Jewish Theological Seminary did encourage traditional liturgical music, and the Reformers continued to sing the works of Europe's great Jewish composers. Occasionally individuals, seeking a setting for the prayers, would employ "Oriental" modes (the Oriental was equated with the Jew).

From the aspect of cultural impact the press was most important. In 1925 there were about one hundred periodicals published in English, German, Yiddish, Judeo-Spanish, and Hebrew, including several children's and youth magazines. In 1879 Rosa Sonneschein organized a woman's literary society in St. Louis. In the middle 1890s she began to edit the *American Jewess*, which emphasized literary, social, and religious themes. She kept it alive for about five years. American Jews, both men and women, had an itch to write. There were hundreds if not thousands interested in belles lettres, though few if any were writers of distinction when they turned to poetry and fiction.

Emma Lazarus's sonnet "The New Colossus"—an ode to America as an immigrant haven—is a notable exception in its generation. Isaac M. Wise wrote dozens of German poems and eleven English and sixteen German novels, most as fillers for the *Israelite* or the *Deborah*. The year 1871 witnessed the appearance of Esther Levy's *Jewish Cookery Book*. In brief, Jews were reaching out in all directions. Culture was the totality of all the experiences that impinged on them.

The quadricentennial celebration of Columbus's discovery of America induced the country's elite Jewish female leaders to establish the National Council of Jewish Women in 1893. These women—a superior lot—were interested in religion, literature, social welfare work, and civic advancement. One year earlier the American Jewish Historical Society had been founded by native-born American Jews eager to show the world that they were among the hemisphere's pioneers. In 1905–06 the Jewish Chautauqua Society printed a syllabus on American Jewish history to celebrate the 250th establishment of the Jewish community in New Amsterdam. Isaac Markens, a journalist, had already published *The Hebrews in America* (1888), the first large-scale overall history of Jewish America. That same year the second Jewish Publication Society of America (JPS) came into existence. Its first year book (1899), edited by Dr. Cyrus Adler, and the subsequent volumes add up to an invaluable reference book. Much of the editorial work in the early days was done by Henrietta Szold, later the founder of Hadassah.

The JPS was to have a notable career as one of the country's most important Jewish cultural organizations. It was complemented by the output of Jewish commercial book publishers. By 1925 the JPS had already issued Isaac Husik's *History of Mediaeval Jewish Philosophy*, Louis Ginzberg's *Legends of the*

Jews, the Schiff *Library of Jewish Classics*, and an accurate English translation of the Hebrew Bible (1917). Christian scholars had translated the verse in the Ten Commandments as "Thou shalt not kill"; the Jewish translators rendered it correctly as "Thou shalt not murder" (Exodus 20:13). By 1927 Alexander Marx of the Jewish Theological Seminary and Max L. Margolis of Dropsie College had published their history of the Jewish people. The last lines of the book informed the reader that on April 1, 1925, a Hebrew university had been opened in Jerusalem in Mandate Palestine. Judah L. Magnes, an American rabbi, became the chancellor. Through Marx and Margolis's scholarly work, thirty-five hundred years of Jewish life and history were unveiled to all who desired to learn.

Scholastically and culturally, American Jewry has never been orphaned; there were truly learned men in this country even in colonial days. By the 1830s individual scholars trained in the new historicocritical method had begun to settle in the United States. In antebellum days, too, competent Talmudists had made America their home. Marcus Jastrow, the Talmud lexicographer, settled in Philadelphia in 1866. Dr. Max Lilienthal organized a rabbinical literary association and edited a scientific magazine in the years 1880–82. Alexander Kohut, a world-famous rabbinic scholar, arriving here in 1885, continued to publish his important Talmudic dictionary. America's most important cultural work was the twelve-volume *Jewish Encyclopedia* (1901–06). This was literally a monumental achievement; there was nothing comparable even in Europe. Though most of the contributors were Germans or European-trained, it was truly an American production. Today, after almost a century, it is still an indispensable reference work.

Moving forward culturally, doggedly, men skilled in Jewish learning began to teach in various universities, in California, in Chicago, and at Harvard. Dropsie College for Hebrew and Cognate Learning, a postgraduate school, opened its doors in 1909, and in 1910 it began to publish the *Jewish Quarterly Review*. In the 1920s, sponsored by the Conservative movement, the American Academy for Jewish Research came into being and soon began to print its *Proceedings*. The *Hebrew Union College Annual* made its initial bow in 1924. Cultural advances are often the work of gifted individuals who blaze new paths. Kaufmann Kohler of the Hebrew Union College recruited distinguished scholars for his faculty. The men who taught at Dropsie were recognized for their contributions to the field of history, rabbinic literature, and Septuagint studies. The Rabbi Isaac Elchanan Theological Seminary led by Dr. Bernard Revel, a Dropsie graduate, worked to effect a blending of modernity and rabbinic studies. The Hebrew Theological Seminary of Chicago brought an intensive study of the Talmud to the Middle West. Led by Solomon Schechter (ca. 1848–1915)—scholar, essayist, personality—the Jewish Theological Seminary of New York assembled a most distinguished group of teachers. Outstanding even among its notables was Louis Ginzberg; no one in the field of the science of Judaism was more learned. In 1916, when European Jews were being harried during World War I, Jacob Marcus, a student at the Hebrew Union College, wrote an article for Wheeling, West Virginia's *Jewish Communal Bulletin* expressing the hope that America would now work to become the "spiritual home of international Jewry." A short generation later, American Jews dominated world Jewry culturally, spiritually, and politically.

Jewish Education

By 1852 the East European Jews were just beginning to make their presence felt in New York City culturally and Jewishly (their impact is described in a later chapter). For almost all Jews, public school education was primary, a Jewish education secondary. For the old-timers, the native-born and the acculturated central Europeans, there were very few changes in Jewish education. The rebbe and the heders—private Hebrew teachers and private schools—had been and were always available. For the affluent there were private all-day schools, at least ten of them in New York City, which were on the whole excellent. For the typical Jewish shopkeeper, the middle-class Jew, there were declining numbers of all-day schools, but attendance at congregational afternoon schools and Sunday morning schools was growing. The future belonged to the synagogue. Hebrew free schools were opened in New York in 1864 to match the allurements of the Christian missionaries. After a fashion these were communal schools. Other towns followed suit.

There was a burst of interest in higher learning in postbellum days. Temple Emanu-El opened a seminary of sorts in New York, while Leeser in Philadelphia established his short-lived teachers' training and rabbinic Maimonides College. In 1890 the present—and permanent—Jewish Publication Society of Philadelphia published its first book, *Outlines of Jewish History* by Lady Magnus. The last chapters were revised by Henrietta Szold because the original English edition had given American Jewry twelve lines, an indication of the author's contempt. The Union of American Hebrew Congregations, dedicated to the furthering of child education, was established in 1873. Two years later the Hebrew Union College, a rabbinic school, opened its doors. Twelve years later New York's acculturated traditionalists met the challenge by founding the Jewish Theological Seminary. The curriculum of both seminaries was influenced by the Breslau seminary; among the core courses taught were Bible, Talmud, rabbinical literature, and Jewish history. The elementary schools, seminaries, and publication societies were reinforced by Jewish public libraries in New York City, by the YWHAs, the fraternal orders, the literary societies of the adolescents, and the preaching of the rabbis in their pulpits and in the small towns they visited. The UAHC was later to employ rabbis as circuit riders. The National Council of Jewish Women, a large and successful organization of elite women, inaugurated study circles and opened Sunday schools for the East European youngsters in the big-city ghettos. In this effort the council was joined by the Reform temples, which always welcomed the Russian, Polish, and Rumanian children. That same year, 1893, the Jewish Chautauqua Society set out to educate America's Jewish youth and adults. Patterning this new organization on the Christian Chautauqua Movement (1874), Rabbi Henry Berkowitz of Philadelphia and his colleagues created a Jewish educational institution that published books and syllabi, organized study circles, and called together a general assembly that met annually in Atlantic City. They even launched one of the first courses to train Jewish social workers. Their budget was pitifully small, but they held on for decades.

The elementary schools, whether communal, congregational, private, or parochial, all taught the same Jewish subjects: Bible, biblical history, catechism (theology), religious customs and practices, ethics, Hebrew reading, and the singing of hymns. There were, of course, textbooks for all subjects taught, as well as almanacs and literary annuals. Above all, there was a press of about forty periodicals in English, German, Hebrew, and Yiddish (1900). Ever since 1871 magazines for youth had circulated, although not all the writers of these papers knew how to appeal to youngsters. Gratz College, a teachers' training school, opened in 1897. The pedagogical approach was completely modern and progressive, covering all phases of Jewish life and literature. In 1909 Jacob H. Schiff, the banker, gave a large sum to endow teachers' training schools at the Jewish Theological Seminary and the Hebrew Union College. The Cincinnati College's pedagogical institute was only moderately successful, but the one established in New York under the tutelage of Rabbi Mordecai M. Kaplan was exemplary. Jewish education had now obviously become so important—even as a profession—that Alexander M. Dushkin saw fit to earn a Ph.D. in this field at Columbia in 1917.

American Jewry had attempted to cope with the challenge of Jewish education on a national scale since 1841. The Reformers took up the challenge in 1886 when they founded the Hebrew Sabbath School Union to coordinate the work of all the schools in the Union of American Hebrew Congregations. In the early twentieth-century Rabbi George Zepin of the UAHC administered the Department of Synagogue and School Extension. He made progress, especially in 1923 when he hired Dr. Emanuel Gamoran, a Columbia University student and one of Samson Benderly's "boys." In the course of a few years Zepin and Gamoran created the largest and best corpus of materials for the country's Jewish schools. New approaches to Jewish elementary education had been appearing since the turn of the nineteenth century, and now modernist pedagogical advances were embraced. It was commonly believed that there could be no survival of Jewry without Jewish education, but Louis Marshall went farther: The Jewish ethical message is indispensable if civilization is to be furthered. Did Jewry score any successes in its schools for youngsters in the years 1865-1924? Content was taught—this is certain—and identification with Jewry and Judaism was very probably intensified. Despite the fact that professional educators tend to ignore the Jewish pedagogical literature, about 350 textbooks were published in the United States between the years 1766 and 1919, in English, German, Hebrew, and Yiddish. Many enjoyed numerous reprintings. A Bible history prepared by Rabbi Maurice Henry Harris went through twenty-six editions.

THE ECONOMIC LIFE OF THE NATIVES AND THE GERMANS

In many states of the Union there were Jews—individuals and families—who were very successful. Their names became household words. On the Pacific Coast the Magnins and Levi Strausses were active as entrepreneurs. In the Southwest there were large-scale merchants and outfitters such as the Ilfelds, the Staabs, and the Nordhauses. In San Antonio, Texas, the Oppenheimers financed many through their private bank. The Kempners of Galveston prospered in sugar and finance. The Sangers operated department stores in the Lone Star State. Rich Arkansas Jews had huge farms. The Godchauxs of Louisiana operated plantations and refined sugar. Hardly a city east of the Mississippi lacked a Jewish-owned department store; R. H. Macy (the Strauses) was one of the largest. Even in the middle decades of the nineteenth century the number of Jewish blue-collar workers was not impressive. Very few were day laborers, miners, steelworkers, or farmhands. Though there were Jews who were skilled artisans, more and more were entering into the professions, law, medicine, engineering, and teaching, though the universities were still reluctant to recruit them for their faculties. Jews were in light industry and were important as garment manufacturers. Henry Sonneborn, a German immigrant, employed two thousand workers and turned out some three thousand men's suits a day. Jews were not wanted in public banking, communications, transportation, insurance, and the utilities, and employment agencies were often hesitant to help Jews find jobs.

The Industrial Revolution opened new vistas for huge numbers of Jews, most of whom had been born disadvantaged. An unusual but not utterly atypical story is that of the Kahn family. Joseph Kahn, a humble German, came to these shores about the year 1881 and worked hard to eke out an existence. Some of his boys—he had six—had to hustle as teenagers to help feed the family. At least four of them achieved national recognition. Julius, a charming, refined gentleman, created the Truscon Steel Company, which pioneered in erecting steel-reinforced concrete factories. Moritz was sent to Russia by the company when it became one of the chief designers of the Soviet Union's industrial program. Felix built the first American underground parking facility and was one of the partners of the Six Company's Inc., which built the $49 million Hoover Dam, one of the great engineering marvels of the West. Albert, the greatest of them all and the founder of the family business, has been called the world's most famous industrial architect. His commercial buildings are found on five continents and in 124 cities in this country. He designed and built more than a thousand factories for the Ford Motor Company alone.

The Florsheim Shoe Company shipped ten thousand to twelve thousand pairs a day from its Chicago factory. With seven thousand dealers, its products were found in nearly every American town and city. Some Jews were innovative. On March 30, 1858, Hyman L. Lipman of Philadelphia secured the first patent for a pencil with an attached eraser. Lipman did not merit mention in Morais's voluminous *Jews of Philadelphia*, but imagine the inconvenience of working with a pencil without an attached eraser? Isador Kitsee invented more than two thousand devices and processes, including a refrigerator car. Louis Benedict Marks helped perfect the arc lamp. David Belais, a jeweler, developed the untarnishable platinumlike "white gold." Otto Eisenschiml (1880–1963), a Civil War buff who attempted to demonstrate that Lincoln had been the victim of a conspiracy hatched by Secretary of War Edwin M. Stanton, was the man who invented rustproof barbed wire and window envelopes.

There were always a handful of magnates: Schiff in banking, the Guggenheims in mining, Julius Rosenwald (Sears, Roebuck & Company) in the mail-order business. In 1920 Sears shipped more than $150 million of wares to its millions of customers. Jews, as we shall see, were concentrated in commerce and trade, but there was no vocation where they were entirely absent. In 1860 Philadelphia's Jews made a living in dozens upon dozens of different trades and callings. Most American Jews were retailers, shopkeepers, and petty businessmen, yet their contribution was very important inasmuch as every community—especially the towns and villages—was completely dependent on local suppliers of foods and goods. One cannot overemphasize the contribution of Jews in "reconstructing" the economic life of the South after the Civil War. In Arkansas at least a dozen hamlets were named after Jewish businessmen. Abraham G. Hutzler of Baltimore opened a small store in the 1850s. Because he was not yet of age, he was compelled to do business under the title of M. Hutzler & Son. Years later, after the firm had prospered, it set up a restaurant for its employees: A ham sandwich cost 3 cents, a sirloin steak 7 cents. Though William Thalhimer had already opened his place of business in Richmond in 1842, he still found time to serve as a voluntary leader of the service at Congregation Beth Ahabah. Slowly the business began to grow, and in the late twentieth century, Thalhimer's had more than twenty branches in a department store empire that extended into North Carolina and employed a work force of over thirty-five hundred. Writing in his *Spectator* in 1712, Joseph Addison had said of the Jews: "They are like the pegs and nails of a great building, which, tho they are but little value in themselves, are absolutely necessary to keep the whole frame together."

New York had thousands of pushcart and city peddlers, and rural peddlers plied their traffic in many states. Most, after a time, graduated from pack to wagon or bayou boat to become "merchants." Peddlers flourished throughout the nineteenth century. Louis Mayer, a German who worked out of Chicago, was exceptional. An avid reader, he lent his customers books and picked them up again on his next visit. Solomon Dewald, a peddler, preached on Sunday in Georgia villages. The people of Rutledge, Georgia, loved him and named a Masonic lodge after him. The German peddlers were slowly succeeded in the last decade of the nineteenth century by thousands of capital-poor East Europeans.

New York City was of course America's most important marketplace. In the 1880s the Jews were highly visible as jobbers and wholesalers in meat, leather, liquor, tobacco, jewelry, glass, paints, and furniture. They were very active as realtors and builders and dominated the apparel trade: "The Jewish needle made America the best dressed nation in the world." In Los Angeles in 1860, every Jew in town was in commerce—except for one lawyer. In 1871 every member of Kansas City's congregation B'nai Jehudah was in some form of business. Allan Tarshish, in his doctoral dissertation on American Jewish history, estimated that in the early 1880s about 2 percent were in finance, 4 percent in liquor, 4 percent in jewelry, about 6 percent in tobacco, and at least 50 percent in the apparel trade. Making a survey for the United States government in 1889, Dr. John S. Billings came to the conclusion that over 70 percent of some ten thousand Jewish families he surveyed were in commerce; 85 percent were white-collar workers. As late as the second quarter of the twentieth century, the independent retail store still accounted for about 70 percent of the nation's business. By that time, however, improved roads, interurban bus and rail lines, and cheap automobiles were driving Jewish retailers out of the smaller towns and villages.

And the women? They made little progress in commerce, although substantial numbers were to be found in the clerical and sales forces. Some were domestic servants; a handful were musicians; an increasing number were milliners and dressmakers. Hattie Carnegie (née Henrietta Koeningeiser), a Viennese immigrant apparently of Jewish origin, built one of the country's best-known women's fashion houses in the early twentieth century. A designer, retailer, and daring entrepreneur, she employed more than one thousand in her various enterprises and created a multimillion-dollar empire. By 1890 Zerlina and Laura Rosenfeld had established the largest stenography, typing, and translating service in the United States. American women were constantly turning to the professions, teaching, law, and medicine. If not always welcomed in the large medical schools, they could turn to the women's medical colleges.

THE JEW ON THE AMERICAN CULTURAL SCENE

Jews made a living because their businesses were patronized by their neighbors. The contacts were constant and the impact of American culture was often shockingly rapid. Yet though Jews are essentially American, they have often lived in at least three cultures: the English, the German or Yiddish, and the Hebrew of their liturgy (which most did not understand unless they turned to the accompanying translation). Nearly all Jews were constantly confronted and challenged by the fine arts, the local press, and, above all, the public schools their children attended. In Boston in 1906, English was the language of communication for the children of immigrants, and 30 percent of the Ben Franklin scholarship medals awarded in the grammar schools went to Jewish children. During the same year, of nine Harvard men who graduated summa cum laude, four were Jews.

The nineteenth century was a man's world, but some cultural opportunities were open to Jewish women. Fannie Bloomfield Zeisler (1863–1927) was the country's best-known woman pianist. Julia Richman, a district superintendent of public schools in Manhattan, influenced the destinies of some twenty-three thousand children. Annie Nathan Meyer helped establish Barnard College. Nina Morais Cohen wrote for the *North American Review*. One of her articles was on the "Limitations of Sex"; she wanted more rights for women. Jessica Blanche Peixotto became a professor of economics at the

University of California (as a student she had urged the girls to shorten their skirts to the shoe tops!).

Jews were symphony conductors and players, and America could boast of a Jewish piano virtuoso as early as the 1850s. Foreign-born Jewish impresarios in the field of music had few rivals. They brought the best music in Europe to these shores. By the second decade of the twentieth century, Otto Kahn, a banker, was the major stockholder in the Metropolitan Opera House. There were opera houses in many towns, and some were owned by Jews. In the world of the theater, the Klaws, the Erlangers, the Shuberts, David Belasco, and the Frohmans were all powerful, though their empire began to disintegrate when the cinema came over the horizon. Jews were also very much interested in literature and were eager to be recognized. Jewish women had been writing and publishing poetry ever since the early nineteenth century, though they were not counted among the great. Jewish notables, proud of their achievements, began to write autobiographies. Lillian Wald, for one, wrote of her experiences in the Henry Street Settlement. Henry Marcus Leipziger (1854–1917) of New York City became supervisor of an adult educational system of lectures that brought information and enlightenment to literally hundreds of thousands of men and women. The first college president of Jewish antecedents was Ephraim M. Epstein (d. 1913). A Baptist preacher, he was a founder of the University of Dakota, where he taught sixty-three students. He was the only instructor and was paid $700 a year.

Abraham Flexner (1866–1959) of Louisville was secretary of the Carnegie Foundation for the Advancement of Teaching. He later became the director of Princeton's Institute for

Advanced Study and is known for furthering medical education. His brother, Simon, was in charge of the laboratories at the Rockefeller Institute for Medical Research. James Loeb of the Kuhn, Loeb banking family underwrote the Loeb Classical Library, texts and translations of Greek and Latin writings of antiquity. The Brentanos, originally an Austrian family, were noted booksellers. Quite a number of Jews established publishing houses of importance. Alfred Boni and Horace B. Liveright reprinted the best of the world's literature in their Modern Library. Walter Lippmann (1889–1974) may well have been America's most influential publicist in the days after World War I. By the turn of the century Joseph Pulitzer (1847–1911) and Adolph S. Ochs (1858–1935) were important newspaper publishers. Pulitzer distanced himself from Jewry, whereas Ochs was devoted to his coreligionists, though he maintained a low Jewish profile in his *New York Times*. His descendants, less apprehensive, would not hesitate to emphasize Jewish news—after all, there were at least one million Jews in the city! The *Times* was a cultural medium read by hundreds of thousands. A generation before Ochs bought the paper, Dr. Edward Morwitz (1815–93) owned or controlled about three hundred periodicals, including eight dailies, many of them foreign-language (German) papers.

There were numerous Americans of Jewish descent who achieved distinction and were respected for their accomplishments. Architects Louis Sullivan and Frank Lloyd Wright had worked in the office of the Chicago architect Dankmar Adler. Edwin R. A. Seligman, the Columbia University economist, was the editor of the *Encyclopaedia of the Social Sciences*. Leo S. Rowe was director general of the Pan-American Union. Julius Bien, the lithographer, was one of the best mapmakers of his day (he became the international president of B'nai B'rith). Alfred Stieglitz was one of the country's most distinguished photographers. George Blumenthal was president of the Metropolitan Museum of Art. Wealthy New York Jewish businessmen had magnificent collections of paintings; their works now adorn this country's museums. Jacques Loeb of the Rockefeller Institute for Medical Research was a highly respected biologist and physiologist who taught that the human being was a chemical mechanism. No anthropologist was more respected than Franz (Feibes) Boas (1858–1942), who threw light on the relations between heredity and environment and emphasized the distinction between race and racism. In 1877 Emile Berliner (1851–1929) developed a microphone that worked, thus making Bell's telephone a commercial reality. Later, he invented the gramophone, an improvement on Edison's phonograph. Before coming to New York, Carl Koller (1854/57–1944) pioneered in Austria in the use of cocaine as a local anesthetic (his friend Sigmund Freud called him Coca Koller). Albert A. Michelson (1852–1931), the first American to become a Nobel laureate in science, was a physicist who "meted out heaven with the span" (Isaiah 40:12). Like many other notables, he was versatile; he was a violinist and a watercolor painter. Joseph Erlanger (1874–1965) taught medicine at Johns Hopkins, but when he made little advance in rank he went on to the University of Wisconsin where he became a professor. After he was crowned a Nobel laureate in his chosen field of physiology, Hopkins invited him back to receive an honorary doctorate. When the 1924 Immigration Act closed the doors to most of Europe's Jews, American Jewry numbered 4 million out of some 115 million souls. The cultural achievements of this relatively small group were and are impressive.

CHARITY

In the colonial period the Jews were expected—indeed compelled—to take care of their needy, and even today Jews nearly always provide for their own poor. Some early communal social welfare agencies were Protestantized, and as Christian organizations were unacceptable to Jews; not only Jews but Catholics, too, avoided the local charities for religious reasons. For decades almost every Jewish charity was autonomous, but as the Germans arrived in large numbers beginning in the late 1830s, solicitations of funds by the different charities became an intolerable nuisance and the federation of such organizations became a necessity. Federations multiplied in the postbellum period. The large city philanthropies were now prefixed with the adjective "United."

By the 1890s the effort was made to have one all-purpose fund-raising drive a year, so the base was broadened to include everyone in the local Jewish community. It was not long before some federations not only raised the necessary funds but also attempted to monitor the expenditures of their client societies. By 1899 lay and trained social workers had established the National Conference of Jewish Charities. Soon the professionals set up their own association where classes were provided for educating full-time personnel. In the course of time the once derided social workers became communal leaders rivaling and outdistancing the rabbis. Indeed, the federations would ultimately become more prestigious than the synagogues. The efficient, newly trained practitioners were frequently looked upon with suspicion by their clients. Shearith Israel in the early days of the eighteenth century had spent £30–40 a year to help the poor; in 1924 the New York Federation collected about $4 million to aid the impoverished.

The disbursements of the Jewish community must not be confused with the largesse of the Jewish industrial and mercantile tycoons. Jacob H. Schiff of Kuhn, Loeb & Co., the Strauses of R. H. Macy, the Guggenheims of the American Smelting and Refining Company, and Julius Rosenwald of Sears, Roebuck gave sizable sums to the Jewish and general communities. Rosenwald donated millions in matching grants to help blacks build schools and churches of their own. Simon Guggenheim and his wife were the donors of the John Simon Guggenheim Memorial Foundation, which provided (and still does) large numbers of fellowships for scholars, scientists, and artists. Nathan Straus, a generous supporter of Palestine Jewry, was in 1923 crowned the outstanding citizen of Greater New York. (Former President William Howard Taft said of him: "Dear old Nathan Straus is a great Jew and the greatest Christian of us all.") Straus was cited in particular for insisting on the pasteurization of milk, an imperative measure if the infant mortality rate was to be reduced.

The revolution in the administration of the charities in the nineteenth and early twentieth centuries affected the women who had done yeoman work in the various ladies' aid societies. The federation in effect destroyed their achievement. Women attempted to adapt themselves to the new techniques so they could aid the professionals. Ultimately, however, their Sisterhoods for Personal Service faded away and became synagogueal auxiliaries. Hannah Greenebaum Solomon, Sophie Irene Loeb, and Hannah Bachman Einstein made careers for themselves in the social welfare world. Einstein and Loeb led in inducing legislatures to grant mothers' pensions for widowed and deserted wives who sought to keep their children at home. These sagacious social workers did not believe that congregate care was the answer for helpless children.

REJECTION

By virtue of being Jewish, Jews were always exposed to prejudice. Very few Gentiles did not, at one time or another, look askance at the children of Abraham. Missionaries never stopped importuning the Jews to convert and save their souls—and extinguish Judaism. Sunday laws in about half of the American states imposed compulsory closing regulations on Jewish shopkeepers. Even Lincoln, during the Civil War, enjoined his armies to rest on "the Lord's Day"; he recognized his constituency as a Christian people. The National Reform Association wanted to Christianize the republic. Among its supporters was Governor Benjamin Gratz Brown of Missouri. Brown was named after a Jew who was still living; if the association had prevailed, Gratz would have become a citizen of lesser status. Most American elementary schools were Christian in practice, in Bible readings, in holiday celebrations. Indeed, many Christians conceived of the American school system as a nondenominational Protestant institution to hold the Catholic parochial schools in check. A few colleges had obligatory chapel services. There was constant pressure to amend and Christianize the Constitution, to invoke God and Jesus, in order to stop the advances of secularism. All these efforts failed. The First Amendment had been adopted to prevent such a kulturkampf between the Christian sects.

The postbellum decades confronted Jews with challenges. In the late 1860s several national insurance companies began denying Jews fire insurance, but they retreated when the angry Israelites countered with a boycott. Social prejudice was very much in evidence in the 1870s. The Grand Union Hotel in Saratoga Springs, New York, refused to admit Joseph Seligman, the international banker. From then on the exclusion of Jews from resort hotels became a common practice continuing well into the twentieth century. This was particularly true in states that lacked accommodation laws.

There were social clubs, fraternities, and lodges that would admit no Jews. Jews were excluded from some art associations, housing areas, National Guard units, and commissioned officers' ranks. Admission of Jews to some of the best American universities became problematic in the early twentieth century and continued well into the 1950s. Some distinguished Americans—members of the presidential Adams clan, for instance—nursed an intense dislike of Jews. In 1888 Telemachus T. Timayenis, a cultured Greek immigrant, established the Minerva Press in New York and began publishing anti-Semitic paperbacks. His material, imported from France, was distinguished by its crudity and viciousness: Jews are arsonists and criminals, they murder Christians, and their women are prostitutes—if the acquisitive John D. Rockefeller is not a Jew, he certainly acts like one!

During the unhappy 1890s, with a four-year-long depression, some Populists associated Jews with the evils of capitalism. That same decade witnessed the arrival here of two leading German anti-Semites, Hermann Ahlwardt and Pastor Adolf Stoecker. But they accomplished nothing, since American

Jew-haters preferred their own nativist concoctions. When Ahlwardt asked for police protection, Theodore Roosevelt, president of New York City's Board of Police Commissioners, sent a detachment of Jewish policemen. The Baltimore *Katholische Volkszeitung* solemnly informed its readers that forty Jews by the name of Rosenfeld had appeared at the ceremony in 1901 when Theodore Roosevelt took the oath as president. They were Roosevelt's Jewish kinsmen! As the funeral cortege of the East Side chief rabbi Jacob Joseph passed the factory of R. H. Hoe & Company, the workers showered the mourning Jews with pieces of scrap metal (1902). Summoned to quiet the riotous scene, the Irish policemen clubbed the Jewish victims, who had not voted for Tammany in the last election.

The new silent movies of the early twentieth century rarely portrayed Jews in a negative light—there was no profit in antagonizing good customers—but the vaudeville stage frequently caricatured the Israelite. The stage Jew had been a popular scoundrel type in English drama since the sixteenth century. In the dozens of plays in which he trod the American boards in the nineteenth century, he had appeared most often as a villain or buffoon, though on occasion he was portrayed equally unrealistically as a shining example of almost startling nobility. The daily press, catering to the masses, often tended to identify Jewish malefactors. A Sandersville, Georgia, editor, commenting on a pogrom in the Balkans, wrote: "We only wish this killing had taken place in Georgia." It is true that the Italians, African Americans, and Irish were also attacked and lampooned, but this was cold comfort to the Israelites.

Distinguished American litterateurs, in general, were not much given to portraying villainous Jews in their writings, though there are certainly anti-Jewish images in the writings of

Nathaniel Hawthorne, Henry James, Frank Norris, and Edith Wharton, among others. Outside belles lettres, too, in 1910, for example, an American firm published an English translation of Houston Stewart Chamberlain's *Grundlagen des Neunzehnten Jahrhunderts* (Foundations of the Nineteenth Century). This Anglo-German anti-Semitic work appealed to Americans already convinced of the inferiority of the Jew. In 1913 the Order of B'nai B'rith established the Anti-Defamation League, primarily to stop the denigration of Jews in the daily press. In this effort it was largely successful. That same year Leo Frank, an Atlanta businessman and a person of education and repute, was charged with the rape and murder of a young girl, one of his employees. He was found guilty, imprisoned, and—with the connivance of the prison authorities—taken out and lynched (1915). There is evidence that Frank was not guilty, and his trial was eminently unfair. But Frank represented everything that the impoverished rednecks of Georgia resented: a Northerner, a businessman, a college graduate, and a Jew. The prosecutor, Thomas Edward Watson, determined to ride into office in a hearse, was soon elected governor. He whipped the masses into a frenzy and went to the United States Senate. The Frank Affair was a "victory" the South was determined to win over the North. Decades later a witness, terrified by the actual murderer, would exonerate Frank.

In 1920 a respectable American publisher issued the *Protocols and the World Revolution*, supposedly the minutes of a meeting of the Elders of Zion, depicted as a secret international Jewish body in control of the world and responsible for global sufferings, upheavals, and evils. The book, a forgery, had been concocted by the Russian secret police in the late nineteenth century to explain away the unrest of the Russian people.

These *Protocols* have been translated into many languages and millions were persuaded to believe in their authenticity. Henry Ford was among the believers and that same year, 1920, published the *Protocols* in his Dearborn *Independent*. He spent millions in a national campaign to convince the people of the United States that the Jews were a menace. It was not until 1927 that he backed off and made a public apology. He may or may not have changed his mind, but he definitely feared American Jewry's relentless boycott of his automobile. Myriads, however, had been exposed to his anti-Jewish attacks in *The International Jew, the World's Foremost Problem*. In 1922 President Abbott Lawrence Lowell of Harvard University announced that he would limit the number of Jews admitted in the future. (A very substantial number of Jewish students had already matriculated.) Lowell was ready to do openly what most Ivy League schools were already doing covertly. Not that he and his fellow presidents were necessarily Jew-haters. For them a college was a socioeducational institution, and they preferred affluent white Anglo-Saxon Protestants, so-called WASPs. If high school grades alone guaranteed entrance, they feared that their institutions might be swamped by intelligent and achieving Jewish youngsters. All these Jews might keep the Gentiles out. Three years later the Harvard *Lampoon* cracked: "No religious discrimination at Harvard. Three Gentiles elected to ... Phi Beta Kappa." There was an outcry against Lowell, but it probably accomplished little. Many big schools sought one way or another to limit the number of Jewish entrants. By the mid-1920s the old Ku Klux Klan had revived and become a powerful political force in American life. The Klan, though primarily anti-black and anti-Catholic, in some areas made life miserable for individual Jews. Its mass following enabled it to elect gov-ernors and send its friends to Congress. It was not long before this new Klan collapsed, however, due to its irresponsible, often corrupt leadership.

Not only proletarian racists but also labor—led by Samuel Gompers, an immigrant Jew—distinguished sociologists, historians, litterateurs, and muckraking journalists urged the closing of America's portals against immigrants. Anti-Catholic sentiment in the United States was also virulent. A restrictionist once cried out, "to Hell with Jews, Jesuits, and steamships." American Jewry reeled yet survived the numerous attacks to which it was subjected, but it could not cope with the immigration restrictionist forces. Congress—i.e., the people of the United States—set out as early as 1882 to limit the foreign influx. It did not rest until it had effectively stopped immigration from eastern and southern Europe and from Asia. The American people as such have always been xenophobic. In 1911 the United States Immigration Commission published a forty-one-volume report that tended to support the prejudice of the masses. Eastern and southern Europeans, it was claimed, are not good immigration material. The crucial Immigration Act of 1924 was, in part, literally anti-Semitic. In the thinking of the time, Jews were "Semites," biologically inferior. They came from Eastern Europe, so immigration from those areas had to be stopped—and it was. And while the Nordic racists were attacking America's non-Nordic Russian and Polish Jews, the children of the immigrants here in this country were bent over their books. Ultimately several of them would be awarded Nobel prizes.

ACCEPTANCE

WHAT THE UNITED STATES DID FOR THE JEWS

The Jews here knew that anti-Jewish prejudice was no real threat to their well-being. They did not have to suffer the vicious literary attacks to which the Catholics were constantly exposed. Every time a Gentile attacked a Jew he made a Jew! The Jews persisted in seeing America as the freest country in the world. Unlike Russia, the United States government had not set out to crush Jewry. America was a land where nobodies became somebodies. Yes, they lynched the Jew Leo Frank, but from 1882 to 1936 Gentiles lynched 1,289 non-Jewish whites and 3,383 blacks. From that perspective, it seemed evident that America accepted Jews.

By the 1860s and 1870s North Carolina and New Hampshire had finally opened all political offices to Jews. Congress in 1911 abrogated the 1832 treaty with Russia because the czar's government would not recognize the passports of Jews who were American citizens. Jews held commissions as officers in the armed forces. They served as governors of states and were dispatched to foreign lands as ministers and ambassadors. They sat in the Senate, in the House of Representatives, and, as of 1916, on the Supreme Court. The Congress and the Supreme Court refused to breach the wall between church and state. In the early days of World War I, the United States collier the *Vulcan* carried American Jewry's gift of tons of food to the hungry Jews of Palestine, and in 1919 the Americans at Versailles helped convince the European powers to give East European Jews equal rights and to look sympathetically upon the restoration of a Jewish homeland in Palestine. When in the years following the Civil War snobs besmirched the good name of Jews, Henry Ward Beecher, the famed Christian churchman, came to their rescue. The Greeks, he said, gave the world beauty and the Hebrews a hunger for righteousness. The Greeks build temples and the Hebrews build men. American citizenship was a bond that bound Jews and non-Jews together.

Unitarian ministers preached in Jewish pulpits. Christians came to synagogues to listen to liberal rabbis. There were instances when churches dedicated stained-glass windows to Jewish benefactors. A Charleston, South Carolina, Gentile physician tended the Jewish poor but never sent a bill. Attracted by the glamour of Christmas, Jews often erected Christmas trees and stuffed gift stockings. The Reform prayer books employed more and more English, and most references to Christian persecutions of Jews were elided. With the new twentieth century, peoples' churches established in the large cities invited Jews to worship with them, ignoring differences of creed. Rabbi Gustav Gottheil was invited by the New York Conference of Religion to help prepare a book of common worship (1900), and when the state's Protestant Episcopal churches met together in 1909 they telegraphed the Reform rabbis then in annual session: God "hath made of one blood all men." The response was immediate: "Have we not all one father?" Most Jews appeared well integrated into the two worlds of Americanism and Judaism, though in this give and take of loyalties Judaism was invariably the loser. In the American atmosphere of acceptance and sociability, Jews intermarried, assimilated, and disappeared. Elsewhere too, of course, the history of the Jews is the record of a minority swallowed up by an overwhelming majority.

151

What the Jews Did for the United States

European Jews who came here in the nineteenth century were grateful for America's unique world of religious liberty, intellectual opportunity, and economic benefits. They were determined to be good citizens, and on the whole they were. Joseph Pulitzer gave millions to endow his prizes; three Los Angelenos, a Jew, a Catholic, and a Protestant, gave the land to help establish the University of Southern California. Responding to American kindness and courtesy, Jews no longer looked upon the churches as sources of oppression. Rabbi Morris J. Raphall, the Orthodox notable of the Civil War period, referred to Jesus as "the great teacher of Nazareth." The Central Conference of American Rabbis decades later attacked the Turks for massacring Armenians. When Lincoln died, New York's Shearith Israel—America's bastion of religious Orthodoxy—recited the kaddish (the Jewish requiem, one might call it) for the martyred president.

Wherever Jews lived they participated actively in the communal life of the towns and cities that sheltered them. More often than not they became leaders in the villages, building the hamlets that carried their names. Henry Heppner of Heppner, Oregon, rode through the countryside collecting funds for the first public school. Wherever they dwelt—and remained—the economy flourished. Because of what America did for them they became fervent patriots. Three sons of Milwaukee's Nathan Pereles emerged as Benjamin Franklin, James Madison, and Thomas Jefferson Pereles. Many Jewish patriots, believing that there could be but one political loyalty, rejected Zionism. This was true of Cyrus Adler, one of the country's most influential Jewish communal leaders. It would be wrong to imply that Jews experienced no anxieties in this privileged land; seventeen hundred years of Old World abuse had taught them to be wary even in the New World. Jews were but a tiny minority in the 1920s, and they were never to become as much as 4 percent of the total population. Some of New York City's Jewish dignitaries maintained a low profile. They objected to the teaching of classical Hebrew in City College, though Latin and Greek were of course acceptable (1908)! Jews insisted on full rights, and as egalitarians they served as a goad to democracy, the barometer of constitutional liberties. By the 1890s American Gentiles had begun to realize that self-respecting Jews preferred to be known as Jews, not Hebrews.

America's National Historical Publications Commission recommended the publication in some form of the papers of sixty-six notable Americans. Five were men of Jewish antecedents who lived during the eighty years between 1840 and 1920: Judah P. Benjamin, Samuel Gompers, Albert A. Michelson, Joseph Pulitzer, and Adolph S. Ochs. The first four were foreign-born; the fifth was the American-born son of an immigrant. Ochs, however, was the only one of the five who evidenced interest in Jews and Judaism. It was "German" Jews like him who organized American Jewry on a nationwide basis. They were the ones who first created a union of congregations, civil defense organizations, and countrywide lodges; federated the charities; developed religious schools; and established a permanent rabbinical seminary.

THE RELIGIONISTS, 1900–24

THE ORTHODOX

As late as the first quarter of the twentieth century, most American Jewish religionists were Orthodox. The Reformers were still a relatively small group, while the masses, now East European immigrants, were nominally Orthodox. Only the socialists and anarchists fell outside these boundaries. (The Russians and Rumanians are treated in a later chapter.) Even many of the old-line native-born and the Americanized German immigrants were traditionalists. Influenced by their Christian neighbors, they had introduced German or English sermons, and decorum was now rarely a problem. Some of these acculturated Orthodox—Sephardim and Ashkenazim—had felt threatened by the aggressive Reformers and organized the Union of Orthodox Jewish Congregations of the United States and Canada in 1898. Their confession of faith was Maimonidean, uninfluenced by modernity. Though committed without reservation to the authoritative rabbinic codes, they kept their distance from the East Europeans and their rabbis, and flirted with the thought of calling a synod that would have the authority to introduce modernist changes. The original leaders in this traditionalist union were men of culture and advanced education. In later decades they could boast of a women's branch and a modest Hebrew Teachers' Training School for girls. Despite their summary rejection of Reform, these traditionalists were ineluctably being pushed to the left by the American ethos.

The Reformers

The Reformers were well organized with congregational and rabbinic unions, brotherhoods, and sisterhoods, all of which came in time to serve as models for the Conservatives and the Orthodox. In 1922 Rabbi Stephen S. Wise, the Reform maverick, established New York City's Jewish Institute of Religion in opposition to Cincinnati's more staid Hebrew Union College.

His seminary was pro-Zionist and friendlier to the émigré East Europeans. In general, however, Reform at this stage did not succeed in building a strong bridge to the Russians, Poles, and other newcomers. The Reformers had not dared adopt a formal creed that would inevitably split their movement. They emphasized their "mission" to preach universalism but were opposed to intermarriage. They were determined to survive as a disparate Jewish group. Reform rabbis were divided among two groups: The radicals favored Sunday services but were egregiously unsuccessful and could muster no more than four or five sizable temples; most rabbis continued to hold Sabbath services even if for only a handful of regular worshipers. Some also lectured on Sunday to relatively large audiences of Jews and Christians, but the occasion was not primarily a religious service. The Christian visitors, after listening to a liberal rabbi, had to come to terms with their own otherworldly theology.

The Reform rabbi was a preacher, educator, officiant at rites of passage, and "a light to the Gentiles," often exchanging pulpits with liberal Christian ministers. Conscious that the Jews constituted a small minority in America, the Reform clergyman did not discourage his followers from maintaining a low profile. He was no pioneer in teaching social justice. His congregants were staunchly bourgeois and also resistant to promoting women in the congregational hierarchy. When, however, women were given the franchise in 1920, congregational leaders felt they had little choice but to begin co-opting women as officers. The rabbi—a male, of course—was the star performer in the service. Congregational participation was somewhat limited. Singing was encouraged, but the rafters did not ring. On the whole, Reform services lacked warmth; "decorum was a cruel substitute for devotion."

Anti-Zionist Reformers, proud of their achievements, were at ease in their American Zion. Though few in number, they were affluent, commanded prestige, and dominated much of American Jewish communal life. They believed that their product was good enough to export, and in 1912 Rabbi Israel Mattuck went to London where he helped build a small but vigorous Liberal Jewish movement.

THE CONSERVATIVES

The roots of Conservative Judaism reached back to antebellum days when a few well-trained—and even university-educated—rabbis began coming to these shores. Some believed that the Reformers had gone too far, too fast. Sabato Morais, who led the Jewish Theological Seminary in 1887, was staunchly Orthodox. His school was on its last legs by 1900, the year that Isaac M. Wise died. The elite Reformers of New York and Chicago thought the time had come to move Wise's Cincinnati college to a metropolitan area, preferably New York, where the native-born Conservatives and Reformers could unite and move as one to deorientalize the metropolitan East European immigrant masses. (Mergers were in the air in religions as well as in steel, oil, and railroads!) The Cincinnatians indignantly rejected the prospect of such a fusion, and they were right—uniting Reform and what was still in essence Orthodoxy was totally unrealistic. *"Wir haben auch Lokalstolz"* (We, too, have local pride) sputtered Bernhard Bettmann, the board chairman of the Hebrew Union College. The New York communal leaders—Reformers—would not be denied. They imported Rumanian-born Solomon Schechter from England to revive the moribund Jewish Theological Seminary in New York. Schechter was scholarly, acculturated, a brilliant essayist, a charismatic personality, and a fervent Jewish traditionalist. He was not to make any real impact on the East Side masses, too far removed from him, but ultimately the Conservatives won over the next generation of East European stock and became America's largest Jewish denomination.

In his effort to build a great seminary, Schechter had the help of Cyrus Adler (1863–1940), a Johns Hopkins Ph.D. in Semitic languages and a brilliant administrator who would in time head or influence Dropsie College, the Jewish Publication Society, the American Jewish Historical Society, the American Jewish Committee, and, after Schechter's death, the seminary as well. Adler was an observant Jew staunchly traditional and staunchly Americanistic. He had been born in Van Buren, Arkansas, on the edge of Indian territory, and Americanism oozed out of his every pore. The newly rebuilt Jewish Theological Seminary continued to stress the importance of the Hebrew liturgy, the dietary laws, and the traditional Sabbath. It brought together a faculty of notable scholars.

By the 1920s the Conservatives had become a distinct Jewish denomination. They adhered to Orthodox practice but as modernists wholeheartedly embraced Western culture. Preaching was always in English. Like the Reformers, they, too, adopted no credo, but their modernism would ultimately push them to the left theologically. Orthodox practices deemed unacceptable were discreetly neglected. Unlike the Reformers, the Conservatives never rejected rabbinic law, the halakah. However, the movement now had to cope with Rabbi Mordecai M. Kaplan. This observant yet humanistic Jew taught his disciples at the Jewish Theological Seminary that Judaism was more than a religion—it was an organic culture, a religious civilization that could encompass almost every man or woman who identified as a Jew. Kaplan's philosophy, which owed little to the halakah, was later to emerge as the fourth Jewish denomination, Reconstructionsim.

During the 1920s the Reformers, Conservatives, and Orthodox found themselves moving somewhat closer together in part because of certain basic beliefs and practices, but even more because of the common need to help Jews abroad and to fight anti-Jewish prejudice here. The inescapable impact of Americanism was the cement, the strong bond that held them together, but even more important was their image of themselves as a distinct people. (Later I describe and analyze this new community for the period 1925–90s.)

Many changes were in store for the next two or three generations: The quota laws of the 1920s would destroy the ethnic particularism of the Germans and East Europeans, and Americanization would proceed very rapidly, so that by the 1960s practically all American Jews had merged in a communal sense. Jew hatred would impel them all to huddle together for comfort; Zionism would emphasize Jewish nationalism and pride; and Jewish education, all of one piece in most schools, would make for a degree of unity. The joint effort to aid oppressed Jews everywhere would bind most Jews together tightly into a feeling of *klal Yisrael*, the oneness of all Jewry.

Part IV
The Challenge of the
East European Jews:
1850–1924

9. The Creation of a Community

THE EAST EUROPEANS COME TO AMERICA

What led the Reform rabbinical leaders to meet at Pittsburgh in 1885? They were aware that the well-established American Jewish community was about to be overwhelmed by East European newcomers; thousands of the "Russians" had poured in during the years 1881–85. The Pittsburgh Platform was meant as a declaration to the American world: We modern Jews are acculturated Americans. Don't confuse us with the immigrants now flooding our shores, though they, too, are Jews. (One long generation later—in 1918—these invading "vandals" would force the American-born and their "German" leaders to come to Canossa. The immigrants would dominate American Jewry, if only temporarily.)

Who were these East European Jews? Poles, Balts, Russians, Galicians, east Hungarians, Rumanians, Balkan émigrés. As early as 1852, enough had arrived to establish an Orthodox synagogue and study center on the Lower East Side of New York City. By the 1870s, there were dozens of such conventicles in the city, and by 1924, nearly two million Slavic and Rumanian immigrant Jews had been admitted to the United States. In 1914 alone, more than 138,000 landed; all the central European Jews who debarked during the years 1837–1924 never equaled this number. Most of the Eastern European Jews who came to these shores passed through New York's Castle Garden or Ellis Island.

Why did they come here? It is simple: They had little future in their native lands. They hated the Russian rulers who oppressed them, denied them civil rights and economic opportunity, and then had them murdered in sporadic pogroms. The Russian civil war years 1917–21 saw Jews butchered in over a thousand towns and hamlets. President Wilson found it necessary in 1919 to send former Ambassador Henry Morgenthau to Poland to report on the Jewish tragedy there.

The Slavic and Balkan Jews came to this land because America spelled opportunity, equality, a new life—this last most important. The United States was a country with a future for Jews. Because the émigrés began most often as sweatshop workers, they learned to curse Columbus for discovering this continent. They also learned to love America as a *goldene medineh*, a glorious land of possibility. Though a few went back to Europe because for them America did not measure up religiously, the vast majority stayed to make their peace with this strange land.

The newcomers frightened the old-timers. These refugees were labeled "Russians." Their Orthodoxy was not at all the Orthodoxy of American Jewry, so they were deemed "uncouth." The fact that so many were impoverished threatened the status of the Jews already here, or so the native-born thought. In 1882, the year after the first bad pogrom in Russia, thirteen thousand landed and confronted a relatively small Jewish community of about three hundred thousand. The Jews already settled in this land felt they had every reason to be disturbed. What was to be done?

In the preceding decade, the 1870s, when the East Europeans started arriving in substantial numbers, representatives of America's Jewry had met with western and central European Jewish notables in three different international conferences. These leaders all worked together to induce the Eastern European rulers to emancipate their Jews, but for the next hundred or more years the effort to export American political values to those lands was, on the whole, a failure. Jews were not emancipated or integrated into the citizenry of Poland, Russia, and Rumania. Pressured by the B'nai B'rith and the Union of American Hebrew Congregations, American secretaries of state and consular officials ever since 1860s had been urging recalcitrant East European governments not to mistreat their Jewish subjects—we, here in the United States, do not seek immigrants who have been compelled to leave their homeland—but Secretary John Hay's note in 1902 to the European powers asking them to caution the Rumanians to behave with integrity was a wasted effort. (Moreover, the implication in the Hay note that the fleeing Jews were less than desirable was no compliment to the Chosen People.)

The central and western European states also did not welcome the few East European Jews who filtered in. The mostly unspoken comment of the German, French, and English Jewries was: Send them somewhere else! American and European Jewish philanthropists encouraged prospective immigrants to turn to Ottoman Palestine and establish colonies there, but despite generous help, the colonists barely survived. Predominantly Moslem Palestine was no haven or refuge. The Russian and Polish Jews' eyes were set on the New World, the United States, so they poured in. They met confusion and hostility, but in the long run American Jewry helped. It had to. What would the Gentiles say if Jews here turned their backs on fellow Jews? Many an American Israelite was unhappy that some of the educated newcomers were anarchists, Communists, union organizers, strikers, and lovers of Zion. The specter of "dual loyalties" was a real problem for the native-born, if not for the immigrants.

Helping the new arrivals was a gargantuan task. Jewry here was in no sense affluent, but a Hebrew Emigrant Aid Society was founded in the 1880s to help the newcomers, and similar organizations were established in numerous towns and cities throughout the land: These newcomers are fellow Jews, not schnorrers and beggars; they have a right to turn to us. Michael Heilprin (1823–88), a native Pole and a distinguished scholar and encyclopedist, did what he could to aid the arriving hosts. Emma Lazarus, a patrician from New York's Spanish-Portuguese synagogue who had become something of a Jewish nationalist, was eager to help them. She gave the Goddess of Liberty in New York's harbor words to greet the incoming émigrés:

> Give me your tired, your poor,
> Your huddled masses yearning to breathe free,
> The wretched refuse of your teeming shore,
> Send these, the homeless, tempest-tost to me:
> I lift my lamp beside the golden door.

Large numbers of Jews continued to arrive, determined to stay, and American Jewry had no choice but to cope. The leaders came up with a tripartite solution: Get the newcomers out of the large East Coast cities and set them up in colonies; scatter them on farms; ship them out to the cities, towns, villages, and hamlets of the immense hinterland. A new Jewish peasantry will be American Jewry's Exhibit A to charm the Gentiles! Colonization fired the imagination of the country's urban Jewish native-born. Already in the 1870s the Union of American Hebrew Congregations had embraced the prospect of colonizing the newcomers. Beginning in the 1880s more than one hundred small and inconsequential colonies were established. Not a single one proved truly successful. Few of the colonists knew how to farm. They had no capital, were exploited, and often had to pay usurious rates of interest. Their leaders were most often incompetent. There were no nearby markets. They were settled on infertile lands and then had to brave fires, drought, hail, and rising rivers, not to mention intramural competing ideologies. Moreover, the four decades between 1881 and 1920 included twelve years of depression or panic. Even experienced Gentile Americans were leaving farms. The only colonies that managed to survive, to a limited degree, were a few in south Jersey that were close to markets and offered creature comforts, synagogues and a social life, even libraries (which the colonists rarely visited). They survived because these colonists were able to become agroindustrialists. They made and sold products, like the twentieth-century kibbutzim in Palestine and Israel—and they had the financial support of a European philanthropist, Baron de Hirsch, who built them a Jewish town, Woodbine, and set up a school there to train farmers. Even so, the Baron de Hirsch Agricultural School (1894) did not train a generation of yeomen, though it did produce several notable soil chemists. Yet after a generation the children in the south Jersey colonies left for the neighboring cities. They had no real future on the soil.

The colonies were a failure, a brief romantic episode. But if Jews could not build successful colonies, there was nothing to prevent them, as ambitious individuals, from becoming successful private farmers. Hundreds homesteaded in the Middle West, especially in the Dakotas, although Jewish farmers were to be found in all the states of the Union. Some did better than others when they specialized in growing tobacco, setting up dairies, and raising poultry, all good cash crops. Simon Fishman (1878–1956), an immigrant, broke more than one hundred thousand acres of virgin soil to the plough in the Kansas-Nebraska country, but even he did not die a rich man. Some of New York's East Side denizens, would-be farmers, moved to the Catskills and took in summer boarders whom they charged $5 a week for good kosher food (a few even advertised, "Hebrews only"). There were at least a thousand of these minuscule enterprises. The hotel business thrived, catering in the twentieth century to hundreds of thousands and producing a number of multimillion dollar corporations. American Jewish farmers set out at length to organize themselves and created a Federation of Jewish Farmers, a Yiddish paper *(The Jewish Farmer)*, credit unions, and an annual exhibition of their products that they proudly set up in New York City. Many Jews managed to hold on to their farmsteads with the aid of the Jewish Agricultural and Industrial Aid Society, *(JAIAS)*, which gave them loans and offered advice. This was succeeded by the Jewish Agricultural Society in 1922, but even this last was not destined to survive. How many Jews lived on rural farms in the second quarter of the twentieth century? There are no accurate figures, only estimates of between fifty thousand and one hundred thousand farmers who may have owned between six hundred thousand and one million acres—unimpressive figures considering that there were between three and four million Jews in the land. Individual Israelites in Arkansas owned twenty thousand to thirty thousand acres of farmland, while Las Jaritas, the Florsheim ranch in Springer, New Mexico, could boast sixty thousand acres. As in the colonies, the children of Jewish farmers tended to look to the cities for a better life.

As mentioned, the fact that at the beginning of the century some of the colonists and farmers managed to eke out a bare existence was due to the efforts of Baron Maurice de Hirsch and his wife. Hirsch, a native German, had made a huge fortune building railroads. After his only son died, he said: "My son I have lost but not my heir; humanity is my heir." Eager to help his fellow Jews because they had been oppressed for a thousand years, in 1891 he chartered the Jewish Colonization Association with a capital of about $40 million. He offered to rehabilitate Russian Jewry on its native heath, but the Russian authorities refused to cooperate. He then set out to settle thousands of East Europeans on the Argentinean pampas; his successes there, too, were limited. That same year he organized the Baron de Hirsch Fund to aid the Russian and Polish Jews who were coming to the United States. Thus some three hundred years after the first Jew landed on the Carolina coast, Jews were still dependent on European largesse. (Fewer than twenty-five years later, during World War I, American Jews, through their Joint Distribution Committee, exerted themselves to rescue the endangered Jewish communities in the East European lands and spent millions in the attempt.)

Baron de Hirsch had a plan, a grand design. He and his wife wanted to put Jews on the land, to further vocational training, to fit Jews for industry, to educate them in civics, to Americanize them, and to resettle them in the distant reaches of the trans-Mississippi country. It was Hirsch money that funded the Jewish Agricultural and Industrial Aid Society, and it was Hirsch money that sparked the work of the Industrial Removal Office in 1901. "Removal" was always on the mind of the baron and the American Jewish patricians who advised him. Eager to divert immigration from New York City, Jacob H. Schiff financed a plan to dispatch Jewish émigrés from Europe directly to Galveston. Aware that the north German Lloyd Steamship Company sent vessels with empty holds to pick up cargoes of cotton in Galveston, Schiff suggested that in the outbound voyage to the United States the ships fill their holds with cash customers: immigrants. The company liked the idea and Schiff took it from there.

Schiff and his friends proposed to syphon the newcomers from Galveston into the Midwest. Over a period of eight years, from 1907 to 1914, about ten thousand Jews came through Galveston. Schiff was aided by the English writer Israel Zangwill, who had organized the Jewish Territorial Organization when the Zionists refused to set up a Jewish homeland in east Africa. Zangwill wanted Russian Jews, who had suffered long enough in Europe, to find a new home. In the end, however, the Galveston movement had to be counted a failure. The immigration authorities in Washington and Galveston were not helpful, and the America-bound Jews preferred New York to sparse settlements in the American interior. Rabbi Henry Cohen (1863–1952), the charismatic Galveston rabbi, pitched in to help but finally threw in the towel. It was hard work, a thankless task, and World War I put an end to the experiment anyway. The Industrial Removal Office of New York dispatched about seventy-four thousand Jews out of town, to seventeen hundred cities and towns. Some refused to stay put and came back, but many did remain to become the core around which little communities agglomerated. Colonization, farming, and removal as policies accomplished very little, but the hinterland did experience very substantial growth. There were always more Jews outside of New York City than lived in that metropolis. Large Jewish communities emerged in Baltimore, Boston, Chicago, Cleveland, Detroit, Newark, Philadelphia, Pittsburgh, and St. Louis. In all these cities Jews could eventually hope to have a home of their own—and a backyard, too. A Jew did not have to live in a tenement house.

Most Jews chose big cities, especially New York. To be sure, after landing many stayed in this metropolis because they had no money to travel farther. Schiff, one of the richest Jews in America and a brilliant financier, wanted to push the Jews into the backcountry where their visibility would be diminished, and he hoped they would do well. But these penniless Jews proved wiser than Schiff. They remained in New York, in a "city and mother in Israel," where there were jobs, synagogues, theaters, Jewish foods, hometown societies, friends, large Jewish neighborhoods, and guarantees of Jewish survival. By 1930, almost 70 percent of American Jewry had settled in the northeast and middle Atlantic states.

THE ECONOMIC LIFE OF THE EAST EUROPEAN NEWCOMERS

PEDDLERS AND OTHER SMALL BUSINESSMEN

The thousands who had moved into the Lower East Side since the 1870s were poor but not beggars. They were eager to work, to make a living and improve themselves. Many became peddlers, haunting the tenement houses to sell notions for the most part, or hawking their wares from pushcarts. There was almost literally no commodity that was not offered for sale on these tiny mobile shops. Hundreds—if not thousands—engaged in this traffic. Peddlers swarmed in the inland towns, too; Milwaukee in 1910 had five hundred householders who peddled, while five hundred other families were craftsmen or petty retailers. The rag peddlers there had an association of their own, as did the itinerant junk dealers and the wholesalers with their junkyards. The grocers, the fruit dealers, the cobblers, and the butchers also had organizations that held them together. Some of these groups may have been mutual aid societies; others were for protection against rowdies who harassed and even clubbed the humble businessmen. In 1896 and later decades, Cleveland peddlers also organized themselves to ward off violence.

Up in the Minnesota backcountry, in the Northfield area, Moses Menahem Zieve managed to make a living as a wagon peddler. It took him six years to save enough money to bring his wife and four children to this country. Zieve kept strictly kosher, did his own cooking, and spent the Sabbath with a friendly farmer who alerted him when the Sabbath was over, thus permitting him, as an Orthodox Jew, to smoke. On Sunday morning Zieve preached to the German farmers in his Yiddish idiom; they understood him and called him Holy Moses. Peddling in the city or in the rural districts was a hard life, but these petty merchants hoped ultimately to improve themselves—though in this they were often disappointed. Even so, their children, with rare exceptions, moved up the economic ladder to become salespeople, bookkeepers, and shopkeepers of an infinite variety.

Both in the metropolitan cities and in the towns west of the Hudson, customer peddlers managed to do rather well.

They were royalty, carrying no wares but referring customers to wholesalers. It was the customer peddler's task to collect from the humble buyers—in effect, an installment business. One of the Schiffs of Cincinnati was a customer peddler. His sons opened shoe stores, and ultimately the Schiff Shoe Company became the Shoe Corporation of America with nine manufacturing plants and seven hundred stores. The Edison Brothers, also émigrés from Slavic Europe, built an even larger shoe empire.

THE NEEDLE TRADES

Many immigrants were artisans—tailors, locksmiths, cobblers, painters, barbers, carpenters, blacksmiths, upholsterers, masons, bricklayers, ironworkers, and cigarette makers—who had learned a trade in their native lands. When James Duke, the founder of the American Tobacco Company, began manufacturing cigarettes in North Carolina, he employed Russian Jewish cigarette makers in his factory. Most East European Jews who came to New York gravitated to the apparel industry, where more Jews were employed than in any other trade. As workers, contractors, subcontractors, and manufacturers, they dominated the men's and women's clothing industry, the "rag trade." In 1880 production in the industry was already in the many millions; by 1924 it had risen into the billions. But newcomers who practiced a craft were, for the most part, a one-generation proletariat, neither the children nor the parents of blue-collar workers, and their sons and daughters moved up to white-collar jobs.

In 1890, it is estimated that 60 percent of the laborers—mostly Jews working for Jews—were in the garment industry. About 8 percent were artisans, while some 30 percent were shopkeepers or tradesmen. Conditions in New York City's factories and workplaces during the 1880s and 1890s were deplorable. The goods in the apparel industry were mostly produced in sweatshops. The hours were long, the pay was poor, and sanitation was inadequate. Thousands of children were employed and never went to school. In 1907 there were still many thousands of boys and girls laboring in New York's tenement workshops (not all of them, of course, were Jews). In Pittsburgh little girls worked from dawn to dusk for a pittance. When the inspectors came, they were hidden in the cellars. The children wanted to be caught and sent to school.

Because working conditions were so bad in the apparel industry, strikes were inevitable. The leaders were usually socialists committed to a political philosophy of voting the capitalists out of office and establishing a Marxist—a messianic—state. (A similar ideal would inspire the Labor Party in Palestine when it called the new State of Israel into existence in 1948.) At a Socialist Labor convention in 1895, a banner strung across the hall proudly proclaimed: "We are not Jews; rather we are all Yiddish-speaking proletarians" (this despite the fact that the rank and file in all the unions then and later were humble East Europeans sympathetic to, if not always practitioners of, traditional Orthodoxy). In the 1890s one of the most active of the socialist ideologues was the highly educated and committed Daniel De Leon. An assimilated Jew who denied his Jewish origins, he established a separate federation of socialist labor unions that published a paper of its own. Strikers in the 1880s and 1890s won victories occasionally but did not systematically build unions. It was the party that came first, not the union.

De Leon's Socialist Labor Party was challenged in 1901 by the Socialist Party. Over the years this new political party was fortunate to have dozens of competent, devoted leaders, a number of whom helped build great unions in the apparel industry. Some of these union leaders had been influenced in their native Slavic lands by the "bund," a Jewish political party and workers' organization. The four American "Jewish" unions that they created and that affected labor relations were the International Ladies' Garment Workers' Union (ILGWU); the Cloth Hat, Cap and Millinery Workers; the Furriers; and the Amalgamated Clothing Workers of America. Among the leaders in the new Socialist Party was Victor Luitpold (Louis) Berger of Milwaukee, the first Socialist to be elected to Congress, but he was not primarily interested in close ties with the apparel unions. The socialist leaders in New York City who did aspire to guide the rebellious workers were Morris Hillquit (1869–1933), Sidney Hillman (1887–1946), and Abraham Cahan (1860–1951), editor of the *Forward*.

Perspective is imperative. The socialist leaders who set out to organize the masses from the top down were Jewishly schismatic. They were not traditionalists, though the masses still were. Maverick anarchists even held parties on the eve of the Day of Atonement. They set out—successfully—to annoy the religionists, but it is important to recognize that socialism was never a mass movement in the United States, not even among the Jews. A Jewish Socialist Federation in 1912 numbered but five thousand Jews in a Jewry of about two million. Yiddish was the cement that held all Jewish émigrés together, and when in 1915 the workers' Marxist leaders joined the new Joint Distribution Committee to succor Jews in Europe, they tied—or retied—themselves irrevocably to the Jewish people. Later, in the 1930s, the socialist leaders of the Jewish unions, moving to the right, capitulated to Roosevelt, the New Dealer, who had cut the ground from under their feet by giving the workers, his allies, what they wanted.

THE JEWISH UNIONS

Tough-minded immigrant leaders took a step forward in the 1880s when they organized a Yiddish-speaking federation of unions, the United Hebrew Trades (UHT). The Gentile labor federations did not want these Jews, and the Jews in turn certainly wanted to be on their own, so that ultimately the UHT embraced at least one hundred unions and more than two hundred thousand workers. That took time, of course, and these newcomers wandered in the capitalist wilderness for almost thirty years before they approached the Promised Land. In November 1909, the shirtwaist workers met to voice their problems. When they hesitated to go on strike, a young worker, Clara Lemlich, sparked the final decision: "I offer a resolution that a general strike be declared now." It passed, and what is known as the Uprising of the Twenty Thousand was underway. Charles K. Harris, the Jewish songwriter, encouraged the young women with his strong, "Heaven Will Protect the Working Girl"—they needed divine intervention. Magistrate Olmstead told the young women brought before him: "You are on strike against God and nature." When the strike was settled in February 1910, the Jews emerged with a fifty-two-hour week and, apparently, a pay increase—not an overwhelming victory. That same year, in July, when the cloakmakers of the ILGWU went on strike in New York and more than fifty thousand workers walked out, American Jewry was disturbed—Jews were fighting Jews. A. Lincoln Filene, the Boston department store magnate, intervened, as did Louis D. Brandeis, the corporation lawyer, and Jacob H. Schiff and Louis Marshall of New York

City. The victory in September—and it was a victory of sorts— involved the adoption of the Protocol of Peace, a document that provided for a Joint Board of Sanitary Control, prohibited the employment of subcontractors (sweatshops), and established a system to deal with grievances and a compulsory resort to arbitration. The striking workers won a fifty-four-hour week.

Though it took years, the unions made progress despite the internal dissension between the socialists and communists and the determination of the Jewish employers to make as few concessions as possible; a successful strike always cost the owners millions. There were mass general strikes in the men's clothing industry in Chicago and New York between 1910 and 1912, and again the strikers won: fewer hours and more money. The men's clothing union in those days was the United Garment Workers, but unhappiness with the leaders—Gentiles, for the most part—induced the Jewish members to secede and form the Amalgamated Clothing Workers of America in 1914. Their president, Sidney Hillman, had been one of the leaders of the 1910–11 strike against Hart, Schaffner & Marx, the Chicago company that finally agreed to arbitrate all future differences. This, too, was a gain.

Hillman became the Jewish unions' most notable leader. He had begun life in Russia as a rabbinical student, became an intellectual and a revolutionary, went to jail, and immigrated to the United States at the age of about twenty in 1907. Leaving Chicago, he went to New York, where he helped administer the Protocol of Peace (1914) before he was called to lead the Amalgamated Clothing Workers. Before his career came to an end in the 1940s—this was a long haul—he had unionized the men's dress clothing industry and raised the standard of living of the workers. By 1939 his union could boast about 250,000 members in hundreds of locals throughout the country. The union's in-house newspaper was published in seven languages. Wages were constantly raised and hours were constantly lowered. Hillman worked closely with the employers, preferring not to see them as the "enemy" but to help them stay in business. Of course, he wanted the unions to have a say; this was "industrial democracy." Hillman was also concerned with workmen after they left the shops. The Union pushed for education, recreation, cooperative cheap housing, and insurance as well as unemployment benefits. This was the new unionism. Hillman went into politics and, in the 1930s and early 1940s, was an important labor leader in the Roosevelt administration, occupying prestigious posts on the Labor Advisory Board, the National Industrial Recovery Board, the National Defense Advisory Commission, and in the Office of Production Management during World War II. In 1938 he was one of the architects of the Congress of Industrial Organizations (CIO), a rival of the American Federation of Labor (AFL). Despite the fact that Roosevelt eased him out of office in 1942, Hillman remained loyal to the astute president and led the political action committee to help reelect him and make Truman the vice president. This was quite a career for a Russian lad who had once swayed over his lectern to chant a page of the Talmud.

Hillman lived to see many changes in the life of the Jewish unionists. Where workers once labored almost sixty hours a week, the time came when they spent but thirty-two and a half hours. The men and women employed in the apparel industry did better than millions of blacks and many whites, both in the city and on the farms. The union Americanized and educated them and encouraged them to read their Yiddish paper. It is worth bearing in mind that many of the immigrants had never had the opportunity to read a Yiddish paper in their homeland. In Rumania, for example, except for a very brief period, there was no Jewish daily. While the first Yiddish daily did not appear in Russia until 1905, there had been one in New York City as early as 1885. When the steel workers went out on strike in 1919, three Jewish unions contributed more in relief than twenty-four other international unions. America gave immigrant Jews the political immunities and economic opportunities denied them in the East European lands, taught them the meaning of democracy, and disciplined them. The sons and daughters had it better than the parents. Jewish apparel workers made America the best dressed nation in the world. They undermined the visible distinction between the classes and thus advanced democracy.

The Jewish Unions as a Jewish Movement

It is obvious from the solicitude of the Jewish unions for their members that they were concerned with more than wages and hours. The labor movement was so extensive that it constituted something of a cultural, spiritual, social, and class enclave. The ties that bound the workers together were strengthened by the United Hebrew Trades, their umbrella organization. Nothing that concerned the welfare of a member was alien to the ideologues who guided the destinies of their labor organizations. Indeed, there were some unions whose services were of a mutual aid nature, providing sickness and death benefits. In the year 1900 a group of non-Zionist socialists close to the unions created an order they called the Arbeter Ring (Workmen's Circle). Later, in 1912, the Zionist socialists established a separate fraternal order, the Jewish National Workers' Alliance (Farband Labor Zionist Order). The unions provided the bread and butter; the auxiliary organizations guaranteed sociability and intellectual stimulation. The devotion of the unions to their followers is best reflected in the Union Health Center. The ILGWU took it over in 1913, and by 1942 it was serving forty-two thousand men and women. This institution, an ambulatory diagnostic health clinic, was first envisioned by Dr. George Moses Price (1864–1942), who served as its chief. Price's career is interesting and enlightening. After landing in the United States in the 1880s, he was faced with the need to earn a livelihood. In the course of the next six or seven years, he made baskets and paper collars; worked in a chair factory; labored in a paper mill, a boiler factory, and on a farm; dug ditches; ran a grocery store; collected tickets on a railroad; handed out money as a bank clerk; managed an apartment house; taught public school; and edited a weekly journal—all this before receiving his M.D. degree in 1895. His associates were all Jews. His own religion? He was a member of Felix Adler's Ethical Culture Society.

The Immigrant Jewish Woman in a Man's World

Pauline Newman (b. ca. 1889) served as educational director in George Price's Union Health Center. Much of the life of this courageous woman was spent organizing labor. The other women engaged in this task had much in common. All were foreign-born, socialists, and unwavering in their devotion to their jobs. They were beaten by thugs as they walked the picket lines; their fellow unionists, even the leaders, were not always cordial and helpful. But rare women made careers in the movement. Dorothy Jacobs Bellanca (1894–1946) headed her local at the age of twenty and sat on the executive board of the Amalgamated Clothing Workers two years later. In 1911 146 workers—mostly young women—perished in the Triangle Shirt-waist Company fire. Rose Schneiderman (1882–1972) was called upon to make the memorial address: "The life of men and women is so cheap and property is so sacred," she lamented. At the age of thirteen, Schneiderman was already working in a department store, a genteel job that paid her $2 a week. Needing more money—if not less gentility—she went to work in a factory making caps. Like Bellanca, she served on the board of her international union and before her career had run its course became national president of the Woman's Trade Union League, an officer on two prestigious New Deal committees, and finally, in 1937, secretary of the New York State Department of Labor. Bellanca had been born in Latvia; Schneiderman, in Poland. Rose Harriet Pastor Phelps Stokes (1879–1933) was also a native of Poland. Put to work at the age of four to help her mother make a living, Rose sewed bows on slippers. When she grew up she became an English columnist for New York's Yiddish *Tageblatt*. While on a journalistic stint, she met and married James Graham Phelps Stokes, scion of an aristocratic New York family, and from then on she was dubbed the Proletarian Cinderella.

The 1880s and the 1890s, with their almost eight years of depression, were bad years for all of America's workers, but the newcomers—indomitable and industrious—survived. The children helped. Lincoln Steffens tells this story of an eleven-year-old child: When Mama, in charge of a large tenement house, took sick, her little girl took over. At home, she did the cooking and washing and looked after five younger children, including an infant. Another girl handled the running of a large apartment house, collected the rents, and conducted the interviews with the Board of Health. Stokes was a Socialist and Communist;

Emma Goldman (1869–1940) was an anarchist. Stokes, though a devoted liberal, was little more than a dilettante; Goldman, self-educated, was a brilliant, cultured, knowledgeable woman. Because of her radical social justice views, she was in prison more than once, but she never betrayed herself. Loyal to her ideals as she understood them, she was a feminist, an individualist, a universalist who preached her gospel: No polity offers freedom; salvation lies only in a cooperative ethical society. She had little use for a capitalistic Christian civilization that tolerated the lynching of blacks (who were Christians). Her Jewish identity? Goldman was in the biblical prophetic tradition. She wanted a better life for every man and woman. Ruth Katz of Chicago was no union organizer and no intellectual, not even a socialist. She was the biblical "woman of valor" whose job it was to help her husband make a living (or if necessary, she would be the chief provider). She started out doing piecework—garters and suspenders—working twelve hours a day for seven cents a dozen (to make $10 a week, she had to finish 1,716 pieces). Katz married, ran a ladies' and children's shop, lost everything in the Great Depression of the 1930s, sold bakery goods, delicatessen, and cigars, and finally acquired some real estate that sustained her in her old age. These are the not so simple annals of the lower middle class. Jennie Grossinger (1892–1972), put to work at thirteen, made $1.50 her first week. Before she died, she and her husband had built a resort in the Catskills. The resort covered 1,200 acres with 600 guest rooms, had its own post office and a 1,700-seat auditorium to serve 150,000 guests some years, and, in a good year, enjoyed a $7 million turnover.

Most immigrant women were as eager to become somebodies socially and financially as immigrant men. They were not enamored of a proletarian way of life and had no desire to remain garment workers, cigarette makers, salesladies, or servants. They wanted to be lawyers, doctors, dentists, writers, or the wives of professionals, and many achieved their goals. Jennie Loitman Barron (1891–1969) became the first woman in Boston to serve as a judge in a local court (1937), seventeen years after women received the vote. Belle Lindner Israels Moskowitz, the daughter of a Polish immigrant, was a competent social worker and, as a person concerned with the welfare of society, had much in common with Lillian Wald (1867–1940) and the Russian-born Sophie Irene Loeb (1876–1929). Some historians believe that Loeb was responsible for more beneficial welfare legislation than any other woman in the country. By far the majority of Russian and Polish women who worked in the clothing and dress factories stayed home and raised families after marriage. They wanted to leave the Lower East Side—and they did, moving northward in Manhattan till they reached the Bronx or crossed the Williamsburg Bridge to Brooklyn. They were looking for better housing, a bathtub, and more room, but they were equally determined to retain the familiar ghetto atmosphere. Most of them hoped, someday, to become part of the attractive middle class.

An Amorphous Middle Class

A dictionary defines the middle class as "a fluid heterogeneous socioeconomic grouping composed principally of business and professional people sharing common social characteristics and values." American Jews prove that the dictionary is right, although it is not easy to determine the confines of the immigrant middle class. A successful carpenter who renovated old houses might well be deemed a prosperous businessman. Owners of myriads of Jewish shops of all sizes, selling general or specific commodities; small- and large-scale immigrant manufacturers, real estate speculators, and building contractors; Jews active in show business as comedians, actors, and musicians—all these might fit within the limits of an amorphous middle class. Many of the newcomers—or their sons—achieved acclaim and cash as professional boxers. A goodly number of Jewish immigrants, yearning to join the middle class, made their way into the early Jewish *Who's Who* volumes and the *Who's Who* "mug" books in which one could write one's own more or less embroidered biography. Climbing up the economic ladder was hazardous, but those who fell—as many did—could start all over again.

Many of the newcomers at one time or another nursed hopes of becoming white-collar workers, professionals. It was not so difficult even in the decades before 1930 to secure a college education. Tuition was very modest, and one could nearly always work one's way through school, though it might take years to obtain the coveted diploma. Thousands went into dentistry, pharmacy, accounting, engineering, law, medicine, journalism, music. The elementary schools did not reject Jewish teachers, though the colleges did. By 1926 and 1927 11 percent of the students enrolled in the University of Pittsburgh were Jews, for the most part Slavic immigrants or their children. If one were to pick a page or two from the 1926 (Jewish) *Who's Who in America*, the high percentage of professionals would be obvious. Pages 9 and 10 list eight individuals: one born in the United States, one in Palestine, and six in Eastern Europe; four were rabbis, while a Hebrew educator, a neurologist, a calligrapher, and an orthodontist comprised the other four. Among the notable professionals who stood out in early twentieth-century America were two statisticians, students of social security legislation and old age pensions: Dr. Isaac M. Rubinow (1875–1936) and Abraham Epstein (1892–1942). These pioneers in this field were recognized authorities, even though when the 1935 Social Security Act was written, their views did not always prevail.

Out of thousands of other biographies of émigrés, the following six (chosen more or less arbitrarily) document the middle-class status of Jewish immigrants. All are interesting. All but one were notables in their generations.

David Lubin (1849–1919) prospected for gold in Arizona in 1868, established a successful dry goods emporium in Sacramento, California, built up a large mail-order department, united a number of California's fruit growers, and finally organized the Italian-based International Institute of Agriculture, which was meant to inaugurate, as it were, a "United States of the World."

Sol Levitan (1862–1940), a Lithuanian immigrant, was a brilliant, shrewd, successful Wisconsin politician, who quit peddling and storekeeping to run for office. He was close to the great American liberal Senator Robert M. La Follette: "I sold him a pair of suspenders and I supported him the balance of his life." "Uncle Sol" served several times as the Wisconsin state treasurer. When his opponents sniped at the aged officeholder, he answered that he was looking for the Golden Gate not the Golden Calf.

Aaron Marcus (d. 1933) was no notable. Markelson (his name in Lithuania) was a farmer who was conscripted and served the czar for about five years. (The captain appropriated Markelson's pay when it fell due.) He left for America via Hamburg, where he adopted a good German Jewish name. In New York in 1889 Marcus worked in a brick factory and baked matzos. He became an apparel worker but was fired when he sewed two left sleeves on a jacket. Picking up a basket of notions, he peddled his way to Pittsburgh, worked in a modest machine shop for a man named George Westinghouse, peddled again during the depression of the 1890s, opened a store in Homestead next door to the Carnegie Steel Works, made money, moved back to Pittsburgh, started a little department store, went bankrupt in the next depression, moved to West Virginia, and settled in the hinterland, the only Jew in thirty-six square miles. He finally made enough to retire—on an annual income of about $1,500—and spent his last days in Pittsburgh, his core city, where he joined a decorous Conservative synagogue. Marcus, who always voted the straight Republican ticket, had no use for socialists or communists; a bottle of rye whiskey would last him a whole year.

Col. Harry Cutler (1875–1920) came to the United States at the age of eight after his father had been murdered in a pogrom. As a child he worked in a Providence canning factory for 90 cents a week. At the ripe age of fourteen he was a foreman in charge of a dozen other boys. Saving his money, Cutler bought a defunct jewelry factory for $150, did well, became a state assemblyman, colonel of a militia regiment, president of a synagogue, a founder of the American Jewish Committee, and a delegate dispatched by American Jewry to Paris when the Treaty of Versailles was being written. The delegation was instructed to further a homeland in Palestine and to seek emancipation for the Jews of Russia, Poland, and Rumania. The French awarded Cutler their medal of honor. He died at the age of forty-five.

Israel Baline (1888–1989), the son of a Russian cantor, was brought to the United States in 1893. In his early days he worked as a singing waiter in a Chinatown saloon. Renamed Irving Berlin, he married an heiress—granddaughter of a successful Irish miner—and wrote nearly one thousand songs, including "God Bless America" and "White Christmas." In the 1920s he was already a millionaire. Jerome Kern, composer of *Show Boat*, said of him, "Irving Berlin has no place in American music; he is American music."

Golda Mabovitch (1898–1978) never made millions. A Milwaukee schoolteacher, she had been born in Kiev and brought to the United States as a youngster in 1906. A fervent Zionist, she settled in Palestine at the age of twenty-three. Forty-eight years later, as Golda Meir, she became the prime minister of the State of Israel (1969).

A handful of Slavic Jewish newcomers became wealthy. But, historically, how important are the rich? If in 1924 there were, say, a hundred or so émigré millionaires among 3,500,000 Jews, what was their impact, if any, on Jewish life? History, after all, is the story of the entire people, not the paltry few. True, rich immigrants document the opportunities available in these great United States. (Parenthetically, some able Jews rose to wealth and power even in stepmother Russia: The Baron Guenzburg and his clan were notable bankers; the Brodskis were sugar magnates; the Wissotsky name became a synonym for a good cup of tea.) Ultimately, the rich deserve a line in a history only if they pay their way, if the Jews and the larger general community are the better for their presence. Louis Borgenicht ("Don't Borrow!"), a Galician who started his life in America presiding over a pushcart full of pots and pans, became the "King of the Children's Dress Trade" with his sales running into the millions. This innovative manufacturer had built a better mousetrap; the garments he designed and produced were beautiful. Isaac Gilman (ca. 1865–1944), sixteen when he came to this country, was a peddler and a cigar maker before he established the

Gilman Paper Company. Around the year 1907 he bought out a paper mill in Fitzdale, Vermont, and before long had erected the largest paper mill in the state. Fitzdale soon became his and, because of him, a model factory village. He gave Fitzdale a fire department, waterworks, and a railroad station. In gratitude the villagers changed the name of the town to Gilman.

Louis J. Horowitz (1875–1956) was one of the few Jewish Poles who came to the United States with a good "high school" education. Only seventeen when he landed, he soon made a name for himself in the building industry and in 1903 was hired by Thompson Starrett Company, a firm then in trouble. Seven years later he was president of the corporation, which under his direction became one of America's largest construction companies. Horowitz built the Waldorf-Astoria and the Equitable and the Woolworth buildings; few men have done more to change the New York City skyline. When he died, he left millions of dollars to New York University.

Akiba Horowitz (1860–1928)—no known relative of Louis J.—decided that his Jewish name was a liability and changed it to Conrad Hubert, which for him was a good American name. He invented a flashlight, established the American Eveready Flashlight Company, and amassed a fortune. The administrators authorized to divide his estate were a Catholic, a Protestant, and a Jew.

Louis J. and Akiba Horowitz both made millions; Louis Blaustein (1869–1937) and his son Jacob (1892–1970) did even better. They built the world's largest oil refinery. Louis began as a kerosene peddler carrying his stock in a one-horse tank wagon. He pioneered in setting up gasoline stations for the newfangled automobile. The firm he built, the American Oil Company (AMOCO), became an American household word.

Jacob carried the firm to even greater heights and distinguished himself as one of the country's outstanding Jewish communal leaders, dominating the American Jewish Committee, Jewry's most influential organization in his day.

One of the Baltimore contemporaries of the Blausteins was a Lithuanian immigrant by the name of Jacob Epstein (1864–1945), not to be confused with the expatriate American sculptor. The Maryland Epstein founded a mail-order house that catered only to retailers. This able wholesaler, who later obtained recognition as an art collector and philanthropist, employed about one thousand workers in his business in 1910 when his sales ran around $1 million a month.

Two successful entrepreneurs made their mark in Louisiana. Abrom Kaplan (b. 1872) and Samuel Zemurray (1877–1961) both followed a traditional path, beginning their lives in this country as peddlers. Kaplan peddled in New York City and Connecticut and then in Louisiana, where he turned to rice farming. He drained swamps, set up irrigation systems, built rice mills, and finally emerged as the largest producer of rice in the United States. His headquarters was in Kaplan, his own town, which would one day shelter five thousand souls. Like Gilman in Vermont, Kaplan became a model community reflecting luster on its founder. Zemurray came to this country in 1892, a year before the depression started, and peddled bananas in his adopted Louisiana. His initial challenge determined his future. Before he stopped pushing his way to the top, he controlled the United Fruit Company with its five hundred thousand acres in Central America and fifty-two ships to transport its harvest. Zemurray gave liberally to charity and initiated welfare programs on the company's plantations, though for many of America's liberals the United Fruit Company was anathema.

The kaleidoscopic variety in the enterprises of immigrant achievers was fascinating, almost startling. Iser Hiram Nakdimen (b. 1871), a Slavic Jew, peddled tinware on foot in Arkansas and Oklahoma. He settled in Ft. Smith and in time built a small railroad, purchased newspapers, and established numerous banks in his part of the country. On one occasion he bought well over a million dollars' worth of Oklahoma bonds—it may well have been the bank's money he invested. Nakdimen was concerned with the welfare of Oklahoma's Native Americans and was friendly to organized labor.

On the upper peninsula of Michigan, with headquarters in Ishpeming (twenty-nine Jewish souls in 1937), the Cohodas brothers built one of America's largest produce companies. The family had settled originally in Wisconsin, and after Papa Cohodas died his widow and children struggled to survive. The young boys peddled milk, sold newspapers, and worked as clerks behind the counter. By 1915 the firm had pulled up stakes and moved on to the tiny towns of Michigan's upper peninsula, where at the end of the world the family built its own business empire.

Abraham Slimmer (ca. 1835–1917) never became a millionaire, but he was decidedly successful. This native Pole settled in the village of Waverly, Iowa, where he made a fortune placing mortgages for insurance companies. Once he had amassed a competence, he began giving it away. Helping Jews and Christians through matching grants, he built hospitals and homes for orphans and the aged. Isaac Shwayder came to Colorado in 1879 with a wife and eleven children whom he supported as a clerk and grocer. Jesse (1882–1970), the leader among the children, started a small luggage company in Denver in 1910. Eventually the Shwayder brothers' Samsonite luggage company was reputed to be the largest of its type in the world.

THE CINEMA

Several Jews of East European stock—a glove salesman, a furrier, a junk dealer, owners of a bicycle shop—were among the pioneers of the cinema industry, which had had an unimpressive start in the 1890s as penny peepshows in arcades. To hack out a living, some Jews were always ready to crawl into interstitial spaces. That same decade saw the beginning of primitive silent movies. It was not until the early 1900s, however, that the first nickelodeon opened, and within a year there were eight thousand more. Sheriff Bronco Billy's shows were among the most popular. The "sheriff" was Max Anderson (né Aronson), a Jew. How Jewish was he? He refused to eat pork, but that was about the extent of it.

By World War I, America already dominated the new film industry, and Hollywood, California, became the preferred spot for the production of pictures. In 1927 Al Jolson, an actor and singer, starred in what was in part at least a talking—at any rate, a singing—movie. The singing voice heard was not Jolson's but belonged to the incomparable Joseph (Yossele) Rosenblatt, America's greatest cantor.

Among the Jews in the industry were writers, directors, and a few actors, but it was as producers—excellent merchandisers—that they stood out. This was important if the new type of show business was to thrive. By the 1920s these adventurers had established several of the country's greatest cinema corporations. When these entrepreneurs hit their stride, they began building magnificent theaters. The orchestras and accompanying organ music were often of symphonic character and the staged gala openings of new pictures were artistic triumphs. By the 1930s, out of a total of eight important companies Jews owned three and exercised partial control in three others. What did these moviemakers do for the America that had given them home and opportunity? They helped develop a major facet of the entertainment industry. By the 1920s they were beginning to employ thousands of people and, ultimately, would put hundreds of thousands to work. In that same decade thousands of movie theaters were opened in the United States. What had begun as a five-cent industry in 1905 was grossing billions by the 1940s.

The cinema the Jews helped bring to birth was on the whole probably an influence for good. Imagine the world without it! These Jews educated people, gave them vistas of life they were never to experience themselves, and even on occasion moved them to action. The cinema made hundreds of millions of men, women, and children happy, giving them what they wanted, or had learned to want: cowboys, Indians, gangsters, intrigue, mystery, beautiful women, courageous men, a moment to weep, and above all, the conviction that always, *always*, virtue would be rewarded. The movies furthered what would become the chief form of entertainment for the American people and, soon enough, for almost every human being, even in the farthest corners of the world. Their appeal was and is universal, and it cannot be deemed a sin to have entertained the world.

Were these Hollywood impresarios Jewish? Most of them belonged to synagogues, even if they rarely frequented them. The founders had been raised in Orthodox homes and surroundings, but their real religion was not one of home and synagogue—it was to produce motion pictures that sold. They had set out to bring heaven down to earth, and they succeeded.

MAKING IT—AND NOT MAKING IT—IN AMERICA

Lena Himmelstein (1881–1951), an immigrant from the Slavic lands, came to this country in 1897 when she was sixteen. Opening a small dressmaking shop in New York in 1907 she became one of the first in this country to design a maternity gown. In 1916 she incorporated her firm under the name of Lane Bryant, Inc. A year later the sales in her business exceeded $1 million, and by 1968, with the firm having grown to more than one hundred branches, sales had risen to $200 million. Starting out with maternity dresses, Himmelstein then added special sizes.

The wise author of Proverbs (31:30) had written: "favor is deceitful and beauty is vain," but Helena Rubinstein (ca. 1871–1965) was not disheartened by the biblical admonition. "Beauty" was her specialty, and as a result she became one of the country's richest Jewish businesspersons. This extraordinarily successful cosmetician had come from an impoverished Galician family, immigrated to Australia, manufactured a cold cream there, and made some money before moving on to London in search of new worlds to conquer. She opened beauty salons in the English capital, in Paris and other cities, and from all indications was consistently successful. The coming of World War I led her to shift her base to the United States. Rubinstein became one of the country's most important and innovative manufacturers of beauty products. At her death she left a large personal estate, and the business was later sold for $142 million.

In 1914 Meyer London (1871–1926), a New York ghetto denizen of foreign birth, defeated the Tammany candidate and was elected to Congress on the Socialist ticket. Socialists, trade unionists, and other admirers sent him to Washington. This East Side Jew was loved and respected. A man of honor and a true humanitarian, he had no interest in traditional Judaism but was devoted to Jews. Like Hillquit and Berger, London was a staunch Socialist, an internationalist who nursed messianic hopes and had little sympathy for Zionists and their nationalism. Indeed, he refused to introduce a resolution in Congress endorsing the movement and its hopes for a reborn Jewish state.

The hundreds of victims of the 1917 Espionage Act included several Jews. One of them was Jacob (Jack) Abrams, who in 1918, along with some of his friends, had distributed English and Yiddish pamphlets protesting the intervention of American troops in Russia and Siberia. There had been no declaration of war against the new Soviet regime in Russia, but six Russian Jews, among them a young woman, were arrested in connection with this protest. One, tortured and badly beaten in jail, died of injuries; the woman was sentenced to fifteen years' imprisonment; three others, including Abrams, received sentences of twenty years. When in 1919 the case was sent to the United States Supreme Court, the sentence was affirmed, though Holmes and Brandeis dissented. Four of the offenders, finally released in 1921, had to leave the country and went to Russia. Unhappy, Abrams soon fled the Soviet state and found refuge in Mexico.

Kiev-born Samuel Paley (1877–1963), son of Isaac and Zelda Lapatofskey, was brought to this country as a child of eleven. When he grew up, he went into the cigar business in Chicago and made a fortune. His brand was La Palina, named of course after himself. Moving to Philadelphia, he joined the elite Jewish city and country clubs, but his synagogue was a traditional one. The millions he made in cigars became the seed money he and his son William used to build the Columbia Broadcasting System.

David Sarnoff (1891–1971) was nine when he came to the United States. In 1906, after a few years of public school, he went to work as a messenger for the Commercial Cable Company. When the High Holy Days came around, he took three days off not only because of the sanctity of the occasion but also because he was the soloist in the synagogue choir and wanted to make some extra money. The company fired him. Sarnoff then became an office boy for the Marconi Wireless Telegraph Company and later a telegraph operator (1907). In 1919 the company was taken over by the Radio Corporation of America (RCA), and he was appointed one of its junior executives. Two years later he was made the general manager, and in 1926 he established the National Broadcasting Company and in 1930 was named president of RCA. Sarnoff developed coast-to-coast broadcasting and later pioneered in color television. In 1960 RCA, one of the largest electronic companies in the world, was a $2 billion corporation employing one hundred thousand people.

RELIGION

The newcomers who landed at Castle Garden and, later, Ellis Island went at once to the ghetto on the Lower East Side. It had always been the ghetto. It was there in the 1840s that a group of Germans established Temple Emanu-El with $28.25 in the treasury. The ghetto had synagogues, Hebrew schools, kosher meat shops, a mikveh where the women could take their monthly ritual bath, a Jewish bookstore. The Irish in this ghetto area savored their many saloons, but when the Jews started crowding in, the saloons moved out. In the Jewish areas the common language was Yiddish. The newcomers brought their religion with them, Orthodoxy, belief in God, the Messiah, the

Ten Commandments, a traditional universe of customs and rites. Their book of common prayer was the siddur, as old as the hills. The rites of passage were all observed, from circumcision to the days of mourning for their dear ones. Except for the sophisticated radicals, all kept kosher. Manhattan's P.S. 9 served the Jewish youngsters—two thousand strong—kosher lunches for 3 cents.

The most important institution in the Jewish quarter was the synagogue. The Russians had opened a House of Learning in 1852 and soon had a spiritual leader who looked upon himself as their chief rabbi. The typical ghetto synagogue was a rented one-room affair, and anyone could serve as a reader there. By 1880 about thirty such conventicles had been established in town. (In 1917 New York City had at least seven hundred, and there were said to be at least two thousand of these chapels in the United States in the 1920s.) Even tiny Burlington, Vermont, had a small synagogue. On the High Holy Days, Sergeant Max Pilzer of nearby Fort Ethan Allen brought in twenty-five Jewish soldiers to worship there. The fort's Jewish cavalry troopers had a society; they called themselves the Knights of Zion. And the Sabbath? Many, unfortunately, had to work on that day, which is why the meticulous thought America an unkosher land. With a modicum of prosperity, ambitious officials of large synagogues imported noted cantors, hazzanim, men with glorious voices. A good cantor brought in members, and members helped pay off the mortgage.

Nearly every town that sheltered Jews had a ghetto of its own. New York's, of course, was the largest, but as early as the second decade of the twentieth century only 23 percent of the city's Jews lived in the ghetto. The settlement house workers—often Gentiles—wanted to change the ghetto ambience, and the Jews wanted to change their address. By 1907 Brooklyn had at least ninety synagogues and prayer rooms; there were already some hundred thousand Jews in this suburb. With the influx of the immigrant masses the need was felt in New York City for an organized chief rabbinate. All efforts in the 1870s and the 1880s to federate the Orthodox synagogues and to impose a "chief rabbi" on the masses failed. Rabbi Jacob Joseph of Lithuania was elected in 1887–1888, but he had no control over the kosher meat industry. In effect, he was ignored, though the East Side did give him a great funeral and even named an all-day school after him. The émigrés never failed to honor their dead.

Annoyed by the advance of the Reform synagogues and their union of congregations, many of the tradition-minded Jewish native-born and "Germans" met in 1898 to establish the Union of Orthodox Jewish Congregations of the United States and Canada (UOJC), undeviatingly Orthodox in belief and practice. Four years later, however, the East European immigrant rabbis founded a national society of their own, the United Orthodox Rabbis of America. They wanted nothing to do with the acculturated Orthodox of the UOJC or the new Jewish Theological Seminary. Their rejection of the UOJC was primarily ethnic, not theological, since both groups accepted the twelfth-century Maimonidean credo as their confession of faith, but these militant rabbinical newcomers could not compete with their Orthodox predecessors who preached in English or German. Ultimately the Yiddish-speaking leaders and Talmudists had to make their peace with America or lose all their youth. A few even learned to speak and publish in English. No one hewed more to the traditional line than Rabbi Bernard L. Levinthal of Philadelphia, but he and his circle knew that

Hanukkah had to compete with Christmas. On Hanukkah, his son Israel was given toys, a sled, games, and a policeman's or fireman's uniform.

In 1919 American Jewry published an edition of the Talmud and began sending copies to war-devastated Europe. The immigrant East Europeans were paying off their cultural debt to their native lands. Under the impact of American mores, devoted Orthodox laymen in 1912 established a national organization that soon came to be known as Young Israel. The members insisted on decorum as well as devotion and encouraged an edificatory lecture on Friday eve. By 1915 the East European traditionalist rabbis had appointed Bernard Revel (1885–1940), an American Ph.D. and a competent Talmudist, head of the Rabbinical College of America, which had been established in 1897. East European Orthodoxy was now rapidly acculturating itself. By 1921 the Agudath Israel, a far-right-wing-group, was educating Jewish girls. The following year Mordecai M. Kaplan, a Conservative rabbi, saw to it that his daughter, Judith, was called to read a portion of the Law in the synagogue—the first bat mitzvah ceremony. The women, too, were coming into their own religiously.

JEWISH EDUCATION

HEBREW SCHOOLS

Surveys made in New York City before 1917 disclosed that relatively few Jewish children were receiving a Jewish education, at one time only about 23.5 percent. The heder, the traditional one-room Hebrew school, was most common. Youngsters learned to read—mechanically—the Hebrew that they could not translate (but that God surely understood!). That was considered important, as the ability to read Hebrew (i.e., to read the Hebrew alphabet) made for identification as a Jew. Thousands of the children of immigrant East Europeans in the big cities of the country went to Jewish-sponsored schools designed to compete with the schools of missionary Christians and the Sunday schools of the Reform synagogues where little or no Hebrew was taught. Relatively few attended the Orthodox congregational afternoon schools, and even fewer went to the all-day schools, of which there were only four in all of New York City. A handful of first-class schools for children functioned—primarily in New York City—but they were in no sense typical.

Corporal punishment in the elementary schools? For the most part violence was recognized as self-defeating. Long gone were the early days when, as at Harvard, the college head, Nathaniel Eaton, wielded a heavy cudgel to control his charges.

The better afternoon school in the larger towns was the Talmud Torah (Study of the Tradition), usually a private tuition school operated under semicommunal auspices. Girls were accepted in a few of these Talmud Torahs. The curriculum included some understanding of the Hebrew classics. The most innovative experiment dated from 1909 when the kehillah (Jewish community) of New York City—an attempt to organize the Jewish institutions of the Lower East Side—established a Bureau of Jewish Education. Modernist in every sense of the term, the bureau was headed by Dr. Samson Benderly (1876–1944) and encouraged by a small group of Jewish leaders determined to effect a synthesis of tradition and modernism. In brief, using a few pilot Talmud Torahs, Benderly pressed for a graded and varied curriculum, employed trained teachers, and

197

urged the attendance of girls. Modern Hebrew speech was stressed, and Palestine, the biblical homeland, was looked upon as a spiritual center. In effect, these new schools were very up-to-date, Zionist, and American.

Benderly leaned heavily on his "boys" and "girls," university-trained helpers, some of whom had earned Ph.D. degrees. Several were to become notable, among them Dr. Emanuel Gamoran (1895–1962), who in 1923 was appointed head of the commission on Jewish education of the Reform movement and produced a series of excellent textbooks serving as paradigms for the other Jewish denominations. Benderly was given full rein by the head of the kehillah, the charismatic Rabbi Judah Leon Magnes (1877–1948). Magnes in turn had the support of many members of the faculty of the Jewish Theological Seminary, including Rabbi Mordecai M. Kaplan, who was to become the founder of the Reconstructionist movement, American Jewry's fourth religious denomination. (Reconstructionism continues today as a religiohumanist-tinged movement respectful of tradition and emphasizing both Zionism and diaspora nationalism.) In the long run, Benderly and the bureau failed to popularize the American concept of community responsibility for education. There was no official "community" and could be no compulsion. Congregations ultimately controlled Jewish education, certainly until the rise of all-day schools in the 1960s.

YIDDISH SCHOOLS

By 1910, a separate school system had arisen, independent of the many different Hebrew schools, emphasizing Yiddish almost exclusively. Secular institutions, these schools were sponsored primarily by three fraternal orders and met in the afternoon after public school hours. The Jewish National Workers' Alliance School was Zionist and taught some Hebrew, while schools of the Workmen's Circle (Arbeter Ring) were socialist, internationalist, and anti-Zionist. Communists, members of the International Workers' Order, also established Yiddish schools and summer camps (1930). Their Jewish content was negligible, but they had a large following. There were also Yiddishists, folkists who tended to negate political affiliation, loved Yiddish for its intrinsic appeal, and were known as the Sholem Aleichem group.

Some of these Yiddishists had camps where families could spend the summer and indoctrinate their youth. What did these school leaders want? They set out to further Yiddish culture—as they interpreted it—and to bind the children to their families and their culture. Yiddishism almost took on the quality of a religion. Some of these lovers of Yiddish may not have realized that devotion to the language made them indubitably Jewish. The children in the afternoon Yiddish schools, and even the Yiddish campers, were fully American. They attended the public schools during most of the day.

YOUTH AND ADULT EDUCATION

Professional Jewish educators with an axe to grind lament a Jewish education that is "an inch deep and a mile wide." This was not so true in the smaller towns of the hinterland where social pressure often induced parents to give their children some Jewish education. On the whole the youth of East European stock found very few institutions that catered to their special needs, but they frequented the YMHAs and YWHAs, settlement houses, synagogue centers, and Jewish community centers where they were made welcome. They flocked as well to Jewish teachers' colleges all over the country. A diploma was a chance to improve oneself financially, and there were at least nineteen such colleges in the country by 1926. Hebraists for their part organized Hebrew literary societies in several cities. The socialist Workmen's Circle established Yiddish and English lecture courses in many towns. Men with some Talmudic training enjoyed the sociality of the *hevrahs*, small intimate groups where they could read psalms or the rabbinic classics.

By 1930 even the Orthodox, rarely enthusiastic about educating women in Hebrew, had opened schools to train their female teachers. American concepts of pedagogy and school organization were regnant. The Torah-true Jews crowned their efforts to further adult Jewish education when in 1915 they appointed Bernard Revel president of the Orthodox rabbinical seminary in New York City. The new college took over a teachers' school, established Yeshiva College in 1928, and constituted itself Yeshiva University in 1945. Additional yeshivot, typical Talmudic academies, sprang up in New York, Brooklyn, and Chicago. The Orthodox, entrenched in antiquity and tradition, nonetheless met the American challenge. And they survived.

AMERICAN JEWISH CULTURE: THE PLACE OF HEBREW

The Yiddish school movement was a cultural enclave. There were, in fact, several Jewish ethnic groups. Some spoke Russian, others Hungarian or Ladino (Spanish-Portuguese), primarily the mother tongue of those Jews from the Turkish Empire who were descendants of the Spanish exiles. There were two Hebrews, the classical and the modern. For most American Jews, the Hebrew of the Bible and the rabbinic codes added up to a holy tongue. And not only for Jews: In 1911 an aged Christian minister enrolled in a Hebrew course at the Hebrew Union College; he wanted to be able to speak to God when he entered Heaven. Hebrew had been cultivated here in North America ever since the early 1600s, and all through the nineteenth century Jewish writers of prose and poetry employed this classical tongue. Scholars in the seminaries and in the teachers' colleges wrote books in rabbinic Hebrew on the Bible, the Talmud, the medieval poets, philosophy, history, the codes, lexicography, and bibliography. It was, however, in the nineteenth century that a new Hebrew appeared, a modern Hebrew roughly analogous to modern Greek, which differs from the classical tongue. This new Hebrew had been cultivated here in the United States since the mid-nineteenth century by Maskilim, men who embraced the Haskalah (Enlightenment) movement that originated in late eighteenth-century Europe. The Maskilim set out to modernize the East Europeans by bringing the best in the world's culture to the Russian and Polish Jews. The instrument they employed was modern Hebrew, to which they turned as a medium because so few in Russia had access to the public schools. The Haskalah never attained its goal as a mass educational movement in Europe, but some of the enlighteners came to the United States no later than the third quarter of the nineteenth century. They realized speedily that they had no future in this land, for the whole wide world of American education was open to the children of the immigrant Slavs who were welcomed in the public schools and state colleges alike. Faced with this reality, the cosmopolitan Maskilim, oriented to the world at large, did an about-face and, as nationalists, cultivated a modern Hebrew that they hoped would be the language of a future Jewish Palestinian state.

Modern Hebrew did have a modest following here. Poets began to use the new medium, and by 1883 admirers of this new language had created a Hebrew-speaking literary society in Chicago. By 1920 more than twenty modern Hebrew periodicals had appeared—and speedily died for want of a market. New York's youngsters had a Hebrew-speaking club. Quite a number of its members, all of Orthodox background, moved on to the Hebrew Union College and most of them became well-known rabbis; their leader was Abba Hillel Silver (1893–1963). The Hebrew periodicals of the twentieth century survived—though most of them only briefly—through the generosity of one or another Maecenas. By 1921 *Hadoar* (The Post) had appeared, first as a daily and then as a weekly. It would enjoy the patronage of the Histadruth Ivrith, the Hebrew Federation, a national overall society founded in 1916 that initiated a publishing program, encouraged the teaching of modern Hebrew in public high schools, and looked sympathetically on the establishment of Hebrew-speaking summer camps.

The following decades saw these Hebraists create a small but vigorous modern Hebrew literary movement of poets, short story writers, novelists, and essayists. Americanization posed no problems for them. This land and its ethos impressed them deeply, and they wrote in Hebrew of the blacks and the Indians. As votaries of the new-old tongue, they translated America's great poems and some of Europe's literary classics into modern Hebrew. Their output was relatively large. Zionism and its hope for a reborn state and the challenge of a new language encouraged these creative litterateurs, though their impact on the American Jewish masses was limited.

Some of the earlier Hebraists who had immigrated here were colorful personalities. Two, at least, were renegade Jews who came to start a new life. America's maw was big enough to digest all newcomers. Henry Gersoni (1844–97), who served as a rabbi, tutored Stephen S. Wise in Hebrew and Arabic and translated Longfellow's "Excelsior." Arnold Bogumil Ehrlich (1848–1919), a brilliant biblical exegete, wrote many volumes in Hebrew and German. Naphtali Herz Imber (1856–1909), author of "Hatikvah," today the Israeli national anthem, led a most undistinguished life in this country after he landed in 1892. Like Stephen Collins Foster, the American folk song writer, he was a heavy drinker. Judah David Eisenstein (1854–1956) republished numerous Hebrew classics, edited a ten-volume Hebrew encyclopedia, and translated the American Constitution. What did this notable Russian-born Hebraist do for relaxation? Did he read a page of the Talmud or write a new Hebrew book? No, he played the piano and rode horseback! Gershon Rosenzweig (1861–1941), "the sweet satirist of Israel," parodied the ages of man in the third-century *Sayings of the Fathers:*

> A child five years old should peddle Jewish newspapers
> . . . six, toilet paper, seven, writing paper, eight, candles
> and matches. At nine he should peddle candy, and at ten
> English newspapers. When he is eleven he must be strong
> enough to carry up ice to the top floor, and at twelve he
> should know how to harness a horse. At his [bar mitzvah]
> confirmation he should deliver a speech in true gamin
> fashion, and at fourteen he must already be behind bars to
> remain there until he comes of age.

The rise of the State of Israel crushed the modern Hebrew literary movement in the United States, since all but very few of the outstanding litterateurs moved to Israel. On the eve of the twenty-first century, however, so many Israelis have now settled in North America that at least two of the Israeli dailies publish an air mail weekend American edition, and resident Israelis in the United States issue Hebrew periodicals of their own.

AMERICAN JEWISH CULTURE: THE WORLD OF YIDDISH

THE YIDDISH PRESS

If Hebrew was the language of worship, Yiddish was the language the East Europeans lived in. Menahem Mendel Dolitzky (ca. 1855–1931), a Hebrew poet of international repute, survived here in America only by writing Yiddish potboilers. He had no more than a few hundred readers of the Hebrew poems he published, but there were probably two million Yiddish readers in New York City and other areas in the United States. Next to the synagogue, the Yiddish press was the most important East European institution in the United States. By constantly telling its readers what an honor it was to be a citizen, the Yiddish press played a crucial Americanizing role, helping East European immigrants make the transition from an agrarian and protoindustrial culture to a sophisticated urban industrial one. One must always remember that in their native Russia and Rumania these men and women had been little better than pariahs. The press brought them news from Eastern Europe, where family members still lived, and informed them about the unions and job opportunities. It was also a prime source of culture, publishing Yiddish translations of the best in American and European literature. It was this beloved tongue that tied the diaspora newcomers to one another.

The Yiddish press reflected and promoted numerous ideologies: traditional Judaism, Zionism, socialism, anarchism, communism, and the bourgeois good life. The left-wingers wanted to change and save the world, the bourgeois wanted to improve it, and the nonradical periodicals favored Republican, Democratic, and liberal opinion. America's first Yiddish paper appeared in 1870, and by 1874 Kasriel Hersch Sarasohn (1835–1905) had begun publishing a successful weekly. In 1885 he gave the Yiddish-speaking world its first daily, *Yidishes Tageblatt* (Jewish Daily News). The radical press began to flourish in the 1890s, and on the whole the periodicals were of a high quality. The editors were well-educated ideologues. Most, if not all, of them were anti-Orthodox and (except for Zion's Laborers, the Poale Zion) anti-Zionist. They were also schismatic, unconcerned with Jewish survival, though the ravages of World War I induced many to moderate their views. The socialist *Forverts* (Forward) appeared in 1897, and for many years—a half century!—Abraham Cahan remained its editor. Cahan as novelist, short story writer, and journalist had honed his skills working for years in the English-language press. The *Forward* was destined to become the largest foreign-language paper in this country, with two hundred thousand subscribers and numerous special editions dispatched to America's metropolitan ghettos. Not all its readers it were socialists; many non-socialists subscribed to it because it was brilliantly edited, and many enjoyed in particular its "Bundle of Letters"—Bintel Brief—written to the editors (1906). Cahan encouraged his readers to vent their emotions and tell him their problems. The Bintel Brief was no "advice to the lovelorn" column; it was a mirror to American Jewry's social pathology: "A tuberculosis victim, compelled to go to Denver, discovers that during his absence his wife had sold the store and taken the children, and run off with a stranger. What shall I do?" The *Forward* made money and succeeded in building a skyscraper on East Broadway—socialism American style.

Der Morgen Zhurnal (Morning Journal), Republican in its political loyalties, made its appearance in 1901. It appealed to many "solid" Jewish merchants and to workers who scoured its classified ads in their search for jobs. Louis Marshall, one of America's distinguished communal leaders, was well aware that the Yiddish papers carried translations of the world's literary classics, but he was not always convinced of the probity of the publishers. His skepticism induced him to subsidize a daily, *Di Yidishe Velt* (The Jewish World, 1902–05), in the hope that its editor, Zevi Hirsch Masliansky (1856–1943), would publish an exemplary paper. Marshall was disappointed. But in 1914 Herman Bernstein (1876–1935), journalist and translator from the Russian, brought out the first issue of *Der Tog* (The Day), a newspaper much more satisfactory to Marshall. It was welcomed by many who were convinced that its standards would be high, but the masses remained loyal to the *Forward*. In 1921 the communist *Freiheit* (Freedom) made its appearance; with the czarist collapse and the 1917 Bolshevik revolution many American Jews thought that the messianic age was just over the horizon.

In many respects the best in the Yiddish press was reflected in the weeklies and monthlies published from the 1890s on. Most of the editors were intellectuals who had studied in good European universities. More than eighty American Yiddish periodicals of diverse hue, among them several dailies, had appeared or disappeared by the year 1900.

America tolerated, if it did not glory in, this foreign-language press, which appeared in fifteen hundred papers in thirty-three languages with eight million readers. By the 1920s a daily Yiddish paper was appearing in Boston, Philadelphia, Baltimore, Cleveland, and other towns; Chicago alone supported three. It has been estimated that about six hundred thousand people in this country read the daily Yiddish press in the year 1915. By 1923 a decline had set in, though New York still had five dailies, three of them bourgeois, one socialist, and one communist.

As the earlier waves of Jewish readers died off, the Yiddish periodicals began to disappear. Readers became increasingly limited in number with the enactment of the immigration acts of the early 1920s. Nevertheless, in 1925 there were still some thirty Yiddish and Yiddish-English publications. The dailies had all vanished by 1983, but at least twelve Yiddish-English periodicals were still being published in the 1990s. The Yiddish spirit dies hard!

Yiddish Literature

The classical writers of modern Yiddish literature lived and remained in Russia—all except Shalom Rabinovitz (Sholom Aleichem: peace be unto you), who came to the United States in 1914 and died two years later. But by 1920 New York City was the world's Yiddish literary center. The total corpus of this vast literature runs to millions of pages, although the *Oxford Companion to American Literature* polishes it off in three lines in the entry on "Jews in America." The eight-volume *Biographical Dictionary of Modern Yiddish Literature* discusses in detail the work of at least seven thousand notables, many of them American. Even as late as 1993, six national organizations dedicated themselves to the advancement of Yiddish culture. A major role in this endeavor was played by the YIVO Institute for Jewish Research, housing millions of pages of archival material in New York City. Since so much of Yiddish literature had appeared originally in Yiddish magazines and newspapers, which ran the gamut of ideologies, Yiddish literature is very definitely not of one piece; it obviously reflects diverse philosophies and a variety of stylistic approaches. Two main literary streams were manifest in Yiddish writing: the art of high seriousness and *shund*, "trash" or kitsch. Good literature included editorials, feuilletons, essays, humorous sketches, translations, plays, poems, short stories, and novels, much of it the work of masters. All Yiddish newspapers, however, published thrillers—potboilers built circulation. The real literature of the masses may well have been the *shund* literature reflecting their needs. For many, *From the Throne to the Gallows* or *Murder for Love* would certainly have had more appeal than Tolstoy's *War and Peace* or Buckle's *History of Civilization in England*. Those relatively few in search of the best could always turn to Druckerman's Yiddish bookstore in New York, where judicious purchases could lead one to become truly educated. Reading Druckerman's catalogs was an education in itself.

Notable Yiddish Poets and Writers

Much of Yiddish literature is poetry, and poetry preceded the press. The poets began writing in the 1870s, before the appearance of the first Yiddish daily. The proletarian poets who slaved in factory and sweatshop made their appearance in the 1880s; several folk litterateurs—socialists, anarchists, revolutionaries—preached the gospel of a world without exploitation. Morris Rosenfeld (1862–1923), the best-known though perhaps not the most gifted of this group, wrote of the sad lot of the sweatshop worker. He attracted the attention of a Harvard professor, who published a thin volume of Rosenfeld's proletarian verse in transliteration. For a few years Rosenfeld was popular with the country's literati, but it was the Jewish multitudes who loved his verse—Jewish, simple, intelligible—and turned his poems into songs. There were also many sophisticated writers, journalists, and college-trained individuals who were anything but propagandists. They took it upon themselves to explain the sciences to the masses who had never attended even elementary secular schools in Eastern Europe, helping readers catch up with the twentieth century.

One cannot begin to list all the important writers. Dr. Charles Spivak (1861–1927) published a dictionary that threw light on commonly employed Hebrew and Aramaic words and phrases. Spivak's collaborator was Yehoash (né Solomon Bloomgarden, ca. 1871–1927), who translated the Hebrew Bible into Yiddish. Few readers did not chuckle as they read the adventures of Hayyim, the customer peddler, narrated by Israel Joseph Zevin (pseudononym: Tashrak; 1872–1926). Abraham Cahan, editor of the *Forward*, influenced millions with his fiction as well as his journalism. As the twentieth century advanced, two groups of literary artists made their appearance. The first, known as the Young Ones *(Di Yunge)*, construed Yiddish culture as an end in itself. This made them new and "young," and so they named their anthology *Yugend* (Youth). Among their leaders were a popular novelist and short story writer, a poet, a farmer who had worked in the Northwest, and a dramatist and poet who had languished in trans-Ural exile. They were not propagandists but writers devoted to image, tone, and form. One of them even wrote an epic on Kentucky. These Young Ones—men and one woman, too—wanted to be part of the republic of letters. They were not Jews writing to further Jewry; their medium "simply" happened to be Yiddish.

The second coeval school was the Inzichisten, the Introspectionists, who published a journal called *Inzich* (Within Oneself), in which they thought to reflect their psychic experiences. They too believed in art for art's sake and did not see themselves as preaching. Most of their leaders (like the Young Ones) could claim college training; they were not sweatshop workers. For them the poem was an outward sign of inward grace.

Unique after a fashion was Leon Solomon Moisseiff (1872–1943), a distinguished bridge builder of national repute. Yet in 1915 this engineer found time to lecture on Yiddish literature to a group of uptown Jewish intellectuals. Moisseiff published a Yiddish radical magazine, supported the work of the Jewish Publication Society, and furthered the new Hebrew University in Palestine.

After the gates of America were closed to East European émigrés in 1924, Yiddish began to languish for lack of new readers. Yiddish then—and this is interesting—entered into its classical phase. Its poets, storytellers, novelists, and critics were inching into a Golden Age. These classicists sprang full-blown from the body of a culture soon to decline. Best known to non-Yiddish readers were the writers whose works have been translated into English. Some entered into the halls of bestsellerdom. Israel Joshua Singer (1893–1944) is known to American readers for his masterly novel *The Brothers Ashkenazi*. Isaac Bashevis Singer (b. 1904) portrayed the world of the weird, the grotesque, the satanic. In 1978 he was awarded the Nobel Prize for his Yiddish stories. Sholem Asch's (1880–1957) translated works include *Three Cities, East River,* and a trilogy on the early Christians: Jesus *(The Nazarene)*, Paul *(The Apostle)*, and *Mary,* works written during the years that German "Christians" were destroying Jews. These three "New Testament" novels did not receive a cordial reception from American Jewry, but Asch was recognized as a writer of distinguished achievement nonetheless.

Novelist and dramatist Leon Kobrin (ca. 1872–1946) adapted Tolstoy, Goethe, and Shakespeare for the Yiddish stage. Abraham Reisin (1876–1953) was a folk poet and short story writer. Abraham Liessin (pseudonym: A. Walt; ca. 1871–1938) translated German and Russian poets as well as Walt Whitman. The plays of David Pinski and Peretz Hirschbein also were produced in English. Among the writers famous in their day were the great poet Jacob Glatstein, the poet H. Leivick (rescued from Siberia), novelist Joseph Opatoshu, critic Samuel Niger, David Ignatov, Mani-Leib, Z. Libin, M. L. Halpern, and Isaac Raboy, who had once been a Dakota cowboy. The nonpareil Chaim Grade came to the United States after World War II to bring new life to a dying Yiddish literature. At the close of the twentieth century, most of these writers are scarcely more than names, but they were once vibrant personalities. It is difficult even for the critical historian to refrain from sentimentalism: Is there no immortality beyond the printed page?

There were women among the Yiddish writers struggling to make a place for themselves in their new American home. They were active as journalists, columnists, poets, and fictionists. Although a great many Yiddish-reading women didn't go to public schools in Eastern Europe, they were highly intelligent and perceptive. Eager to increase their circulation, the dailies catered to the daughters of Eve, enticing them with romances and domestic science hints. In no sense, however, did this appeal to women indicate that the ghetto world was moving toward gender egalitarianism. The Jewish Lower East Side was still a man's world, and it was not easy to modify a patriarchal system that was as old as society itself.

On the eve of the twenty-first century, is there still a pulsating, living Yiddish literature? The answer has to be no. Were any of the nineteenth- and twentieth-century Yiddish writers comparable to America's great, a Mark Twain or a Robert Frost? Let the critics who know the Yiddish works only through translation answer that question, though writers such as Israel J. Singer, Sholem Asch, Jacob Glatstein, and Chaim Grade surely possessed extraordinary credentials. Yiddish—the language, not this literary heritage—lives today in the humble homes of America's Hassidim, in religiocultural enclaves which, like those of the Mennonites and the Pennsylvania Dutch, are separatist and may well survive for decades, if not centuries.

The Yiddish Theater

The roots of the Yiddish theater go back in Europe for centuries. The story of the biblical Joseph who rose from slave to prime minister and the almost miraculous delivery of Persian Jews as related in the book of Esther were standard themes of folk plays dished up for the delectation of the ancestors of modern theatergoers. In nineteenth-century Russia the *badhan*, the bard or the minstrel, with his impromptu verse and tunes amused the masses on festive occasions. Eliakum Zunser (ca. 1843–1913), a distinguished minstrel, came to the United States in 1889 but found no mass following here. Apparently audiences had come to prefer full-scale theatrical productions.

The father of the modern Yiddish theater was Abraham Goldfaden (1840–1908), who produced his first play in Rumania in 1876. He worked with a plot and did not rely wholly on improvisation. His plays, operas, operettas, and adaptations from the classics became standard for decades. Gobs and gobs of history were tunefully served up; Goldfaden was a composer of merit, and what he could not conjure up he borrowed from others. His productions had but one goal: to amuse the throng. Typical fare included song and dance, buffoonery, humor, romance, sentiment, and pathos. Goldfaden's was the *shund* prescription, but is that not some evidence for the true Golden Age of the theater? This, after all, is what the people demanded and enjoyed. History is a fraud if it does not reflect the interest of the masses.

A determination to please the multitude also characterized the many dozens of plays of Joseph Lateiner (1853–1935) and Moshe Hurwitz (Horowitz; 1844–1910), which dominated the East Side Yiddish stage from the 1880s on. Let it never be forgotten that the men and women who flocked to the Yiddish theaters on the Bowery and Second Avenue had little secular schooling; their aesthetic standards had never been cultivated. A parallel was the "opry" house in almost every town in Gentile America. The average American at the beginning of the twentieth century was clearly not much more advanced in taste over those who delighted in *shund*. Peter Jackson, a black bare-knuckle fighter, boxed three rounds with Joe Choynski in a theatrical production. Every red-blooded American glowed and wept as he followed the fortunes of the honest gal and the city slicker. It is well to remember: "Rags are royal raiment when worn for virtue's sake."

The melodrama was dominant in the Yiddish theater for decades, but there was also another stream—realism. The outstanding protagonist of this approach was the Russian Jacob Gordin (1853–1909), who came to these shores in 1891. His dramas were a challenge to the serious-minded and the

213

intellectual. His followers were offered Shakespeare, Tolstoy, and other adaptations from Europe's best writers. Ibsen in Gordin's day spoke with a Yiddish accent; devotees of the Yiddish theater had a choice of two Hamlets, one by Shakespeare and the other a Jewish adaptation. By 1900, if not earlier, New York City stood out as world Jewry's most distinguished theatrical center. Different groups—small, to be sure—sponsored serious drama, and the works they staged were European classics or dramas by competent Yiddish playwrights who had made America their home. New York Jewry did not flock to the plays of a Leon Kobrin, a David Pinski, or a Peretz Hirshbein, but in their generation these dramatists were respected by the thoughtful few. Very often it was the actors and actresses who made the play. Then as now, stars had devoted followers. Immigrants throughout the United States loved their theater, and the great actors, touring the provinces, were welcomed. A young seminarian in Cincinnati, Jacob R. Marcus, was privileged to attend a performance by Jacob P. Adler (1855–1926). When this immortal Zeus let loose his verbal thunderbolts, Marcus quivered with delight.

The Yiddish Art Theater

Though never truly popular, "good" Yiddish theater had existed in the United States since the 1890s, beginning with Gordin, if not earlier. At the beginning of the century, Yiddish folk theater was a psychological necessity; the new theater, the Yiddish art theater, was an intellectual luxury. Maurice Schwartz (ca. 1889–1960) and Jacob Ben-Ami (1890–1977) nursed the Yiddish art theater in the second decade of the twentieth century. They presented in Yiddish versions the best that Jews and non-Jews had written. Their work was as good as the best on Broadway, but ultimately it proved self-destructive. Those whose taste had become elevated and who appreciated good theater—and knew English—could wander up Broadway where a much larger choice was available.

After the passage of the discriminatory immigration acts of the 1920s, the reservoir of new patrons of the Yiddish theater began to diminish, though the theater would thrive for another generation. Yiddish musical comedy, too, improved in quality and attracted many, but second-generation American Jews no longer flocked to Yiddish performances. It is beyond question that the impact of America raised the level of the Yiddish theater and then destroyed it. With some modest survivals, the whole Yiddish cultural epoch may be said to have lasted a century. Yiddish—the language, the press, the theater with its two thousand plays—began to fade away. There is still a Yiddish theater in New York, but it is dwindling. No culture dies overnight; the historians who wish to study an American Jewry that in a few turn-of-the-century decades grew from two hundred fifty thousand to six million, will see to it that Yiddish never perishes.

SELF-HELP

When the Jews from the Slavic and Balkan lands started coming in sizable numbers to the United States in the mid-1800s and early 1900s, they could not fail to hear the American slogan: God helps those who help themselves. This expressed their own approach. As a body the East European Jews were not schnorrers; they were not addicted to seeking charity. Of the 10,334 Jews who applied to the United Hebrew Charities of New York City for help in 1904, only 35 had been on relief for the preceding fifteen years. The Jewish community as a whole had evolved an elaborate system of aid for all in distress, but the East Europeans speedily established their own self-help network and ultimately set up federations to provide for their Russian-Polish and Balkan clients. Before long, however, the East European immigrant charity federations were assimilated by the larger communal groups. All this took place when the newcomers were finally accepted by the earlier, better-established Jewish community.

HIAS is an acronym for Hebrew Sheltering and Immigrant Aid Society. The newcomers—with some help from old-timers—organized this immigrant aid society in the early 1900s to help newcomers immediately after their arrival. The chief port of entry was of course New York City, but similar support groups were set up in Boston and Philadelphia, and probably in other cities also. Soon enough the HIAS, faced with the problem of helping World War I refugees, set up offices on America's West Coast as well as in Europe, South America, and the Far East. This agency helped Jews threatened with deportation, ran a hospice that offered temporary shelter, and provided some food and clothing. It tried to find jobs for the new arrivals, searched for relatives, and aided the foreign-born to take out their first naturalization papers. The newcomers were urged to move west where, it was believed, acculturation would be speeded up. HIAS is alive and well today; there are always unhappy or needy Jews looking for new homes, and there are always other Jews ready to help.

Once the newcomers had settled into their new communities, the hometown mutual aid society, the landsmanshaft, was probably the most important self-help organization established by the immigrants themselves. Every Russian village sent émigrés, and these men and women found one another and established a landsmanshaft. New York in 1917 had over two thousand such groups; in the 1930s they could boast of one and a half million members (many of these groups were female societies). As late as 1948 Chicago's six hundred Jewish mutual aid societies had forty thousand enlisted in their ranks. For wage earners and petty shopkeepers, insurance was imperative. A landsmanshaft offered sociability, education, free loans, relief, sick and medical care, unemployment aid, and a cemetery and burial, "the last great necessity." Criminals, gamblers, alcoholics, and those with venereal diseases were not admitted, and men and women nearing fifty were not eligible for insurance. Differences between members were arbitrated. After World War I the landsmanshaften sent millions of dollars to help rebuild the devastated European hometowns. Some groups even offered help to their Gentile fellow citizens in moments of national calamity—gifts were dispatched to Galveston after the flood and to San Francisco after the earthquake.

American Jewish women had been organized into ladies' aid societies since 1819. The East European immigrant women moved into the area of mutual aid and developed their own free loan groups, lodges, and landsmanshaften. Their membership ran into the many thousands, and there were literally hundreds of women's landsmanshaften, though the president and the secretary were usually males.

Need and desire led similar groups across the country to create federations *(ferbands)*, which in turn sometimes established synagogues, schools, hospitals, sanatoria, and homes for the aged and the orphaned. At various times Poles, Galicians, Bucovinians, Lithuanians, and "Orientals" created *ferbands*. The "Orientals" were descendants of the Iberian Jews expelled or hounded out of the peninsula in the 1490s. By 1925 there were about twenty-five thousand of these Balkan and east Mediterranean immigrants in this country, and they were mostly very poor.

The Jews who had come from the heart of the Russian empire itself, at least a million or more, were too numerous to federate. The non-Russian East Europeans, on the other hand, hastened to federate, not wishing to be swallowed up by the immigrant majority from czarist lands. These *ferband* men and women were determined protagonists of cultural pluralism, and some of their leaders nursed the hope that all East European immigrants would ultimately join together to build one all-embracing national Jewish body. Indeed there was a Russian, Polish, and Lithuanian tradition of large-scale organization. By the seventeenth century two such federations had emerged in Eastern Europe, but an American attempt in 1891 to fuse all American Jews into one national organization, the Jewish Alliance of America, lasted only a year or two. The next attempt was made in 1922 when the American Jewish Congress, a permanent national association, came into being. But the congress never embraced the East European immigrant masses, who, as they acculturated, joined diverse American Jewish bodies. The *ferbands*, the groups organized along European regional lines, came into being to help the newcomers survive.

There is another form of survival beyond the cultural, the philanthropic, and the religious: this is political affiliation and identification. Jews in the South were almost all Democrats; they dared not be otherwise. Many in the hinterland were Republicans, since that was a highly respected bourgeois political party. New York's ghetto Jews usually went along with Tammany. In 1912 American Jewry as a group gravitated in very large numbers into the Democratic fold and were still there as the twenty-first century approached.

AMERICAN JEWISH LEADERSHIP

In 1881, the year the Russians started beating and killing Jews, 5,692 of these refugees landed in America; a decade later their number rose to 28,639. These newcomers were different. They had their own Yiddish vernacular, prayed only in Hebrew, kept kosher, retained many of the outmoded ceremonies, and wanted to restore the old Palestinian state. They flocked to the large cities, clustering in ghettos. The established Jewish community here was frightened. Let us settle them in colonies or on farms, in the West, beyond the Mississippi.

The "Westerners," the Reformers, headquartered in Cincinnati, were the only well-organized Jewry in America. But they had no effective policy and little vision in dealing with the newcomers. They resisted a suggestion of Jacob H. Schiff, the New York banker, that they reach out and embrace the Young Men's Hebrew Associations. The frightened, parochial Reformers had no real leadership at the turn of the century. True, they attempted to establish modern ghetto synagogues, but the wary newcomers suspected their motives. The established Reform congregations did not open their vestry rooms where the Orthodox might have raised their voices in prayer.

Initially, only the charities made every effort to help and recognize the newcomers as fellow Jews in distress. It was obvious to the eastern elite in New York that the Cincinnatians, the Westerners, could not—or would not—assume effective leadership and speed up the integration of the arriving Russians. These Easterners had no confidence in Cincinnati's Union of American Hebrew Congregations or in the B'nai B'rith centered in Chicago. The Easterners assumed—better, they reassumed—leadership and began pushing hard. They enjoyed the leadership role. It was Easterners who had established the Board of Delegates of American Israelites in 1859 and labored in the 1870s at Europe's Jewish conferences to accelerate the emancipation of the Slavic and Balkan Jewries. These New York leaders—Schiff, Cyrus Adler, Cyrus Sulzberger, the Lewisohns, Louis Marshall—were devoted Jews. Most had been reared in Orthodoxy, and they felt obliged to help the newcomers at their doorsteps even though the inpouring masses had no intention of submitting to the authority of the old-timers and would never become their submissive clients. What Schiff, Marshall, and their confreres offered the Slavic and Balkan Jews was Americanization, occidentalization, and effective leadership. These New Yorkers were all able men and eager to meet émigré needs.

AMERICANIZATION

The emphasis in those early days was on Americanization, not Judaization. The newcomers were, on the whole, "good" Jews, observant Jews. Turning to their charges, the self-appointed leaders encouraged them to conform to America's social mores, to stop speaking Yiddish—in public at least—and to avoid radical political ideologies. Pattern yourselves on us, the native-born and the acculturated, the old-timers! In order to further the integration of the newcomers into American society, these leaders established vocational schools, night schools to teach English, and classes in domestic management for the women. The Jewish fraternal orders and the National Council of Jewish Women stood ready to be of service. The proletarian lodges

established labor lyceums and a variety of educational programs. Yiddish papers introduced English columns. Most
children of Russian and Polish origin did not have to be
encouraged to go to the public libraries. The Chatham Square
branch in downtown New York lent a thousand volumes a day,
especially books about history and science.

Two very popular Jewish Americanizing agencies were
the Educational Alliance on New York's Lower East Side and
the Jewish People's Institute in the Chicago ghetto. These new
social institutions were settlement houses offering a variety of
services. (It is interesting that uptown New York Jews forbore
to give their settlement house a Jewish name.) There were
hundreds of these agencies in the United States. Jews themselves established and financed several such cultural and
educational houses, which sheltered clubs, libraries, lecture
forums, and gymnasiums, and maintained shower baths—the
latter were important! The Milwaukee settlement house taught
basic concepts of housekeeping; in Slavic villages cooking was
of the most primitive type. Out of the instructions on how to
cook a meal and wash a dish came the *Settlement Cook Book*,
which went through more than forty editions and helped
introduce Jewish "soul" foods to a grateful America.

The influence of the Jewish settlement houses was probably limited. It was primarily the young folks who went. The
untutored fathers and mothers did not crowd the libraries, the
gyms, or the lecture halls unless they dropped in to hear Zevi
Masliansky deliver an inspiring Yiddish address on Zionism.
The basic influence exerted on all Jews—with none excepted—
was the American ambience, which touched the entire family
and profoundly influenced the children. What happened to the

sons and daughters of a distinguished American Talmudist? Papa wrote Hebrew disquisitions on the ritual bath required of menstruating women. One wonders whether the scholarly essays of Henry (Harry, Zevi Hirsch) Grodzinsky (1858–1947) had any relevance to the needs or interests of his Omaha congregants, though they may very well have respected him for his rabbinic learning. One wonders, too, what degree, if any, of Americanization would flourish in the home of an old-fashioned European rabbi concerned with Talmudic studies. The answer is at hand: One daughter became a social worker; another a public school teacher; one son, a lawyer, graduated magna cum laude; another became a professor of medicine.

During the early 1920s, with the imminent curbing of immigration from Eastern Europe and the Balkans, the Young Men's and Young Women's Hebrew Associations and the settlement houses realized that they would have to alter their programs. The immigrants and their children had stopped thinking of themselves as Jewish Rumanians, Polaks, Litvaks, and Galicians. They saw themselves now as Americans, and intra-Jewish ethnic hostilities were beginning to recede. A new socioeducational and cultural institution now made its appearance: the Jewish community center. If Jews now went to a settlementlike agency, they went as full-fledged Americans who felt completely integrated into the larger body politic. Thus the community center was essentially a sociocultural, recreational institution for all Jews, whether native or foreign-born. In a way, it was a club for nonrich Jews. There was no longer an urgent need to "civilize" immigrant Jews from across the seas, to teach them civics. Americanization had largely been achieved, and dejudaization was the new threat. The pendulum had swung too far.

OCCIDENTALIZATION

Orthodoxy, the religion of the masses, was slow to change under the impact of a demanding Americanism. Cherishing its sacrosanct customs and values, it hesitated to "modernize" itself. The native-born Jews and their allies believed—rightly or wrongly—that changes were imperative to ensure Judaism's survival in the American milieu. They went to work to deorientalize the newcomers. The Union of American Hebrew Congregations in Cincinnati developed no effective plan to integrate the newcomers into the Reform movement; the gulf between the two cultures was simply too wide. But with about four hundred thousand "Russians" on their doorsteps, the New Yorkers could not ignore the problem of Americanization. Around 1900 Schiff and other New Yorkers of German background conceived a grand design. Isaac Mayer Wise had died in Cincinnati, and the East Coast elite proposed moving the Hebrew Union College (HUC) to New York City. (Emil G. Hirsch wanted to move it to Chicago.) The New Yorkers had nursed the hope of building a modern Jewish theological seminary in their city since the 1860s. If HUC and the moribund Jewish Theological Seminary (JTS) could be joined, there was a possibility of channeling the Orthodox into a type of modern Orthodoxy. The merger of the two schools appealed to the elite bankers, corporation lawyers, and big businessmen who had recently created United States Steel and the Standard Oil Company. The Cincinnatians summarily rejected the proposed merger.

The New Yorkers went ahead on their own, rechartering the Jewish Theological Seminary and bringing Solomon

Schechter to the United States to head the reorganized school. After receiving a good Talmudic training in his native Rumania, Schechter had wandered west and had become a scholar of note, combining in himself the best in modernity and traditional culture. Clever and charming, an English stylist who enjoyed the support of the New Yorkers financing the new JTS (1902), Schechter believed in good afternoon Hebrew elementary schools, instruction in English, and maintenance of the traditional liturgy and ceremonies. He was no Zionist, though years later he was to change his mind. (In the early 1900s, Zionism was deemed by him, as by most, to be a visionary hope.) Patterning his new school on the Breslau model—which had also influenced the Hebrew Union College—Schechter built a great seminary with a great faculty: Alexander Marx, the librarian, bibliographer, and historian; Israel Davidson, the authority on medieval literature; and Louis Ginzberg, America's most distinguished Hebraic polymath. In its approach to classical Jewish sources, Schechter's JTS accepted the canons of critical scholarship and by this act was divorced from Orthodoxy and its myriad followers, who no longer looked on the JTS community as "Yidden," our kind of Jewry.

By 1913 the people and congregations allied with JTS emerged as a new denomination: the Conservatives. It was obvious that they had patterned themselves on the Reformers. They established a congregational federation (1913), a sisterhood, and a brotherhood, and their library at JTS was notable. When Schechter died in 1915, he was succeeded by Cyrus Adler, who could never hope to win the allegiance of the European Talmudists although he was himself a staunch traditionalist. His Ph.D. was from Johns Hopkins, where he received an excellent education in Semitics. Before Adler died in 1940 he had succeeded in establishing himself as one of America's leading Jewish administrators, effectively controlling Dropsie College, the Jewish Theological Seminary, and the Jewish Publication Society; he was also a power in the American Jewish Historical Society and the American Jewish Committee. But he had very little in common with an East European rabbi who had studied Talmud all his life. He was scholarly and kept kosher, but he wore no beard. Ethnos is everything; he had not been born in Kovno but in Arkansas. Since deorientalization was beginning to characterize many of the newcomers—and virtually all of their children—Conservatism ultimately became the largest American Jewish religious denomination in the twentieth century.

Around the year 1902, when they reorganized the Jewish Theological Seminary, New York's Jewish notables succeeded in recapturing the leadership they had once exercised. The Westerners in Cincinnati, comfortable in their insularity and invincibility, did not really contest the advances of the New Yorkers. There was, however, an interesting episode at the Hebrew Union College in Cincinnati in 1907. A group of professors—Zionists for the most part—were encouraged to leave. In all probability these teachers, led by Max Margolis (1866–1932), would have welcomed the resignation of President Kaufmann Kohler (1843–1926). If this coterie had succeeded in deposing the anti-Zionist classical Reformer Kohler, the college may well have moved closer to the East European masses and thereby altered the course of the then dominant Reform movement, but it would be another sixty years more or less before neo-Reform, with its acceptance of Zionism, would emerge triumphant in the Cincinnati seminary. By 1900 most of the Reformers were convinced that the Messiah was just around the corner: God's in His heaven, and this is the best of all possible worlds! Isaac M. Wise, the great organizer of the American Reform movement, had once written: *"Before this* [nineteenth] *century will close* the essence of Judaism will be *the* religion of the great majority of all the intelligent men in this country."

THE SUCCESS OF AMERICANIZATION AND OCCIDENTALIZATION

In czarist days, before the rise of the Soviet Union, brilliant Eastern European Jews often made a career in the rabbinate. In later decades, Talmudists who came to America experienced less acceptance, since rabbinic learning had little market value here. unless accompanied by a Ph.D. degree. University-trained Talmudists like Louis Ginzberg, Israel Friedlaender, and Bernard Revel were highly respected. There was an especially promising future for a Jew skilled in the secular sciences. The typical American Jewish youngster, the child of an East European immigrant, wanted to be a somebody. Public School 188 on the Lower East Side had five thousand students, many if not most of them Jewish. When the thirty-nine boys in one class were asked what they hoped to become, one student had not yet made up his mind, eleven wanted to be businessmen, nine wanted to be lawyers, three dentists, three doctors, and two teachers; one each wanted to become a mechanic, an engraver, a clothes designer, and an electrical engineer. Six, who picked their vocation after watching the building of a skyscraper, opted for civil engineering. Many realized that the world was theirs if they were well educated.

Mary Antin came here at the age of thirteen. She was passionately interested in education, and the cultural opportunities offered her are reflected in her book, *The Promised Land,* an American classic. The push for higher education became even more general by 1900 as the younger "Russians" began to enter the professional schools, where many studied finance, medicine, engineering, law, and dentistry. It is believed that in 1918–19 almost 10 percent of the students in 106 large American colleges were Jewish, and their percentage in the schools of secondary learning was much higher than their numerical proportion in the general population. Most of the Jewish students surveyed in these statistics were either natives of Eastern Europe or children of Slavic and Rumanian Jewish immigrants. There are about twenty-seven hundred biographies in *Who's Who in American Jewry, 1926.* After a fashion they are all notable, and a very substantial number are of East European stock.

Though the new arrivals not uncommonly included individuals of unquestionable capacity and brilliance, few received faculty appointments in the larger colleges and universities. These new Americans had three strikes against them: They were Slavs, they were immigrants, and they were Jews. Of the approximately four million Jews in this country in 1924, a handful did forge ahead despite the barriers to make their way in the American world, especially in the world of music as virtuosi, conductors, composers, and critics, too. As far back as the 1890s, Isaac M. Wise had said that "the Polak will be wiped out [he meant assimilated] in the rising generation." He knew what he was talking about. He had many such students at the Hebrew Union College, and some of them became eminent rabbis to whose Sunday morning lectures Gentiles flocked.

Several Slavic-born clergymen eventually officiated even in New York's Temple Emanu-El, the most prestigious synagogue in all America. Many newcomers carved out great careers. One could summarize their achievement by saying that they were distinguished in their field, but that would be unfair. They deserve a moment in the historian's sun.

Moses Gomberg, professor of chemistry at the University of Michigan, became president of the American Chemical Society. Isaiah Leo Sharfman, who taught at the same school, was an eminent economist. Abraham Arden Brill helped make the United States the world center of psychoanalytic theory and practice. Leo W. Wiener taught Slavic languages at Harvard. Samuel James Meltzer headed the Department of Physiology and Pharmacology at the Rockefeller Institute of Medical Research. Jacob Zeitlin taught English at the University of Illinois. Abraham Cahan may well be deemed America's most distinguished foreign-language journalist. Peter Wiernik, another Yiddish newspaper editor, wrote the first good history of American Jewry. Selman A. Waksman, a soil chemist, was awarded a Nobel Prize for his work in antibiotics. Baruch Charney Vladeck, a Socialist, was a New York City alderman who pushed for slum clearance. Irving Berlin was a great songwriter. Philosopher Morris Raphael Cohen exercised great influence on the Lower East Side youngsters who flocked to City College. David Sarnoff built RCA. Jascha Heifetz was one of the world's most acclaimed violinists. Samuel Reshevsky, a child prodigy, was "concertizing" as a chessmaster at the age of eight. Jacob Epstein, who later settled in England, was a world renowned sculptor (who, like other Jewish artists, found Jesus the Jew a challenging subject for portrayal). Most of these notables were secularists; one was a Unitarian; Reshevsky, however, was an Orthodox Jew. Obviously both Americanization and Occidentalization had succeeded in helping these notables make their marks in American society.

American freedom also made it possible for women of Slavic and Balkan origin to begin realizing their potential long before the Nineteenth Amendment in 1920 gave all women the vote. By 1924 these women were clerks, bookkeepers, and secretaries. Though they did not flock to the colleges in appreciable numbers, since in Jewish tradition women were not encouraged or expected to study, some women were becoming public school teachers. This frightened Burton J. Hendrick in his muckraking days; Christian children should not be taught by Jews! Golda Mabovitch taught school in Milwaukee, before moving on to Palestine where she became Golda Meir. Emma Goldman, anarchist, brilliant thinker, and able lecturer, is important historically as evidence of what a woman can do when given the opportunity to study. Few men could rival the achievements of the foreign-born journalist and reformer Sophie Irene Loeb, who devoted a great deal of her time to social welfare activity and legislation. New York State's pension law for widows owes much to her, and she also worked to provide penny lunches for schoolchildren and strove to keep the city's schools open to serve as community forums. Busying herself with child welfare, Loeb insisted that home life for dependent children was superior to institutional care. Dorothy Jacobs Bellanca, the union organizer, was invited to sit on the executive board of the Amalgamated Clothing Workers of America when she was only twenty-two. Rose Schneiderman, a factory worker and labor leader, served as New York's secretary of labor. Anna M.

Rosenberg, a manpower consultant, held several important government offices before President Truman appointed her assistant secretary of defense in 1950.

10. Years of Crisis

If East European Jews were coming of age in their new home, then it was just in time, for in 1903 the impossible happened. In April of that year a pogrom ravaged the Jewish community of Kishinev in Russia. More than forty Jews were murdered, some five hundred were beaten, and thirteen hundred homes and businesses were looted. The czarist government was privy to all that happened, apparently to distract attention from the economic distress in the empire. The Jew was the favorite scapegoat: If there are problems in Russia, the Jew is responsible! Frightened Jews began fleeing to America, and in the years 1904–08, about 650,000 landed at American ports, confronting a Jewry here whose numbers were nearing 1,700,000. Schiff, eager to help, tried—unsuccessfully—to divert the incoming stream to Galveston and the West.

After Kishinev, protest meetings were held in at least thirty states. Christians joined the protesting Jews (Russia had few friends here), and substantial relief sums were raised. The response to the crisis pulled the newcomers and the native-born Jews closer together: "I am Joseph thy brother." Kishinev was but the beginning of a tragedy that continued for decades, the pogroms increasing in number and violence. When Russia was defeated by Japan in 1905, the empire's workers and their urban leaders rose in revolt. The czar's government had no choice but to grant a constitution, though a counterrevolution was soon instituted. A favorite remedy offered by the czarists to solve their problems was to speed up the mass killings of Jews. They placed great hope on this diversionary maneuver, and between April 1903 and June 1906 there were at least seven hundred civil disorders. In 1903, after Kishinev, Jews raised $100,000 for relief. In 1905, after a massacre in Odessa, they collected over $1 million from eight hundred towns and cities. Terror and distress abroad were creating a united American Jewish community here.

THE AMERICAN JEWISH COMMITTEE

If Jews in this country expected the administration in Washington to protest against the slaughter in Russia, they were mistaken. No American citizens had been killed, and the Russian authorities could always respond that Americans were lynching blacks. In 1906 President Theodore Roosevelt appointed Oscar Straus, a Jew, to his cabinet. It may well be that his appointment was a sop in lieu of presidential denunciation of the czarist state. In 1903 the B'nai B'rith had prepared a petition signed by thousands protesting Russian brutality; the petition was rejected by the Romanov government. The Board of Delegates on Civil and Religious Rights of the Union of American Hebrew Congregations expressed its disapproval to the Russians through its Washington lobbyist, Simon Wolf. Though the B'nai B'rith fraternal order and the UAHC were mass organizations, New York's Jewish elite remained unhappy with these two western groups. The New Yorkers were determined to retain the leadership they had resumed. They wanted a strong, well-financed defense organization that could help provide relief for oppressed Jews in periods of disaster.

American Jewry was inching forward preparatory to the assumption of hegemony over world Jewry.

Most American Jews were now of the opinion that a more effective national organization was needed to cope with the problems that faced Jews abroad and here, too. They wanted an agency that would have the power and authority to influence Washington and other national capitals on behalf of Jews experiencing disabilities. After 1903 there were at least five distinct proposals to create such a central body. A few leaders wanted a synod—a legislative council—of clergy and laymen from all the Jewish denominations, but this was not seen as a serious alternative. In January 1906 European leaders from Russia, Germany, and England met in Brussels to assess the continuing crisis in Russia. The Zionists were among them, and there was talk of creating a homeland, somewhere, for the fleeing thousands. The New York Jews knew of this assembly—which accomplished nothing—and it may have prompted them to take action. They met in February and by May had created a brilliant oligarchy, the American Jewish Committee (AJC). One of the founders of the new elite organization was Louis Marshall (1856–1929), America's most distinguished Jewish layman in the first third of the century. Though a dyed-in-the-wool Republican, he leaned toward democracy. He wanted no rule by the hoi polloi but was certainly no partisan of "the public-be-damned school," and he strove to build a national organization that would include the country's elite. In all his doings Marshall evinced absolute integrity.

Among those asked to serve on the new AJC were leaders of the Union of American Hebrew Congregations and Adolf Kraus (1850–1928), the international chief of the B'nai B'rith.

When the constituent committee first met, Kraus—who himself had landed in America a Bohemian immigrant with 2 cents in his pocket—insisted that it include no "riffraff." Like a similar meeting in Paris in 1806 under Napoleon, the American Jewish Committee was an assembly of notables and co-opted several East European émigré worthies. The president, Judge Mayer Sulzberger (1843–1923), was a learned, observant Jew. The executive committee, which exercised control, included two East Europeans. The country was divided into twelve districts, each of which chose its own members and distinguished East European immigrants were not excluded there either. It is very probable that the new organization hoped to achieve leadership of world Jewry. America already sheltered the second largest Jewish community after Russia, and the latter was a stricken giant. The committee, chartered to serve as a defense and relief agency, proved efficient and successful. It reached out to help Jews in Morocco and Turkey as well as Russian refugees. It struggled with some degree of success to fend off anti-immigration legislation and defeated those forces in the United States that had set out to classify would-be Jewish immigrants as "Asiatics" (the United States had been excluding Chinese since 1882).

THE AFFAIR OF THE RUSSIAN TREATY

America's 1832 commercial treaty with Russia guaranteed United States citizens the same rights enjoyed by Russia's subjects, but since Russian Jews were second-class citizens under the czar, an American Jewish citizen who was a native of the Russia empire was denied many rights if he returned to

Russia, even if only to visit the family he left behind. He was a Jew subject to disabilities, and if he had not served in the czar's army he was still subject to conscription. Starting in 1864 Russian Jews—American citizens—returning to their native land were subjected to discriminatory treatment, which continued until 1917, when the Romanovs were driven off the throne. Most American secretaries of state attempted without success to induce the Russians to accord equality to American Jewish citizens and to respect the American passport when carried by a Jew. Russia's mistreatment of the Jews in the 1880s, 1891, and in the early twentieth century turned enough Americans against the czarists to open the way for American abrogation of the treaty, but American Jews never succeeded in inducing Russia to accord them equality. They were also unsuccessful in their efforts to compel the Rumanians to naturalize their Jews. Following the suggestion of Jacob H. Schiff and Oscar Straus, President Theodore Roosevelt instructed John Hay, his secretary of state, in 1902 to write a note to the European powers, which in 1878, at the Congress of Berlin, had demanded that rights be accorded Jews in the newly sovereign Rumania. Hay wrote that mistreatment of Rumanian Jews had driven them to come to America. Let the powers instruct the Rumanians not to discriminate against Jews. Such a forced immigration was not "acceptable or beneficial." In a way, of course, this note denigrated Rumanian Jewish newcomers, but the Jews ignored this nuance. Grateful for small favors, they were pleased that it had been dispatched. Roosevelt, hoping to retain the presidency in the 1904 election, was eager to win the Jewish vote.

In the years after 1903, Russian Jewry had to cope with many pogroms. After the Bialystok massacre in June 1906, in which 105 Jews were killed and hundreds wounded, Congress passed a joint resolution of condemnation. Seizing the initiative, the American Jewish Committee set out in 1908 to urge the abrogation of the 1832 treaty. But the Jewish leaders moved slowly since some notables did not want to embarrass the Taft administration. On February 15, 1911, a delegation of Jews from the B'nai B'rith, the Union of American Hebrew Congregations, and the American Jewish Committee met with President Taft to discuss the discriminatory attitude of Russia toward American Jews. Taft's approach was pragmatic; he knew it would do no good to cancel the treaty. The meeting with the president accomplished nothing. But on December 4, 1911, Representative William Sulzer of New York offered a resolution calling for abrogation. The vote was three hundred to one, with eighty-seven abstentions. When Taft realized that Congress would terminate the treaty over his veto, he hastened to urge abrogation, and the Senate and the House took immediate affirmative action.

The Jews had triggered the uprising that forced the administration to take action. New York was a strategic state politically, with more than one million Jews. The Jews were very proud of the part they had played. The East European newcomers, the German old-timers, and the native-born had worked shoulder to shoulder to win this victory, and a feeling of Jewish community was generated. Had the American people rallied to help the Jews? Not necessarily. What they wanted was the American passport to be respected. Only ten years later Congress passed the Immigration Act of 1921 limiting the number of Russian, Polish, and Rumanian Jews who would be admitted into the United States.

CRIME IN THE GHETTO

In 1908, the same year the American Jewish Committee set out to urge Washington to abrogate the 1832 commercial treaty with Russia, it confronted a most annoying situation in New York City. In the *North American Review* for September 1908, General Theodore A. Bingham, the city's commissioner of police, made the bald statement that about 50 percent of all those charged with crimes were Jews. Inasmuch as Jews constituted about one-fourth of the city's population, it was obvious that he deemed them an undesirable lot. The Jews protested vigorously, denouncing Bingham and offering statistics to refute him. Bingham apologized for his statement and withdrew the wholesale indictment.

Nevertheless many Jews had been dragged into the courts for both misdemeanors and criminal acts. Myriads of Jews on the Lower East Side were on the edge of poverty, and poverty breeds wrongdoing. It was primarily for crimes of gain, not violence, that Jews were incarcerated. Juvenile delinquency among Jews was not uncommon in all the big towns, and the malefactors were often the children of foreign-born parents. Between the years 1905 and 1916 the New York Jewish community established eight correctional agencies for boys and girls (two had been founded in pre-Bingham days). No later than 1909 the Jews of the city had created a Big Brother Association and that same year the Central Conference of American Rabbis established a Committee on Dependents, Defectives, and Delinquents to minister to the blind, deaf, retarded, dependents, delinquents, farmers, working men, and soldiers! Rabbis visited prisons and conducted religious services. Desertion of families was a most serious problem. The Jews had their own National Desertion Bureau and by 1917 there were about ten thousand cases in the files. Prostitution among the Jews was high, and an alarmed National Council of Jewish Women sent agents to the docks to protect arriving young women from the approaches of procurers. For the years 1907 to 1929 about 21 percent of all who were arrested were Jews; New York Jewry was able to tally its demographic proportion of sinners. Cynical and brilliant is this statement of a Yiddish writer: "Father plays cards; mother amuses herself with the boarders; daughter spends her time in the dance halls; sonny sits in jail." It is amazing that, despite these sobering statistics on juvenile delinquency and crime, this East European immigrant community within the course of two generations developed into one of the most affluent, law-abiding, and prestigious groups of citizens in all America. And the youngsters, either foreign- or native-born? Who would have suspected that some of the little bare-bottomed "pishers" one saw running around would one day become corporation chief executive officers, distinguished lawyers, eminent physicians, pontificating judges, university deans and presidents, and Nobel laureates?

THE KEHILLAH

Both downtown and uptown leaders of the city's Jews recognized that the community had a morals problem. They set out to solve it, and many other problems, through a proposal that was both truly visionary and naive. With the aid of the influential Rabbi Judah Leon Magnes they moved to create the kehillah (the Jewish community) of New York City. As the metropolitan regional division of the American Jewish Committee, the kehillah proposed unifying practically all East European agencies into a tight, well-organized polity, a kehillah or "community." The Hebrew name was nostalgically borrowed from the Russian Pale of Settlement where for centuries the kahal or local Jewish council had ruled—and often misruled. Magnes and his cohorts hoped to organize New York City and other major towns in the country and then federate them into a single entity. New York City was to become a functioning united kehillah and not a mosaic of thousands of autonomous units.

The kehillah cast a wide net: naturalizing newcomers, arbitrating religious disputes, encouraging Sabbath observance, developing an employment agency, maintaining kosher food surveillance, eliminating abuses in Jewish marriage and divorce procedures, furthering philanthropy, recreation, and the unions, curbing crimes, collecting statistics, establishing a bureau of education and loan societies, and coping with anti-Semitism. The concept was grandiose, romantic, impractical, and a failure. Its progenitors should have known better. Since biblical days Jews have rarely if ever built strong communal or national organizations. In America the one exception was the colonial synagogue, the one strong religious organization in town, although when new settlers arrived secessions became the order of the day. The denizens of the Lower East Side never looked upon the kehillah as a crusade. A heterogenous lot, they had in common Jewish birth, a basic religion, the Yiddish language, a mutual wariness, and the realization that their Gentile neighbors looked askance at them. The kehillah could never hope to become an abiding reality. In Europe many Jewish communities enjoyed the active support of the state, but that authority was totally lacking in this country. The East Side butchers, teachers, owners of private mushroom synagogues, and rabbis thumbed their respective noses at the whole world when their own vested interests were threatened. Magnes, their leader, lost what influence he still possessed when he became a pacifist during World War I.

Magnes, who brought the kehillah to birth, deserves more than a passing mention. Close to Louis Marshall, his brother-in-law and one of the most influential Jews in New York City, he began his career as an instructor at the Hebrew Union College in Cincinnati and went on to become a Zionist leader in New York City, a rabbi in the Reform movement's prestigious Temple Emanu-El and then in the Conservative B'nai Jeshurun, and was active for a time in the early Reconstructionist movement. He served as the head of the kehillah, as an organizer and fund-raiser for the American Jewish Joint Distribution Committee, as the first president of the Hebrew University in Jerusalem, and as a determined proponent of binationalism, parity in Palestine for Arabs and Jews. Solomon Schechter disdained him because of his diverse views, but Magnes was a remarkable man, wise enough to envisage the ultimate death of classical Reform and the rise of neo-Reform. This man was not deterred from undertaking impossible tasks. An idealist and an independent thinker, a courageous fighter for what he thought was right and important, he was a charismatic personality, a maverick who never swam with the current, a heroic character constantly reaching out in search of himself. He was dedicated to his people and determined to help them. Those who knew him well thought him a latter-day major prophet.

KLAL YISRAEL: AMERICAN JEWS ATTEMPT TO RELIEVE THE SUFFERING OF JEWS ABROAD

World War I erupted in 1914, with England, France, Russia, Serbia, and Belgium, and in early 1915 Italy (the Allies) facing the Germans, Austria-Hungary, and the Ottoman Turks (the Central Powers). As the armies of Germany, Austria-Hungary, and Russia marched and countermarched across Eastern Europe, close to a million Jews, caught between the warring forces, suffered doubly as civilians and as Jews. Thousands of them conscripted by the Russians had to die for a country that denied them elementary civil and political rights. Because the unfortunate Jews in Eastern Europe desperately needed help, American Jewry rushed to aid them. Almost immediately the Orthodox East European Jews and the native-born federated their efforts. The following year the labor element joined the others to create the American Jewish Joint Distribution Committee (known as the JDC, or the Joint). Since the Orthodox and socialists cooperated in this federation, they obviously realized that blood was thicker than theology and Marxist dialectics. Working for a common cause, even Jewish schismatics had no choice but to return to their people. The campaigns that followed tended to create an informal national American Jewish community—and a world Jewish one, too—united in purpose, gratitude, and affection. More than half of the money raised in the early years of the Joint came from the towns and cities of the American interior.

Palestine Jewry was given special consideration, since the Jews there, mostly pietists, were still dependent on diaspora laymen as they had been for centuries. Early in 1915 American

Jews dispatched the collier *Vulcan* to Palestine with nine hundred tons of food and cash (45 percent of the food had to be given to non-Jews or the distribution would have been forbidden). Though the Palestine Jewish settlements numbered but a minuscule portion of the Old World Jewish millions in distress, at the insistence of America's Orthodox leaders, they received a relatively high percent of all funds sent abroad. The JDC soon became the chief rescue and relief operation for world Jewry. The forging of the Joint confirms the rise of American Jewry to world Jewish hegemony, a hegemony solidly based on numbers, wealth, organizational skills, and devotion to Jewry as a whole. Above all, it was a concomitant of the international power that the United States now exercised.

The United States went to war on April 6, 1917, on the side of the Allies. About two hundred thousand Jews served as soldiers. Of the approximately eight thousand who were commissioned officers, none reached the rank of general, although the Navy had a Jewish rear admiral and the Marine Corps a one-star brigadier general. Thousands of recently arrived East European Jews were conscripted; some died in action before ever enjoying the immunities of their new American home. To encourage Jews in the armed forces, the United States government sanctioned the creation of the Jewish Welfare Board, which provided a variety of services to the Jewish personnel in the Army, Navy, and Marine Corps. After the war was over, the board, looking for a peacetime challenge, undertook to supervise the work of the YMHAs, the YWHAs, and the rising Jewish community centers.

As recently as 1891 the fabulously wealthy Baron Maurice de Hirsch and his wife had established a fund of more than

$2 million to help the East European newcomers who fled to the United States. Less than two decades later American Jewry was pouring multiple millions into Europe to save war-wracked Jewish communities. The goal for 1917 was $10 million, and Julius Rosenwald offered a matching grant of 10 percent. By 1923 American Jews raised more than $50 million. After the war ended and the armies disbanded, the Joint, with Boris D. Bogen as director, carried on a massive program of aid and rehabilitation working closely with Herbert Hoover's American Reconstruction Administration. Jewish Eastern Europe had to be salvaged and rebuilt. In the postwar years conditions in the Ukraine, Poland, Hungary, and Rumania were very bad, and by 1925 the United States was closed as a haven of refuge. Civil war, anarchy, and guerrilla outrages cost the lives of thousands upon thousands of helpless Jewish men, women, and children. The Poles were determined to undermine the position of Jews as an important segment of the country's middle class. Writing to his teacher Gotthard Deutsch at the Cincinnati seminary on April 2, 1920, Rabbi Bernard Cantor reported on his visit to the Galician town of Belz, a famed center of Orthodoxy and Hassidism. Three centuries before, in the 1650s, the town had gone up in flames during the war between the Poles and the Swedes; now in 1920, 600 of the 720 houses in town had been destroyed. Belz alone had six hundred orphans. There was no bread. Forty people were living in two caves. On July 5, just about three months later, Rabbi Cantor and Professor Israel Friedlaender, on a mission of mercy for the Joint, were murdered by bandits.

In the early 1920s the Joint, aided by Baron de Hirsch's multimillion-dollar Jewish Colonization Association, worked together to rebuild Jewry in the postwar succession states of Estonia, Latvia, Lithuania, and Poland. Its instrumentality was the American Joint Reconstruction Foundation, which fed hundreds of thousands, opened schools, old-age homes, and hospitals, trained nurses, and repatriated refugees. Most important, it set up cooperative loan banks and free-loan associations; credit was the life blood of the numerous small-scale enterprises, artisans, and shopkeepers. The average loan was about $20, but these small amounts helped keep petty businessmen afloat. From 1924 to 1938 the American Joint Reconstruction Foundation of the JDC, operating in the non-Russian lands, made more than five million loans and lent over $580 million.

The problem of helping Jews in Soviet Russia in the postwar years was complicated by the fact that the traditional bourgeois society was rejected by the Communists. Jews, declassed, could survive only by becoming proletarians—laborers, farmers, artisans. Joseph A. Rosen, a Russian-born agronomist and administrator, addressed himself effectively to the task. Beginning in 1924 to 1926 he worked under the aegis of the American Jewish Joint Agricultural Corporation (the Agro-Joint), and here, too, the Jewish Colonization Association contributed its millions. More than three million acres of land were cultivated in the Ukraine and Crimea, and approximately 250,000 Jews were settled on the soil. There is no question that the Agro-Joint saved thousands by qualifying them as farmers and artisans. Whole villages were built, machines installed, tractors brought in, livestock purchased, seed supplied, farm and trade schools set up, loan societies and dairy cooperatives organized, agronomists enlisted, and clinics and hospitals established. Civically and economically Jews were integrated into the Soviet body politic. An impressed Herbert Hoover called it a marvelous feat of "human engineering."

After several years the work of the Agro-Joint in the Soviet Union was continued by a new organization composed of a relatively small number of American Jewish notables, all old-line natives: the American Society for Jewish Farm Settlement in Russia, which raised about $7 million to help Soviet Jewry. Julius Rosenwald promised to give $5 million, and help was also pledged by the Soviet government. Rosen continued to guide and advise. (The Zionists, however, were not happy with this emphasis on Soviet Russia; they believed that reconstructed Jewry had no future in Europe. History, alas, justified their apprehensions.) In 1938 the JDC and its affiliates were asked to leave Russia, the Soviet government having decided that they were no longer needed. A great achievement culminated in a tragedy. Just three years later Nazi Germany invaded the Soviet Union and murdered huge numbers of Jews. On September 29 and 30, 1941, almost thirty-four thousand Jews were machine-gunned by the Germans at Babi Yar, a ravine near Kiev. By the time the invading German armies retreated to their native land, some one hundred thousand men, women, and children had been executed and buried in the same ravine. The remaining Jews in the Soviet Union were subjected to forced assimilation in the postwar decades, but the 1980s and 1990s found many thousands of these assimilated Jews opting to move to Israel, North American, and elsewhere.

11. Zionism, Anti-Zionism, and Two American Jewish Communities

THE PLACE OF ZIONISM IN THE AMERICAN JEWISH WORLD, 1760s–1914

Zionism was world Jewry's most important movement in the late nineteenth century. Many dyed-in-the-wool Zionists—those who made aliyah (immigration to Jewish Palestine and the successor State of Israel)—maintain that Jewry has no future in the diaspora. If others laugh at them, they point to the Holocaust, the greatest tragedy in all Jewish history. The Zionism they espoused had not sprung full-blown from the brow of Theodor Herzl in 1896. It was as old as the capture of Jerusalem in 70 c.e. by Titus, as old as the second-century b.c.e. Maccabees and the restoration by Nehemiah and Ezra in the fifth century b.c.e. "By the waters of Babylon . . . we wept when we remembered Zion" (Psalm 137:1). As early as the 1760s American Jews had been asked to help the oppressed Jews of Hebron. An authorized "emissary of the Sages," a collector for Palestine Jewry, had made his appearance in the American colonies in 1775. After the successful revolt of the thirteen colonies against Great Britain, American Jewish worthies had speculated that the descendants of the Twelve Tribes might yet return to the promised homeland. Napoleon's march into Palestine led many to believe that he would restore the Jews and fulfill God's promise. In 1818 Mordecai Manuel Noah, American Jewry's best known layman in his day, became the country's first political "Zionist." Not only had he expressed an interest in restoring the Jews to Palestine, but Noah also set out to build an extensive American Jewish colony. If the Jews established a settlement here in the free democratic United States, it would prepare them ultimately to rule in the Holy Land. With this in mind, he decided to proclaim an American Jewish "state"—under the federal Constitution, of course—on Grand Island near the western terminus of the Erie Canal. The new Jewish polity was dedicated in Buffalo on September 15, 1825. The dedication marked both beginning and end of the project. For decades, however, Noah harangued his Christian, Bible-loving audiences: The Jews will be restored. If necessary, let North Africa's Jewish masses march eastward and drive the Turks out of God's country. The growing American nationalism influenced him profoundly; even the blacks are being restored to Africa, he pointed out. The ideal new state he posited, a state patterned on America, would be preeminent in industry and agriculture. (Nearly a century later, Louis D. Brandeis voiced similar hopes.) The problem of dual loyalties to America and to a sovereign Jewish nation in Palestine rose early. Max Sutro, the rabbi of Congregation Har Sinai in Baltimore, even questioned whether Jews should assemble in prayer on the Ninth of Ab, the traditional anniversary of the fall of the Temple. To do so, he thought, might call into question their loyalty to their American homeland—let us not mourn for ancient Judea; we have our modern America.

The presumptive problem of simultaneous devotion to a Jewish state and to the land of one's citizenship goes back to

French Revolutionary days when Jewish emancipation was debated: "To Jews as [individual] human beings, everything; to Jews as a nation, nothing." Here in America, in the 1830s to 1850s, societies were organized to support Palestine's pious Jewish settlers. But these organizations were doomed; the funds raised rarely reached those for whom they were intended. Isaac Leeser, the country's most eminent antebellum Jewish religious leader, faced the restorationist problem pragmatically: A Palestine refuge had to be established to shelter Europe's persecuted Jews, but there was no need for American Jewry to return there. Palestine was too small, though the rebirth of a commonwealth there would certainly bring a new pride to the community here. We will be respected if we have a government of our own. Instead of peddlers, shopkeepers, and bankers, we will produce farmers and statesmen.

A new wind was blowing in Europe in the 1870s. Ethnic groups in all parts of Europe were seeking national expression. The Jew, Daniel Deronda, in George Eliot's novel of that name, preached the gospel of a national Jewish center. By 1880 the word *anti-Semitism* had been coined in Germany, and its most extreme exponents understood it to mean that all Jews must be exterminated. Russian pogroms led to the establishment of the first Zionist colonies in Palestine and the rise of the Lovers of Zion, Hoveve Zion, in Europe and in the United States. Stealing a concept from the eighteenth-century physiocrats, some Zionists emphasized the primacy of agriculture. Then going a step farther, they declared work on the soil ennobling. It was just this American pro-Zion enthusiasm that in 1885 induced skeptical radicals in the Reform rabbinate to repudiate the concept of a historic Jewish state. In 1891 a Chicago Christian, William Eugene Blackstone, attracted a great deal of attention by petitioning President Harrison to call a conference of European nations to arrange for the purchase of Palestine for its return to the Jews. This was the very year that the Russians expelled large numbers of Jews from Moscow. Clearly, a new haven was imperative. Just a few years later, someone coined a word expressive of the hope that a commonwealth could be established in the biblical homeland of the Jews. The word was *Zionism*. It was in that decade, too, that a Boston Jew designed a Jewish flag: two blue stripes stretched across a white field, and between the stripes a Star of David carried the Hebrew inscription "Maccabee" painted in blue. Why Maccabee? The Jews would have to fight to build a new state. Fully cognizant of what some of the European nations were doing to his people, the decidedly anti-Zionist Isaac Mayer Wise wrote: "the world has sinned more against the Jew than a hundred Christs could atone for on the cross."

In 1894, the arrest and conviction for treason of the French army officer Alfred Dreyfus—an innocent man—persuaded many, among them the Viennese journalist Theodor Herzl, that anti-Semitism was endemic in Europe. To escape the eternal role of scapegoat for society's ills, the Jew needed a country of his own. With this in mind, Herzl published a German pamphlet in 1896, *The State of the Jews: An Attempt at a Modern Solution of the Jewish Question*. Entranced with the prospect of a Jewish republic, Jews from all over the world, including the United States, gathered in Basel the next year to adopt a Zionist platform: A home for the Jewish people must be created, one that would be secured by public law and based on Jewish national sentiment. Zionism caught on like wildfire. Societies were established in all lands that sheltered a Jewish community. There was hardly a town in the United States, no matter how small, that did not nourish a Zionist group. There were even some eminent Reform Jews who were enamored of the prospect of a Jewish homeland. Most Conservatives were enthusiastic Zionists, but the Orthodox were split. A few believed that God, the Holy One, Blessed Be He, should not be pushed. He would redeem Jewry when He saw fit. Though the Orthodox rabbinate was not enthusiastic, most of the Orthodox were in a way automatically Zionists. They prayed for the return daily in their book of common prayer (the siddur). Some Orthodox leaders went their own way, refusing to be numbered among the mostly secular general Zionists and preferring to set up a Zionist organization of their own. These partisans were the Mizrachi. The word, a Hebrew acronym, resolves itself in English as the Oriental Spiritual Center, but the formal name adopted was the Mizrachi Organization of America (1909). The rabbi-led Mizrachis were not obscurantists but had numerous branches, women's auxiliaries, youth groups, a good teachers' college, and afternoon schools open to modernist influences. Another divergent group was the Jewish Socialist Labor Party Organization, Poale Zion (1905). These Zionists were committed secularists, Socialists, non- and even antireligionists, but they wanted to remain Jews despite the reproaches of the Marxists and anarchists who scoffed at Jewish loyalties and savored the gospel of world brotherhood.

What motivated the various groups in the national Zionist federation? Why Zionism? Restoration to the Holy Land was implicit in the Maimonidean articles of faith. Every nineteenth-century ethnic minority hoped ultimately to achieve national independence, and Jews, too, believed that there must be one place in the world where they would always be welcome. Many felt there was no land, no matter how cultured or civilized, that would wholeheartedly accept Israelites; there was anti-Semitism even in the United States. The new Palestine, they believed, could become a romantic, idyllic agrarian Garden of Eden. As Leeser had observed, a country of their own would give Jews status. It was indeed a constant source of pride to many in the diaspora that there were dozens of settlements in Palestine, that the colonists were speaking Hebrew, and that there was a modern academy in Tel Aviv. Many American Zionists lived in two worlds: They were pro-Palestine and wanted a Jewish homeland, but they were also pro-American. They thought in terms of two cultural centers, one in the Promised Land and the other in the United States. These were the cultural Zionists, who had a very large following, though they established no formal organization. They were very much influenced by Ahad Ha'Am (né Asher Ginsberg), whose *Essays* were first published in this country in 1912 and soon enjoyed three more printings. Palestine, so Ahad Ha'Am taught, was to be a national spiritual center that would influence world Jewry. Zion as such a "center" was a far more important concept than the hope of a politically autonomous Jewish settlement. Whether they knew it or not, most American Zionists would have subscribed to Ahad Ha'Am's cultural goals.

At least half of America's Zionist shekel payers (contributors), members of Zionist organizations, lived in the backcountry; some of the societies were even open to women. The Zionist organization in San Antonio, founded by a University of Vienna Lover of Zion, was established in 1897, the very year the Zionists met for the first time in Basel. Twenty years later when the Balfour Declaration was proclaimed by the British, the blue-and-white Jewish flag was flown on one of the city's municipal buildings. In 1910 the Milwaukee Socialist Zionists had 124 dues-paying followers. When solicited for funds, 104 gave 25 cents each, all they could afford—a quarter would buy five loaves of bread.

America's national Zionist organization came into being in 1897 when some thirty pro-Palestine groups in New York City federated. The following year they emerged as the Federation of American Zionists (FAZ), a grouping of various Zionist societies loosely tied together. Its leaders were educated, acculturated men and women; not one of them was a New York ghetto denizen. A Zionist press in Hebrew, Yiddish, and English soon evolved. With the exception of Abraham Cahan's socialist *Forward*, the Yiddish dailies smiled on the new movement. By 1914 the federation included at least two fraternal benefit orders, libraries, clubs, youth groups, men's and women's organizations, associations of college students and urban professionals, middle-of-the-road Orthodox and Conservative Jews—in short, a variety of societies with disparate and conflicting ideologies, but all of them devoted to Zionism.

Zionists had a problem. They had little social status, since most members were humble newcomers from the Slavic East. The affluent early settlers of central European background were, with notable exceptions, bitter opponents of this new Jewish nationalism. But, let it be noted, even the Zionists here had no intention of moving to the ancestral land. The dual loyalty specter had haunted Jewish leaders here since antebellum days. Isaac Harby, the most notable founder of South Carolina's Reformed Society of Israelites, in 1825 had solemnly informed the world that "America truly is the land of promise spoken of in our ancient scriptures." Isaac Leeser, the father of modern Orthodoxy in this country, and the Reform rabbinical leaders all echoed these fears. Rabbi Emil G. Hirsch, American

Jewry's leading religious radical at the turn of the century, denounced some of the Zionist leaders as swindlers. In 1898 after the founding of the World Zionist Organization, the Union of American Hebrew Congregations assured all Reformers that "America is our Zion," and the patrician American Jewish Committee expressed similar views. Ghetto socialists and anarchists were convinced that after the inevitable revolution in Russia and the emancipation of its Jews, there would be no need for a Jewish state. Practically all American English-language Jewish weeklies were anti-Zionist. A Detroit periodical called Zionism "arch treason to the best government on earth," and with brutal frankness Cincinnati's *American Israelite* told the world that Russian Jews—presumably Zionism's chief beneficiaries—were not fit to govern themselves. Still, few if any anti-Zionists were opposed to Jewish colonies in Palestine; Jewish farmers were to be acclaimed!

HADASSAH

No one scoffed at Hadassah, the Women's Zionist Organization of America. It was deemed Zionism at its best. A movement apart, it avoided the political intrigues so typical of the male Zionists. Hadassah is Zionism's greatest organizational success. Its founder, Henrietta Szold (1860–1945), probably belonged to that circle that read and approved of Ahad Ha'Am's cultural views. She may even have helped edit his book of *Selected Essays*, published in 1912, the year that Hadassah was born. In her day this daughter of a Baltimore rabbi was probably the country's most learned woman in Hebraica and Judaica. A stringer for New York's *Jewish Messenger* in the 1880s under the name of Sulamith, Szold taught Russian immigrants in a night school and edited many volumes of the *American Jewish Year Book*. She was no longer young when she became a Zionist leader. A group of Harlem women, Daughters of Zion, became the nucleus of Hadassah, which Szold organized to eradicate malaria, trachoma, typhus, cholera, and tuberculosis and bring healing to Palestine. She provided the Holy Land with visiting nurses, maternity and dental care, pasteurized milk, and health stations and fought juvenile delinquency. Hadassah's clinics and hospitals have treated millions of patients. Hebrew University-Hadassah Medical Center practices the best medicine in the Middle East. Szold gave American Jewish women a cause for which they could work ardently. What Brandeis would set out to do for the Federation of American Zionists in 1914, she did for the women even earlier. In the 1930s, many years after her aliyah to Palestine, she welcomed hundreds of refugee Jewish youth from Germany, whose only hope lay in Palestine. These youngsters were literally brands plucked from the burning. In the 1980s, long after Szold had passed to her eternal award, Hadassah could boast close to four hundred thousand members. Its goals and hopes were always Zionist and it ranked as the world's largest women's organization. Szold was no typical Zionist, despite her position as one of the leading executives of the Palestine Jewish community. Szold and Judah Leon Magnes and a few others marched to the beat of a different drummer. Living in the land when the overwhelming majority were Arabs, Moslems, Szold was concerned that these not be treated as "natives."

LOUIS DEMBITZ BRANDEIS

With the exception of Hadassah, the Zionist movement here in the United States—and probably in other lands, too—was

255

structurally weak and with few resources. Most Zionists were East Europeans, on the whole still an impoverished lot. In 1914 the Federation of American Zionists reported anywhere from seven thousand to twelve thousand members on their rosters. One wonders how many were dues payers—this in a Jewry of three million souls.

Louis Dembitz Brandeis (1856–1941) assumed the leadership of the FAZ. A highly distinguished American of central European stock, he was a legal practitioner who had learned to question the practices of powerful corporations. His support made the Zionist movement acceptable to many, and a coterie of persons, most of them members of old-line families, gathered around him. Brandeis and his friends gave Zionism in this country a status it had never enjoyed before. Through a combination of their leadership and luck, the membership grew to about 150,000 in 1919. Until in his fifties, Brandeis had been a marginal Jew, though perhaps unconsciously—he was very much influenced by his uncle, Lewis Naphtali Dembitz—a "reborn" Israelite. (Brandeis discarded his original middle name David and substituted the maternal family name Dembitz.) In 1910 he helped write the Protocol of Peace, the labor agreement that brought the ILGWU members and their employers together. It may have been this association with Jewish workers that stimulated Brandeis's Jewish consciousness. During the years 1910–1912 he moved closer to Jewry and became a Zionist.

What impelled him to make this move? He was certainly convinced that Zionism was an ideal to which he could give himself. What attracted him was the movement's utopian, democratic, progressive character. He saw it as a potentially fascinating social experiment and one that made no religious demands on him. He could as a Zionist be a Jew *and* a secularist, which appealed to him as he became an ethnic and cultural pluralist and an antiassimilationist. In 1912 this distinguished attorney supported the liberal Woodrow Wilson's presidential candidacy and expected to receive a cabinet appointment. He was not chosen, however, since as yet he had no Jewish following and apparently was not seen as a political asset. Brandeis's public attacks on corporate transgressors, moreover, had saddled him with powerful enemies. In March 1913, just a short time after the new cabinet was appointed without Brandeis, he became active in the New England Zionist movement. There are those, therefore, who say that Brandeis became a Zionist because as a marginal Jew he wanted a leadership role. Others, much more explicit and hostile, maintain that he had no genuine interest in Zionism and set out to buy control of the New England Zionist district in order to secure a ready-made Jewish following for his own political advancement. Former President William Howard Taft, a bitter opponent, said that Brandeis had had himself "metaphorically" recircumcised. But, in fact, there is no proof that Brandeis ever sought adherents to bolster his political status. His conversion to Zion was sincere; it was his great adventure. Even so, it is not improbable that he savored the adulation accompanying his rise to power. He was a disciplined sobersides, but he was a human being. Did he have a *neshomeh*, a "soul," capable of an all-embracing personal compassion and affection? If he did, he was careful to keep it under wraps.

TWO FORCES IN CONFLICT: THE EAST EUROPEANS OPPOSE THE NATIVE-BORN AND THE GERMANS, 1914–22

During World War I, the World Zionist Organization was disrupted because its headquarters were in Germany while the masses supporting it were in an enemy land, Russia. Since it was imperative that the *yishuv*, the Palestine Jewish settlements, be sustained, the World Zionist Organization found it necessary to operate from a neutral land—the United States. In this period of distress, the Zionist leaders in America thought that the creation of a democratically organized American Jewish congress would give them much more authority in their labors to succor their coreligionists abroad and their endeavors to establish a homeland in Palestine.

The concept of an American Jewish congress was not new. Even before the massacre at Kishinev in 1903, the Reformers had begun flirting with the idea. Later, in 1914, when World War I erupted, the Poale Zion, Zion's Workers, began calling for a congress to further Zionist goals in the Holy Land as well as minority rights in the eventual postwar successor states. Many Jews were of the opinion—and they were right—that the Ottoman Empire would be dismembered and that a politically powerful American Jewish congress would be in a position to advance the prospects of a Palestine Jewish state. The Workers of Zion and other Zionists realized that America's Jewish Eastern European newcomers were primarily interested not in Palestine but in minority rights for their dear ones back in Eastern Europe. All this was to be tackled, of course, after the war was over. By linking the Palestine political goals to the minority rights in Eastern Europe sought by the millions of American newcomers, the Zionists hoped that they would have a coalition powerful enough to advance their hopes for a reborn Jewish homeland. Minority rights were imperative, so most American Jews believed. If the prewar empires were to be broken up into successor states after the war was won—Poland, Estonia, Latvia, Lithuania, perhaps the Ukraine, as many expected—the Jews in those new states would have to be protected. Jews needed more than "equal" rights that would compel them to live within parameters set by their frequently hostile Christian fellow citizens. They needed the protection provided by minority rights in the areas of religion, education, and language. Thus an American Jewish congress, as envisaged by the Zionists, would work for minority rights in the Slavic lands and, of course, for a homeland in Palestine.

In order to salvage the World Zionist Organization in 1914, the Zionists moved speedily to organize a Provisional Executive Committee for General Zionist Affairs in the United States. Their leader was Louis D. Brandeis, who soon also became the head of the congress movement. The agenda of the Zionists was clear: protect the Jews in Eastern Europe, and save and build the Palestine settlements, the *yishuv*.

By 1915 the American Jewish Committee and the Zionist congress warriors were locked in a power struggle. It was Brandeis vs. Marshall, the "Russian" newcomers vs. the earlier "German" settlers, the democrats vs. the "oligarchs." The patricians of the American Jewish Committee knew full well that if a democratically elected congress came into being, they could not hope to remain Jewish America's representative group. The committee was anti-Zionist and determined to tolerate no nationwide Jewish congress. The following March, the congress advocates bypassed the American Jewish Committee and in a formal fashion established a congress organization. Among the leaders was Rabbi Stephen Samuel Wise (1872–1949).

Wise, a native Hungarian, was in many respects America's most influential Jewish religious leader in the decades between 1920 and 1949. A Zionist notable, he was also a social worker

259

and a political activist. An outstanding leader, Wise was anything but a typical clergyman. He was a humanitarian concerned with the underprivileged and a very active civic reformer, which made him a politician. Above all, he was an iconoclast. In 1905–06 he turned down the pulpit at New York's prestigious Emanu-El (he wanted absolute freedom of speech, which the board would not permit). In 1906–07 Wise started the Free Synagogue on Sunday mornings in a public auditorium. Hundreds, ultimately thousands, of Jews and Gentiles rushed to hear his nondenominational preaching. Support came from rich admirers, and in a relatively short time he was recognized as one of New York's most distinguished clergymen. In 1922 he took a fateful step, and opened a liberal theological seminary meant to rival the well-established Hebrew Union College in Cincinnati. His new school, the Jewish Institute of Religion, was in many respects the first step in the direction of neo-Reform: the advocacy of Zion, the retention of classical Reform theology, and the return to rituals, ceremonies, and practices associated with age-old Orthodoxy. Wise wanted to train rabbis responsive to the needs of second-generation Jews of Russian and Polish stock. Opening a liberal Jewish seminary was a bold move. He had limited financial resources while the Cincinnati seminary could count on support from hundreds of congregations. This highly distinguished American never became *the* leader of American Jewry because he was too far to the left; religiously he was regarded as a law unto himself. The Orthodox, the Conservatives, and the Reformers all rejected him. The Orthodox, in particular, could not understand his admiration for Jesus. For Jews, "Christ" stood out as the very symbol of a culture that had harassed them for nearly seventeen hundred years. Wise had no rabbinical following until he began training his own men, who adored him.

It was during the last months of 1916 that America's Slavic Jewish community won what seemed to be a decisive victory over its opponents. Having no real choice, the American Jewish Committee accepted the concept of a democratic congress and its program, but it was a hollow victory for the insurgents. The AJC forced the newcomers to agree that the congress would be temporary and would be disbanded after it made its presentation at the peace conference and reported back to its sponsors. Since there was to be no permanent democratically elected congress, the East European Jewish masses thus failed to gain permanent control of America's national Jewish community. True, the native-born went along with the other basic demands of the newcomers: There was to be a democratically elected congress; the great powers at the coming peace conference were to be pressed to accord minority rights—true equality—to the Jews in the eventual successor states; every effort was also to be made to work for a Jewish homeland in Palestine. But the dissolving of the congress meant that the American Jewish Committee would suffer only a temporary defeat. In July 1916, Brandeis, attacked by opponents and sensitive to his position as a Supreme Court justice, withdrew officially as de jure head of the congress and the Zionist forces (he actually retained control of both groups till 1921).

When the new authoritative, inclusive American Jewish Congress appointed an administrative committee in December 1916, it was indeed truly representative. The new leaders ranged from the radical Reform clergy on the left to the Torah-true Orthodox rabbis on the right. Only one woman, Mary Fels, was given a place on the all-powerful committee. Quietly in 1917 Brandeis worked to further the goals of the Zionists. He met with President Wilson, talked to Arthur James Balfour, the British foreign secretary, and to Colonel Edward M. House, Wilson's confidant. He even had the opportunity to see the final text of the Balfour Declaration before it was issued on November 2. In this declaration the British promised that they would favor the establishment of a national home for the Jewish people in Palestine. If Balfour and the British authorities turned to American Jewry, it was because their situation and that of their allies was serious in 1917. The war was not going well. The English courted American Jewry through Brandeis and hoped, too, that the Zionist-motivated Jews in Russia proper—now truly emancipated for a few brief months—would encourage the postczarist government to stay in the war, thus compelling the central European allies to fight on two fronts, the east and the west. The Balfour Declaration was a ploy to win international Jewish support. The British had overestimated Jewish power.

Wilson also was helpful to the Zionists. He had to reward the Jews who had supported him politically. He reviewed the declaration before it was released but made no public statement until the fall of 1918, ten months later. Even then his comment was somewhat equivocal: Palestine was a Turkish province, and the United States was not at war with the Ottoman Empire. Anti-Zionists in the United States, Wilson recognized, were powerful, but so were the evangelical Christians, and they were not happy that the holy places might fall into the hands of the infidel Jews. The American Jewish Committee, too, finally issued a public statement on the "Zionist" Balfour Declaration in April 1918, about six months after the British published it. It was friendly, though carefully worded; the committee leaders were aware that 90 percent of Palestine's population was non-Jewish. Louis Marshall, the prescient AJC leader, made his peace with the concept of a Jewish haven in Palestine. He recognized the growing demand for immigration restriction in America and the need for someplace to which a Jew could turn. American Jews as a whole were elated when they read the Balfour Declaration. Zionism had become respectable. Jews had acquired status and appeared about to have a "country" of their own.

After the compromise between the committee and the congress in late 1916, American Jewry waited patiently till the war was over and the first postwar session of the congress was called to order in Philadelphia, December 15, 1918. (In the meantime, in June 1918, the Zionists had met in national convention at Pittsburgh. Exultant, they paraded with twenty-five bands blaring as three thousand children, dressed in blue and white—the Zionist colors—marched along singing Hebrew songs. The Federation of American Zionists, reconstituted as the Zionist Organization of America, now had close to 185,000 members.) When the American Jewish Congress assembled for the first time in Philadelphia, the delegates compared themselves to the delegates of the thirteen disparate English colonies who had come together in the same city in 1776 to establish the new United States of America. Now the descendants of the twelve tribes of Israel met to take the first step toward a new Jewish national state. The Zionist flag flew over Independence Hall. The congress delegation sent to Paris was given an audience in May 1919. The victorious entente powers listened and the following month incorporated minority rights for East European Jews in the Versailles Treaty. With the full support of the American Jewish delegation in Paris, the Zionist leaders pushed for acceptance of the Balfour Declaration as well, although the British were already chipping away at it. Once the war was over they no longer needed the Jews. On April 24, 1920, at the San Remo Conference of the allied prime ministers, the mandate for Palestine was officially given to Great Britain. In August, when the Treaty of Sèvres was signed, the Turks acknowledged Great Britain as the mandatory power in Palestine. (Earlier that year, in May, the American Jewish Congress, meeting for the second time, had made its report and adjourned indefinitely.)

Disregarding the agreement between the congress and the American Jewish Committee, a rump group reorganized the congress, which was permanently constituted in 1922. It would never become a formidable rival of the committee, although its programs were farsighted. On July 24, 1922, the League of Nations confirmed Britain's control of the Holy Land. American Jewish Zionists were more pleased when the U.S. Congress in September passed the Lodge-Fish resolution favoring a national home for Jews in Palestine. A month earlier the Churchill White Paper had begun the process of delimiting—if not ultimately scrapping—the Balfour Declaration.

In retrospect, it is probable that both the congress group and the American Jewish Committee were fighting for control of America's east Europeans and, even more, of all American Jewry. The United States government in the years 1917 and 1918 was reaching out for world power. Jews here, patterning themselves on Washington, may well have sought to influence, if not to dominate, world Jewry.

THE MORGENTHAU MISSION,
JULY–SEPTEMBER 1919

After the Treaty of Versailles was signed in June 1919, President Wilson sent Henry Morgenthau (1856–1946) on a special mission of enquiry to Poland. Poland was never happy with the minority rights imposed by the powers meeting at Paris in 1919. Intensely nationalistic, the Poles were not overly fond of Jews and certainly had no patience with cultural pluralism. Jews were being murdered in Poland, and American and world Jewry were outraged. On April 5, 1919, thirty-five Jews, meeting to distribute food for the needy in Pinsk, were executed by Polish soldiers. There were reports that the Poles were beating or killing Jews in at least 150 towns and villages. Wilson found it advisable to acknowledge these atrocities. The years 1918–20 were bad years in other areas as well: Thousands of Jews were killed in the Ukraine in the rampaging of Hetman Simon Petlura, and even greater atrocities were perpetrated under the anti-Bolshevik General Anton I. Denikin. Bandits roamed through parts of Eastern Europe adding to the anarchic conditions in those days of civil war between the new Soviet regime and the anti-communist counterrevolutionaries. Conditions in Poland were exacerbated by the boycott the Poles initiated against their Jewish fellow citizens, a boycott even extended to America where Polish miners in Appalachia refused to patronize Jewish stores.

Morgenthau, the German immigrant Wilson chose to investigate the condition of Jewry in Poland, had made a fortune in real estate in New York City and was respected as a philanthropist. He worked closely with Stephen S. Wise in the

Free Synagogue, but Morgenthau was an anti-Zionist, and ultimately the two separated. This brilliant entrepreneur raised substantial sums to finance the election of Woodrow Wilson and hoped to become secretary of the treasury, but Wilson shunted him off to a traditionally "Jewish" post, the Constantinople embassy. After Morgenthau assessed what was happening to Poland's Jewry, he made his report in September. He described the acts of violence but avoided denouncing the Poles—unlike Sir Stuart Samuel, dispatched on a similar mission by the British. Morgenthau's carefully worded recital of events in the Polish republic lost him his opportunity to become an American Jewish folk hero. Angry Jews in the United States were inclined to see his report as a whitewash. Morgenthau wanted to help the Poles rebuild their economy, but his proposals were not accepted. It is not improbable, however, that his appraisal of the situation—and the public scrutiny of Polish actions—induced Poland's rulers to be more sensitive to the needs of their Jewish citizens. In addition, Morgenthau probably realized that Wilson was eager to help the new Slavic republic. There were hundreds of thousands of Polish-American voters devoted to their reborn homeland.

ZIONIST LEADERSHIP: THE FIGHT FOR CONTROL

During the years 1918–21 when the American Jewish Congress was riding high and the country's Jews were working to impose minority rights on the new states in Eastern Europe and help Great Britain assume control of Palestine, Justice Brandeis reorganized the Federation of American Zionists. The new Zionist Organization of America was more tightly structured than the old federation. Brandeis wanted a strong national

Zionist association because he was eager to build a strong new Jewish Palestine. In 1918 Brandeis attended the Zionist conference in Pittsburgh and in 1919 visited Palestine, where he was not altogether pleased with what he saw. He returned overseas the following year for a critical Zionist meeting in London and on his way back aboard the *Zeeland* finally refined his plans for the Jewish Palestine of the future. He wanted equal rights for all—women, too—national control of natural resources, Hebrew as the medium of instruction, support for higher education and research, furtherance of the cooperative principle in new economic enterprises, vocational training, and the use of funds from the diaspora to help the country survive. It was imperative that the soil be improved, production increased, the country's meager resources exploited to the fullest, and afforestation intensified. He was eager to co-opt non-Zionists in the building of Palestine. Obviously immigration would have to be increased and commerce encouraged. Brandeis was determined to build a modern state that could be proudly displayed.

In July 1920 the Zionists meeting in London created the Keren Hayesod, the Palestine Foundation Fund. Brandeis was not pleased. He did not approve of an all-purpose agency to embrace both investments and noncommercial activities. Besides, it looked to him like an all-purpose grab bag, something of a slush fund. He was not interested in taking care of the "good old boys," the loyal stalwarts. He was all business. A well-organized state was more important to him than a powerful world Zionist organization. Brandeis's approach was always rational and businesslike—it was the dogged, determined "Germanic" in him. The East European–born Chaim Weizmann was brilliant, highly charismatic, and—unlike Brandeis—never devoid of romanticism. Weizmann was interested in a movement that would embrace world Jewry and all aspects of its folk culture; all Jews would have to be Palestine-oriented. Weizmann distanced himself from Brandeis. When at London the Zionists made Justice Brandeis honorary president of the World Zionist Organization, were they now moving to kick him upstairs? In June 1921, at a Zionist conference in Cleveland, the Brandeis-Mack group that had played a dominant role in world Zionism since 1914 was voted out of office. After a fashion, Cleveland was a replay of the *Yidn* vs. the *Yehudim* struggle, the "Russians" vs. the "Germans." Weizmann and Brandeis were two strong personalities—and viewpoints—in conflict. Neither would or could accept second place; there could be no bridge between Washington and Pinsk! The rejection of Justice Brandeis and Judge Julian Mack and their followers hurt Zionism. Some of the country's ablest and most distinguished Jews were no longer in the saddle, although they continued to implement their original plans. By the 1930s, they had regained control of the Zionist Organization of America.

BRANDEIS THE ZIONIST, 1912–41

It must have been a source of satisfaction to the justice that after several years his Zionist opponents were removed and a pro-Brandeis group once again took over the Zionist Organization of America. Before leaving Germany he had attended a gymnasium, a high school. His early exposure to German culture influenced him more than he realized, teaching him to value meticulosity and to spurn slipshoddiness. Brandeis had built the American Zionist movement and made it respectable. This Boston Jewish Brahmin insisted on discipline and on the proper use of funds, and he told a fearful American Jewry that dual loyalties were objectionable only if inconsistent. He knew that corporate America was anything but an ideal state. The Palestine that he fashioned in his mind was to be a center of Western culture—a reborn, cleansed America on the shores of the Mediterranean where refugee Jews could find a haven and live a good life. For him the political structure of Jewish Palestine was not all-important, as long as the nature of the future culture, its content, its potential contributions were ethical. Classical Americanism, biblical prophetic ideals, and Zionism were equated. Brandeis never went into a synagogue to pray, yet he was a great Jew. His oft-quoted Zionist statement, "to be good Americans we must be better Jews and to be better Jews, we must become Zionists," meant that Zionism had to reflect the best and the highest in social idealism. He seems never to have conceived that America itself could become a great Jewish cultural center, which is interesting in view of the fact that American Jewry had already produced the *Jewish Encyclopedia* and was about to complete the best, most authentic English translation of the Hebrew Bible. He failed to anticipate the potentialities of America's new immigrants and was unable to foresee what secular education would do for American Jewry when harnessed to Jewish knowledge and idealism.

12. The Persistence of Two Jewish Communities, 1850s–1924

In 1920 when the original American Jewish Congress adjourned, a divided American Jewry was back where it had started—although from 1916 to 1920 the Jews had worked together to secure equality for coreligionists in the successor states of Eastern Europe and a homeland of sorts in Palestine. Once again there were apparently two coeval distinct American Jewish communities: that of the older native-born and Germans, still anti-Zionists, and that of the East European émigrés and their American-born children. Nevertheless, ever since 1852 when the first East European community was established in New York City, the newcomers had hastened to blend into the established American Jewish communities. All Jews, of whatever origins, in this land were held together by a consensus: the consciousness of a common past and the belief that America's overwhelming Christian society looked askance at them. In general the East Europeans were ready to renounce Slavic village and town singularities and adopt the American way of life. Both groups in this country recognized the demands of kinship. All Jews here were shocked by the pogroms and the oppressive Russian and Rumanian disabilities, and they were eager to help their coreligionists. With very few exceptions,

Jews here were determined to resist immigration restriction. In one area unity had already been achieved: The two otherwise rival American Jewish communities were working together through the Joint Distribution Committee. It was hard to disdain those newcomers in New York City who were building huge skyscrapers, magnificent apartment houses, and subways. Numerous émigrés were distinguished as lawyers, doctors, and engineers. New York's colleges were filling up with Russian newcomers or their American-born children. A few, if not yet many, joined Reform temples. There was some intramarriage. In short, all Jews here were beginning to blend.

As the newcomers brewed their concoction of Americanism and *Yiddishkeit*, they were moving closer to the earlier Jewish settlers, who had now become completely Americanized by the country's irresistible ambience. All Jews, no matter who they were, were overwhelmed by American cultural institutions; the cinema had an alchemy all its own. In some instances Americanization was almost instantaneous. Russian-born children in a farm colony at Chesterfield, Connecticut, were already proficient in English and playing baseball after a few months in this country. Papa, the Slav, was Americanized by his children, his job, and the Yiddish press. Even the separatist landsmanshaft had an important role in the process of Eastern European Jews becoming one with this land; the Yiddish meetings were conducted according to standard parliamentary rules. The immigrants' standard of living was rising, through the ballot they improved themselves civically, and now for the first time they were entering into a new world of the arts. They even changed physically, increasing in height and weight. As their social vision broadened, they became more discerning. But all the institutions that made for Americanization pale into insignificance next to the public schools, to which the children were devoted. Still, the Jews of this land were not yet one people with a common destiny. Intra-Jewish disparities and hostilities were not easily overcome.

The road to unity was not a smooth one. The native-born, the Americanized central Europeans, and the East Europeans were indeed working together, but perceptible differences remained. The newcomers had their own press, fraternal orders, language, and mutual aid societies. It was the "rich" against the "poor," the old-timers against the many. The Slavic Jews were not made welcome in some of the older Jewish fraternal orders. Prestigious Jewish clubs barred even wealthy "Russians," just as the members of exclusive German Jewish clubs were barred from Gentile societies. This intolerance of Jew for Jew was nothing new in American Jewish history. After a fashion it may well go all the way back, in New York City, to the 1680s. The 1920s still found two groups at different ends of the social spectrum. The earlier settlers—Jewish Brahmins, as they pictured themselves—were determined never to surrender their hegemony, even though they were outnumbered five to one.

American Jews of older stock were convinced that the newcomers were making a mistake in seeking to distance themselves from their "betters." Look what we have done for you. We've assisted you and worked with you as you made the transition from your primitive culture to our advanced American way of life. We are the ones who established most of the important national Jewish cultural, defense, educational, and religious institutions. We created the Board of Delegates of American Israelites, the Independent Order of B'nai B'rith, the rabbinical seminaries, the settlement houses, the Jewish Publication Society, the American Jewish Historical Society, the

273

National Council of Jewish Women! The lion's share of the funds dispersed by the Joint Distribution Committee comes from us. We've kept the door to America open for you. We've helped you synthesize Americanism and Judaism. We're the ones who pioneered the path for your integration into the life of this great country: Be a Jew at home and an American citizen in the larger community! We've given you leadership since the day you landed. We are proud of our achievements, and we wish to continue to help you and to lead you. If United States Jewry is exercising world Jewish hegemony, it's largely because of what we older settlers achieved.

The Russians, the Poles, and the Balkan Jews responded sharply to the claims and complaints of the older, established Jewry. We may have come from obscurantist lands, but we are making our way as scientists, scholars, philosophers, educators, and researchers. Professionals of East European origin now number in the thousands. You disdain us, but we are your peers. We have wealth now and want recognition and power—and no longer to be stereotyped as pushcart peddlers or sweatshop workers. We already have three Jews of Slavic stock in Congress (1922). Look at what *we* have accomplished. Ours is "the greatest collective Horatio Alger story in immigration history"! We believe in *Yiddishkeit;* you "Germans" are assimilationists. This is a democratic land, and we want leadership or autonomy. Thank you, we'll go our own way! The rupture that began in 1914 and reached its climax in 1922, when the permanent American Jewish Congress was reorganized to challenge the powerful American Jewish Committee, was inevitable. Two distinct Jewish communities and cultures were in conflict.

What would ultimately happen to the world of the East European Zionists, to the socialist *Forward,* to the myriad of

Yiddish-speaking Orthodox Jews, to the apparel workers, to the petty shopkeepers? What would ultimately happen to the world of Rabbi Isaac M. Wise, Jacob H. Schiff, and Hart, Schaffner & Marx? What would happened in the decade that followed the passage of the Immigration Act of 1924? Would the newcomers succeed in dominating American Jewish life? Would they impose their cultural and spiritual pattern on the earlier settlers? Would the native-born and the acculturated "Germans" impose their way of life on the newcomers of Slavic and Balkan stock? Would a compromise eventuate?

Part V
Jews in the Modern World: 1925–1990s

13. Forging a Unified Jewish Community

Jews in the United States had come from all parts of the world, from the Iberian Peninsula to the Ural Mountains. Living in America, embraced and overpowered by its ambience, they and their families had become compleat Americans. Jewishly, however, these men and women from a dozen different lands were a motley assembly. Three factors impelled their fusion: the need for them to unite to help overseas Jews in distress; the need to provide a haven, a Zion, a home for the homeless; and Judeophobia, which compelled them to join and work together for defense. Here in the United States East European and Balkan newcomers leaned on the older established communities. Consciously or unconsciously they patterned themselves on the native-born and the acculturated Germans. Melding with the earlier Jewish settlers, all these disparate ethnics created a new Jew—an American Jew—who began emerging in the years from 1925 on. Working together, in need of one another, they succeeded in creating the basis for the new unified community that would dominate the later decades of the twentieth century.

KLAL YISRAEL: HELPING JEWS OVERSEAS

Jews have never failed since the 1700s to respond to the call to help other Jews. One of the major goals of the new Board of Delegates of American Israelites (1859) was to come to the aid

279

of oppressed Jews in foreign lands. In the 1870s, United States Jewry sent delegates to Europe's Jewish conferences with the hope of furthering the enfranchisement of East European and Balkan Jewries. In 1914–15, shortly after the outbreak of World War I, American Jews set aside their ethnic, social, and religious differences to create the American Jewish Joint Distribution Committee and soon the United Palestine Appeal (UPA). The plight of the East Europeans was especially desperate. Later, in 1939, when the Nazi government set the torch to Germany's synagogues and World War II loomed large, the JDC and the UPA decided to forget their differences and to unite in fund-raising as the United Jewish Appeal (UJA). Enormous sums were raised by America's hundreds of local Jewish communities under the aegis of the UJA and the burgeoning charity federations. All in all, the funds collected helped Jewries in Europe, North Africa, Palestine (later Israel), and other Asian lands. Up to 1939 the JDC helped millions in Eastern Europe, though very little could be done to continue aiding them when World War II erupted that year.

After 1939 most of the JDC monies were channeled into Jewish Palestine. After the restrictive immigration acts (1921, 1924) closed America to most Jewish immigrants, it became obvious that the Holy Land was one of the few havens still open to Jewry. But even the Holy Land became an unwelcoming place when in 1939 England, regretting the Balfour Declaration, severely limited or closed Palestine to Jewish refugees. America's Hebrew Sheltering and Immigrant Aid Society (HIAS) did what it could to help Jewish émigrés on their way to the United States. Their leaders and workers, dedicated and able, maintained offices as far east as Japan. In July 1938 thirty-two nations gathered together in the French resort town of

Évian-les-Bains to discuss providing a home for Germany's threatened Jews. Australia graciously admitted fifteen hundred, but nothing else of note was done at the Évian conference to help the desperate Jews. Nazi Germany now knew that the Jews could be destroyed with impunity. On November 9–10, 1938, the Nazis burnt down the country's synagogues (*Kristallnacht*, the Night of Broken Glass). In 1943, after the systematic extinction of Europe's Jews had already been decreed by the Germans and was well underway, the British and Americans met at Bermuda to discuss the fate of a doomed Jewry. Here, too, nothing of consequence was accomplished.

EUROPEAN HOSTILITY TO JEWS THROUGH THE AGES

Why did Hitler and his people do what they did? What prompted the Nazi Party to take genocidal action and the German people to accept its decision? Germany has a Jew-hating tradition. During the Crusades the warriors marching to Jerusalem killed the Jews in the Rhineland cities: Why wait to murder Jewry in the Holy Land when there were Christkillers at hand? During the Black Death about two thousand men, women, and children in Strasbourg were thrown into a huge pit and burnt alive on St. Valentine's Day in 1349. Early in the sixteenth century a tiny Jewish community near Berlin was cremated alive. That same century, Martin Luther, the founder of Protestantism, published a bitter diatribe excoriating Jews and demanding that their synagogues be burnt down, their houses destroyed, and their property confiscated; if necessary, let them be driven into exile. There are few, if any, more heartless attacks in the entire thesaurus of Judeophobia (Luther's attack on the Jews can be purchased today, but only in the bookshops of white supremacist purveyors of antiblack and anti-Jewish writings). In 1750

Frederick the Great of Prussia published a charter regulating the life and activity of Prussian Jewry. His French contemporary, Count Honoré-Gabriel R. Mirabeau, called it "a law worthy of a cannibal."

In the late nineteenth century the Germans developed a racial theory known as anti-Semitism: Jews as Semites, a people without any redeeming trait, have no place in modern society. An anti-Semitic political party came into being, and a huge anti-Jewish literature was spawned in the western, central, and east European lands. This was the tradition that Hitler inherited emerging as he did full-blown from the brow of Satan.

THE GERMAN PEOPLE, THE HOLOCAUST, AND THE JEWS, 1933–45

Between 1933 and 1945 Germany was governed by the National Socialist German Workers' Party (Nazis). As early as 1933 the Nazi regime initiated measures to deprive Jews of their German citizenship, to despoil them of their property, and to force them to leave. The Nazis were successful. The thousands who came to the United States suffered (although of course not as badly as the Jews who were left behind). These émigrés were in a foreign land whose language they did not know. They had no means and, although the Jewish charities helped them, often had to struggle for decades before they became a secure part of America's middle class. Like the Russians and Poles who had come to this land a generation earlier, these refugees set up numerous self-help organizations. American Jews were supportive, but many of them looked askance at the newcomers. Aliens, foreigners, are always subject to prejudice. The newcomers were primarily businessmen, a few of whom even succeeded in developing multimillion dollar corporations. Some were sociologists, psychiatrists, lawyers, physicians, atomic physicists, musicians, Nobel laureates. New York's New School for Social Research made provision for some of the incoming academicians in a "University in Exile." Comparisons, of course, are frequently invidious, but there is no question that there has never been a group of American immigrants better educated or more gifted than these Germans. It is cold comfort to American and world Jewry that the United States injured only itself by doing so little to rescue Europe's endangered Jews.

In 1942–43 the German authorities decided to annihilate the Jews systematically and thoroughly—this was a policy of genocide. The Germans called it the Final Solution of the Jewish "problem"; the nations of the world referred to it in later decades as the Holocaust; Hebrew-speaking Jews employ the term *ha-shoah*, "annihilation." The Holocaust really had begun before 1942, when the Germans invaded Poland and Russia and murdered hundreds of thousands of Jews. In 1931 more than three million Jews lived in Poland; in 1947–48 only eighty-eight thousand Jews were left in the land! Myriads are known to have been executed and buried at Babi Yar in 1943. Scholars and statisticians think that between five and six million Jews were murdered—in one form or another—by the Germans; another five to six million non-Jews were also executed. The German masses knew what its leaders were doing but did virtually nothing to impede this murderous process of exterminating fellow citizens and human beings. How many Germans were shaken by their awareness of what was taking place? Where was German compassion, pity, anger, rage, fury? There was no revolution—no protests—by the German masses. Before World

War II was over it is estimated that thirty-five million men, women, and children were either killed in battle, wounded, or murdered.

THE REACTION OF DEMOCRATIC LANDS TO THE HOLOCAUST

President Roosevelt knew what was happening to the Jews in the lands controlled by the Germans. No later than 1940 he set out to prepare America for war with Germany and the Axis Powers, for he, like Lincoln, realized that the world could not exist half slave and half free. Preparing America for the coming conflict with Germany was his priority. His State Department, Congress, and the American people—typically xenophobic—had no intention of helping Europe's Jews; they were no concern of theirs. Consular officials made the obtaining of visas by Jews so difficult that permissible quotas were not filled. When in 1939 the S.S. *St. Louis* approached America's shores with some nine hundred Jewish refugees, they were not permitted to land. That same year, when the Rogers-Wagner Bill to permit the entrance of twenty thousand Jewish children into the United States was put into the congressional hopper, it died there. Finally, in 1944 a War Refugee Board was established by the president, and some Jews were saved. In addition, 987 Jewish refugees were admitted to the United States and interned in Oswego until the war was over. All in all, the story of American involvement in the saving of Europe's Jews is an inglorious one.

Could the Jews of the United States have done more to pressure the president? As far as it is now known, Judge Samuel I. Rosenman, an intimate and adviser of Roosevelt, did little if anything to move the chief executive. Did Rabbi Stephen S. Wise, deemed a political power in his day, insist that Roosevelt take strong executive action on behalf of Europe's Jewry? There is little evidence that Rabbi Wise pushed the president hard. But all this is idle speculation. The Jewish cinema moguls in Hollywood were certainly in a position through the films they produced to influence the American people on behalf of European Jewry. But they believed that discretion was the better part of valor. And the Zionists in America? Some were diaspora negators in whose eyes there was no balm in Gilead, not even in America. Jewry's future, they believed, lay in Palestine, so their priority was to keep its doors open. The possibility of a calamity like the Holocaust eluded U.S. Jews. They had been outraged in 1903 when forty-some Jews were butchered in czarist Kishinev, but the Nazi annihilation of five to six million? This they could not comprehend (there are still many Jews who do not fully realize what happened). The Holocaust was the greatest disaster in three thousand years of recorded Jewish history. How could this have been allowed to happen in the twentieth century? Even the tragic capture of first-century C.E. Jerusalem by Titus fades when compared with the German death camps and the East European slaughter.

The Holocaust was such a terrible experience that many of its survivors preferred to forget it. They showed no desire even to record its horrors but deliberately blotted it out, even though the details were embedded in their subconscious. The Gentile world, turning to Jews, asked them to forget the past. It was ready to cite Luke 23:34: "Father, forgive them for they know not what they do." What of the anguish of the millions of individuals as they faced destruction? It is difficult for Jews today to wipe out the agony of the men, women, and children as they perished. Is it not probable that the new generation beginning with the 1950s, Jews who have turned to tradition, to the prayer shawl, to the skullcap, have done so not because they are enamored of the old ways but because they have lost faith in liberalism? After a fashion they have turned inward toward each other, turned their backs on modernity, on the world their acculturated fathers cherished.

ZIONISM IN THE UNITED STATES

Looking backward in the post–World War II years, Jewry in America had spent huge sums to rehabilitate fellow Jews in the lands of Eastern Europe. Through no fault of their own, the friends and relatives Jews had saved there since 1914 were destroyed by the forces of evil. American Jewry was more fortunate in Palestine, whose Jewish community, the *yishuv*, had been kept alive despite British indifference and Arab hostility. All in all, the philanthropic efforts of the American Jews were remarkable. American Jewry, immigrants and native-born, blending to become an integrated community, never forgot the obligations of kinship: No Jew should ever stand alone.

If working together to save oppressed Jewries abroad united all Jews here—regardless of ethnic origin—this emotional embrace was intensified when many American Jews set out to secure in Palestine a haven where any Jew could go as of right. Zionism in part at least solved the Jewish problem. Zionism was the Jewish hope, going back at least to the sixth and fifth pre-Christian centuries, when Babylonian exiles had started drifting back to Jerusalem. In later centuries it was believed that a Messiah—an anointed one, a member of the House of David—would inaugurate the restoration. Hardly a century has passed without witnessing the advent of a would-be Messiah. In the early 1990s there were Brooklyn Hassidim who insisted that their leader, the Lubavitcher rebbe, was the long-awaited Redeemer. Most Orthodox, Conservative, and neo-Reform Jews of East European stock in the United States were Zionists even if they were not affiliated with a Zionist society. Why were they Zionists? For many Jews the United States was not God's Promised Land. Too many Jews here had slaved in sweatshops. American society, too, harbored its quotient of anti-Semitism. Relatives languishing in eastern Europe needed a haven denied them here after 1924, but Palestine would welcome them. The culture in the new Palestine would be totally Jewish. There would be no prejudice, no assimilation in a Jewish homeland. Zionism could be—would be—a route to Utopia.

Before 1925 very many American Jews—especially the native-born, the acculturated Germans, and the Reformers—were either non-Zionists or anti-Zionists; you could not be loyal to the United States and to another polity, they believed. There was no need for a Zionist homeland; America was open to the whole world. One may venture a guess: If America had not limited immigration in 1924, a Jewish state probably would never have come into being.

ANTI-ZIONISTS, NON-ZIONISTS, ZIONISTS

After 1925 it was imperative to establish a haven for Jews. The Russians, the Poles, the Rumanians, and those who dwelt in Moslem lands all were exposed to constant hostility. American monies had been pouring into Palestine for generations. Few, if any, native-born American Jews ever frowned on the Palestine colonies as such or on their furtherance. Now, after America showed itself unwilling to admit Jews, Palestine had to be developed as a refuge for those Israelites in need of a new home. Realizing this, Louis Marshall, the leader of the American Jewish Committee and the native-born, in 1929 repudiated the anti-Zionist past and join Zionism's Enlarged Jewish Agency. Palestine had to become the sanctuary America no longer wished to be. The Arabs, anticipating that Jews would now settle in the Holy Land in large numbers, were apprehensive and began to murder Jewish residents; sixty-some were killed in Hebron alone in 1929.

Only a few years after the gates to America began closing, the Reform Jews started modifying their anti-Zionism. A new hymnal carried "Ha-Tikvah," the Zionist national song (1932). A year later, when the German National Socialists came to power and began oppressing and destroying German Jewry, these anti-Semites made more Zionists than Brandeis, Stephen S. Wise, and Abba Hillel Silver had together ever been able to recruit. That same year saw a palace revolution in the hitherto largely anti-Zionist Central Conference of American (Reform) Rabbis. The Zionists among them seized control. Earlier anti-Zionist policies were ignored, and the Conference was now neutral on Zionism (1935). Two years later, in 1937, the British, convinced that they could not pacify the Arabs or the Jews, spoke of dividing the country between the two hostile forces. Meeting in Columbus, Ohio, that year, the Reform rabbinical conference assumed a carefully worded pro-Zionist stance. The non- and anti-Zionist forces in the conference were still powerful and articulate but no longer dominant. The Union of American Hebrew Congregations, too, was now ready to accept Palestine as a Jewish homeland as long as it professed democracy and separated religion and state. After the anti-Jewish violence in Germany in 1938, the need for Palestine as a safe harbor was more imperative than ever for the German Jews. By 1939, when the delegates gathered at Évian offered no sanctuary, the situation was desperate. The British, in their Malcolm

McDonald White Paper declared that even Palestine would be closed to Jews. Now there was no place to go as World War II erupted and once more, as in World War I, thousands—ultimately millions—of Jews in central Europe, eastern Europe, and the Balkans were killed.

All American Jews were determined to help their fellow Jews. If the British would not admit refugees legally, the Jews were determined to penetrate the land illegally. American Jewry sent money and military supplies to the Haganah (defense), a Palestine Jewish underground military organization that fought both the Arabs and the British and helped refugees enter the country secretly. Indignant that no land would open its doors freely to Jews, the Central Conference of American Rabbis now moved quickly and publicly into the Zionist camp. In 1940 it introduced a special Zionist service in its prayer book and two years later opted to support a Jewish army to help the British win World War II. It hoped that this devotion would further the establishment of a Jewish homeland. The CCAR's decision to push for a Jewish army annoyed a large number of its members who believed—correctly—that the CCAR was now completely in the Zionist camp. In their opinion religion should not be the handmaid of politics. In 1942 a substantial minority of these dissident members organized the American Council for Judaism. These non-Zionists, numbering almost a hundred, insisted that the CCAR emphasize religion and emancipate itself from Zionist leadership, but they did not object to the physical rehabilitation of Palestine and the furtherance of its Jewry. These men were rabbis, not anti-Jews. They did not believe that Jews were a "nation," though they accepted the peoplehood of the Jews. (It was of course unrealistic on the part of the American Council for Judaism to oppose Zionism, which offered what seemed to be the only haven for European Jews at a time that they were being exterminated.) In all probability the American Council would not have objected to a democratic state in Palestine embracing both Arabs and Jews and guaranteeing each of them the same rights and immunities. By 1943, with the Holocaust in full swing, the Union of American Hebrew Congregations, which included rich and influential laymen, voted for neutrality in all issues of Zionism but still hoped that Palestine would be open to Jewish settlement.

Essentially the American Council for Judaism set out to stress the anti-Zionist article in the 1885 Pittsburgh Platform. The congregants of Houston's Beth Israel, a Reform congregation, came out with a statement on Basic Principles: They were Jewish religionists of the Caucasian race and were willing to help support the Palestine colonies, though they were strongly opposed to a political establishment. Later Beth Israel ignored its own Basic Principles. Most rabbis left the American Council, and it was taken over almost completely by laymen who were intransigently anti-Zionist; the very thought of a Jewish commonwealth frightened them. Some of these anti-Zionists, however, did yeoman work in the effort to help German Jewish refugees. In following decades the American Council declined sharply as the Holocaust and the rise of the State of Israel undermined this anti-Zionist movement.

In 1942, while Reform rabbis and their lay friends were organizing the American Council for Judaism, the various nationwide Zionist associations were federating in order to increase their political influence. The four most important groups were the Zionist Organization of America, Hadassah, the laborite Poale Zion, and the Orthodox Mizrachi. Aware that the Germans advancing through Eastern Europe were annihilating the Jews of Poland, the Ukraine, and western Russia, the Zionist federation was more than ever convinced that the only hope for Jewry was a commonwealth of its own. In May 1942 the federation met at the Biltmore Hotel in New York and formulated a new program. It hoped that when World War II was won the victorious Western powers would establish a sovereign Jewish state in Palestine (it was through expecting any help from Britain's League of Nations mandate). Needing more political clout, it encouraged the call for an all-American Jewish conference in 1943. (Obviously these Zionists were patterning themselves on the American Jewish Congress of December 1918.) Dozens of national Jewish organizations, meeting in August in the midst of the Holocaust, were carried away by the oratory and overwhelming personality of the indomitable Abba Hillel Silver and adopted the Biltmore Program. (They chose to ignore the fact that non-Jews in the Holy Land outnumbered Jews at least two to one.) The American Jewish Committee dropped out along with the National Council of Jewish Women and the Jewish labor crowd. The Union of American Hebrew Congregations stayed on but did not vote.

As a sop to the Jews who had pushed for an American Jewish conference in the hope that it would establish an overall national authoritative Jewish organization in the United States, the Zionists in control formulated yet another plan for a permanent American Jewish congress. It proved worthless and was never implemented. The conference adjourned in 1949; the Zionists by then had their state, Israel. At the United Nations debate on Palestine in May 1947, Silver spoke eloquently, asking this international body to take over the Holy Land. The British themselves were getting fed up with the mandate. It was no light thing to contend with hostile Jews and Arabs; in 1946

Jewish terrorists had blown up a wing of the King David Hotel in Jerusalem. Since they still controlled Egypt and Suez, their lifeline to India where they had large interests, the British were ready to withdraw. In November 1946 the United Nations General Assembly had voted to partition Palestine into two independent states, one Arab and the other Jewish. The Arabs demanded all of Palestine; the Jews would accept a half portion.

JUDEOPHOBIA AND ANTI-SEMITISM

Jewish kinship strengthened by overseas help to suffering Jews and intensified by Zionism has been heightened by the prejudice against Jewry. Jews draw closer together when attacked. What is anti-Semitism? The term is often used very loosely. Anti-Semitism, a pseudoscientific theory, asserts that Jews—who in antiquity spoke Semitic languages—are culturally and morally worthless and can make no contribution to society. (The final implication is that they should be destroyed root and branch.) Much more accurate terms that may well be employed are Jew-hatred and Judeophobia. Dislike of the Jew is a universal syndrome; Japan has practically no Jews, yet Jew-haters have arisen in that land. Anti-Semitism's greatest victory in the United States occurred when Congress passed the immigration acts of the 1920s restricting the admission of East European Jews (along with eastern and southern European non-Jews) because they were a lesser breed. In 1906 this country had admitted 153,748 Jews; in 1932—a Depression year, to be sure—America admitted 2,755.

THE AMERICAN TRADITION OF HOSTILITY TO JEWS

What are the historical manifestations of Jew-bashing? The Book of Esther in the Bible testifies that Jews were hated and thought deserving of being murdered. Jews who were not citizens were expelled from Rome in 139 B.C.E. Two thousand years later many Americans, xenophobes, nativists, expressed their dislike of Jews. The American Federation of Labor, led by the Jew Samuel Gompers, was eager to keep out East European immigrants, whom they saw as competitors for jobs. Most Jews are "Russians," hence Communists, hence dangerous—don't let them in! Many Jews are affluent: Why should the infidels prosper while a good churchgoing Christian like me must struggle for a living? A well-known source for anti-Jewish prejudice is the so-called *Protocols of the Elders of Zion*, a false concoction of the Russian secret police. The *Protocols* are the alleged minutes of international Jewish leaders who meet secretly to plan how they will proceed to rule and ruin the world. If there is any trouble, the Jews are the cause. The Jews are all-powerful and dangerous. How else to explain the anti-Jewish bias of a number of America's most distinguished nineteenth- and early twentieth-century poets, litterateurs, and social scientists? When Nathaniel Hawthorne began writing in 1828, there were not more than a handful of Jews in all of Boston. He, Herman Melville, Theodore Dreiser, Henry Adams, H. L. Mencken, Ezra Pound, and T. S. Eliot all clubbed the Jews verbally. Oliver Wendell Holmes grew up in a New England that never failed to think of Jews as god-killers, but he, somehow, rose above the prevalent narrowness:

> From these the son of Mary came;
> With these the Father deigned to dwell—
> Peace be upon thee Israel.

Charles A. Lindbergh, who first flew the Atlantic—subsequently an admirer of the Nazis—said the Jews were pushing

America into war. In the end no one knows why Jews are hated by so many people. *Ignoramus et ignorabimus*: we don't know, we will never know.

THE PREWAR YEARS

On September 22, 1928, as the Jews were preparing to celebrate the Day of Atonement, the holiest day of the year, a four-year-old girl disappeared in Massena, New York. The mayor asked a trooper to call the rabbi to police headquarters and question him. The mayor had heard that Jews practice human sacrifice, murdering Christian children. The child, lost in the woods, soon reappeared. Every year, not in one town alone, vandals spray synagogues. Arson and bombings are not uncommon. Scrawled anti-Jewish graffiti are on walls, and hundreds of tombstones are overturned in Jewish cemeteries in all parts of the country. America has a host of professional anti-Semitic organizations. They print and distribute anti-Jewish literature, operate bookstores, and publish newspapers. Some of the anti-Semitic papers, well printed and in color, are expensive productions; obviously they have wealthy patrons. The basic concept, from which everything flows, is that whatever a Jew does is evil. Therefore, he can do no right.

Influenced by the successes of Hitler's National Socialist Party, numerous anti-Jewish groups came to birth in this country during the 1930s hoping to emulate the achievements of the German fascists. For a brief period a German-American bund maintained close relations with the Nazi rulers of the mother country. It has been estimated that in the decade of the Great Depression there may have been in this country fifteen thousand dyed-in-the-wool Jew-haters affiliated with anti-Semitic organizations. With one exception—the Ku Klux Klan in Indiana during the 1920s—no anti-Jewish organization managed to exercise power. Some leaders even were sent to jail. The 1930s were difficult years. Roosevelt's New Deal was not a panacea, and several anti–New Deal populists outbid the charismatic president, offering substantial pensions to the elderly. Senator Huey P. Long, all for sharing the wealth, was ready to guarantee a minimum annual income of $5,000 to every family in need. Among those who aspired to national leadership and who joined forces with the populists was Father Charles E. Coughlin, a Royal Oak, Michigan, Roman Catholic priest. He published a newspaper, *Social Justice*, and worked closely with a thinly disguised anti-Jewish organization, the Christian Front, which had a following in Boston and Brooklyn. Coughlin initially allied himself with the Share-Our-Wealth Clubs, anti-Roosevelt partisans, but their bid for power in the 1936 presidential election proved an egregious failure. It was then that Coughlin turned to the right, and by 1938 he was preaching to millions on the radio, insinuating, as did the *Protocols*, that the Jews were responsible for many of the country's ills. The Jews, for their part, were terrified by this priest who was a magnificent and enthralling orator. Dr. Julian Morgenstern, president of the Hebrew Union College, appealed in vain to the Detroit Catholic prelate, Archbishop Mooney, to silence the "radio" priest, but only when America joined the Allies in World War II and anti-Semitism, a key aspect of the German enemy's program, was determined to be intolerable by Roosevelt, did Coughlin's church superiors act. There was no end to the jabs at Jews during the troublesome 1930s. Members of the House and the Senate, isolationists, conservatives, bigots, antiblacks, and demagogues, raised their voices attacking their Jewish fellow citizens. Senator

Theodore G. Bilbo of Mississippi had no use for "kikes." (In 1947, after he was fatally stricken, Bilbo spent his remaining days in New Orleans's Touro Hospital, a Jewish institution.)

Anti-Jewish bias flourished openly from 1929 to 1941, the years of the Great Depression. America needed a scapegoat, and the Jews had been called on to play this role for centuries. Roosevelt succeeded unwittingly in ameliorating anti-Jewish prejudice. His New Deal social welfare legislation helped take the wind out of the sails of those populists who looked askance at Jews. The new laws helped families with dependents and made provision for the blind, the unemployed, and the crippled. World War II stimulated the economy, bringing prosperity to many; it is hard to hate on a full stomach. Anti-Semitism was equated with Germanism and Nazism, and the Germans in 1941–45 were the enemy. It was important, too, very important, that the hopelessly divided anti-Semitic organizations never succeeded in enlisting competent leaders to unite them. The army generals they approached were always unavailable.

World War II

European Jews who immigrated to the United States found freedom and security—even affluence—here but often paid a heavy price. This bastion of democracy that protected them was cemented by the blood of their children. Statisticians tell us that about eight thousand Jewish Americans perished in World War II. Some 550,000 served in the armed forces. About 20 percent were commissioned officers—many were college graduates—and more than twenty became generals or admirals. On March 30, 1945, Corporal Harold Katz, a youngster from the Bronx, was cited for bravery in action. After two of his comrades had been wounded in an attack on the German town of

Attweilmann, this medical technician exposed himself to enemy fire, gave first aid to his comrades, and was himself seriously wounded. Although unable to move his legs, he pushed the other wounded soldiers to safety. Later he was killed in action. A letter found on his body was sent to his mother. This is what he had written: "Mom, I want you to know that I asked for a combat assignment. . . . I felt that I must risk my life . . . so that I could earn the right for my family to live in peace and free from race prejudice. I didn't think it right to stand by and let others fight for things which would benefit me. I asked for combat for the above reasons. . . . I hope you realize exactly what I am trying to tell you, Mom. I want you very much to be more proud than sorry. I don't want you to think of it as losing a son for no good reason, but rather as sacrificing a son so that all of mankind could live in a peaceful and free world."

Hundreds of Jewish military chaplains served in World War II. Rabbi Alexander Goode, together with three Christian clergymen, went down when his ship, the *Dorchester*, was torpedoed in 1943. No rabbi in the military was more distinguished or more courageous than Abraham Klausner, who struggled against almost insuperable odds to help displaced refugees in the death camps after World War II. With little support—and frequent hostility—from the American military authorities, he salvaged hundreds, if not thousands, who were about to be returned to their original homes in Eastern Europe where they would have been exposed to constant prejudice and harassment.

THE POSTWAR YEARS

After World War II anti-Semitism was in bad odor. The Germans were despised for their views and their atrocities. American fathers and mothers were fully aware that in the war,

297

which had been initiated by these central Europeans, more than one million Americans had been killed or wounded. The anti-Semitic newspapers reappeared after the war, but their combined readership was very small. Polls, however, constantly showed that every fourth American adult disliked Jews. How important are polls? If a carefully crafted questionnaire were presented to Americans asking them what they thought of the British, the French, or the Italians, the answers might well be startling. Polls or no polls, no one knows how many Americans nurse hatred toward Jews.

In the postwar world a more confident American Jewry set out to confront the many prejudices that had existed for generations, and over the next decades Jews made substantial advances. With the help of state and national executives, Congress, and the court system, they curbed the employment agencies that accepted discriminatory job orders; they challenged the apprehensive Gentile suburbanites who did not want to see the landscape scarred by the erection of synagogues; they stopped hotels and places of public accommodation from rejecting Jews; and with a ruling of the Supreme Court they ended the enforcement of restrictive housing covenants. Little could be done at first to hurdle the barrier to the executive suites of the great American corporations. Some city and many country clubs were still closed to Jews. This social exclusion is not necessarily a serious disability, although refusing a Jew the right to join a club where affluent Gentiles congregate may well be an economic disadvantage; if you can't eat with a prospective client, you can't do business with him. Socially, Gentiles in their clubs wanted to be alone. This was true, too, of Jews, who enjoyed making social distinctions, and in many cities the snobbish old-line Jewish families impelled American Jews of East European stock to establish clubs of their own. Snobbery is often the last bastion of socialites who have no other distinction to sustain them.

Jews were always encountering roadblocks to the status to which they were entitled as citizens of a democracy. Before World War II this had been especially true in the halls of academe. Individuals of merit occasionally secured appointments, but they were a handful. It would take another decade or more before they would be accepted as college instructors and this only because they were needed and able. Jews still faced admission restrictions in many colleges. They were at times denied dormitory housing and were nearly always refused membership in the Greek letter fraternities and sororities. Their answer to this snobbery was to establish fraternities of their own, but here, too, social exclusivity played a role and Jews discriminated against Jews. The Menorah Societies, dedicated to the humanities and Jewish culture, were dying out fast. They had never had any élan vital and were replaced by the Hillel associations that emphasized sociability and the Jewish way of life.

As far back as 1928, Yeshiva College—for "Jewish learning and science"—opened the first higher school of secular as well as religious learning that deferred to Jewish religious sensitivities. In 1948 Brandeis University came into being. Were discriminatory practices in American colleges responsible for the founding of this secular Jewish university and the earlier Yeshiva University? The Brandeisians said that they wanted to make a contribution to American culture. This may well have been the rationale, but it is also true that they were patterning themselves on the numerous Protestant and Catholic institutions. Jews wanted Jewish colleges of their own. Let it also be borne in mind: American Jews were just beginning to sense the significance of the Holocaust. They were well aware that the civilized countries of the world were largely indifferent to the fate of the six million Jews who perished at Nazi hands. Jews were retreating into their shell.

In one respect at least, the decade after World War II was a bad one for American Jews. The whole country, it would seem, was hagridden by the fear of Communism. Communism seemed powerful then in Europe and Asia and was regnant from the Baltic Sea all the way east to the Pacific. The Soviets even had the atomic bomb. America had helped rescue the Soviet Union in World War II but now looked upon it as a Frankenstein threatening its very existence. This dread of the Bolsheviks assumed almost hysterical proportions: Anti-Communist laws were passed; a congressional committee investigated un-American activities; Communists were imprisoned; anti-Semites—posing as patriots—impugned the loyalty of the Jews and attacked them as Communists. Though apparently no Jew-hater, Senator Joseph R. McCarthy carried on an anti-Communist crusade implying that the Communists threatened the very security of this country. In 1950, in the midst of this madness, Julius and Ethel Rosenberg were accused of passing on atomic bomb secrets to the Russians during World War II when the Soviet Union had been allied to the United States. Tried and found guilty, they were executed in June 1953, the only Americans ever put to death for espionage and conspiracy. The judge who tried this case was Jewish. His position as a Jew trying a Jewish couple was a most difficult one, and it is not hard to believe that he leaned over backward. A few months after the execution, Dr. J. Robert Oppenheimer was suspended from his position as a government consultant, though he had been in charge of the Los Alamos Atomic Laboratory that produced the first atomic bomb. He was suspended as a security risk because he had communist friends, although he himself was no communist and was highly respected by most of his colleagues. The chairman of the Atomic Commission at that time was a Jew, Rear Admiral Louis L. Strauss, who voted against reinstating Oppenheimer.

The Perforated Wall between Church and State

Maintaining a separation between church and state was a challenge that impinged on the constitutional rights of Jews—as they interpreted them. Actually there was never a distinct separation between the two realms. The Founding Fathers could not resolve the hostilities between the disparate established churches in the different states. They solved the problem by erecting a wall between church and state as a political compromise. Over many decades the Supreme Court and the federal, state, and municipal governments have permitted encroachments on the concept that church and state must not meld. If the Supreme Court has frequently equivocated with the establishment of religion clause, it is because the justices are caught between the Constitution of the framers and the Court's knowledge that America is actually a Christian country. Despite the discreet silence of the Constitution, the U.S. government has not failed to recognize that most Americans are Christian religionists. The Supreme Court bores holes in the wall and lets Christianity (and Judaism, too) seep through. Any breach is feared as ultimately a defeat for Jewry, since it may lead to establishment of Christianity as America's national religion.

The courts and the politicos in power have showered the church and religions with benefits. Church schools are granted bus service and receive lunches, textbooks, and tax exemption, as well as therapeutic and remedial help. Church colleges get government grants. The clergy enjoy parsonage allowances. Schoolrooms are made available after class hours for religious meetings. Children are released on school time to secure religious instruction even if not on school premises. The government provides funds for Christian and Jewish hospitals, for chaplains and hundreds of chapels for the armed forces. Christian holidays are recognized; in some instances, Jewish observances too. Prayers and hymns and Bible readings are allowed in some classrooms. Schools have even banned books in their libraries at the request of some religious groups. Christmas displays, crèches, and occasionally menorahs are erected under governmental auspices. There are few universities that deny graduates the prayerful good wishes of visiting clergy who invoke the Father, the Son, and the Holy Ghost. There are millions of committed Christians who have never lost their determination to make this country a Christian state juridically. There has never been a generation in which the pious have not attempted to change the neutral religious intent of the framers. In the early 1950s Senator Ralph Edward Flanders proposed amending the Constitution: "This nation devoutly recognizes the authority and law of Jesus." In 1966 Senator Birch Bayh offered a resolution proposing that the Constitution be amended to permit voluntary participation in prayer in public schools. Some Jews seeking government support for all-day schools are also quite willing to breach the wall between church and state.

Gentiles and Jews

Did America's Gentiles flock to aid Jews during the Nazi and post-Nazi days? Many Jews felt that the Gentile response to anti-Semitism left much to be desired. America went to war in 1941 to destroy an international menace, not to crush a Jew-hating government in Europe. Labor unions in the United States knew full well that if German National Socialism ever gained a foothold in the United States, the workers would no longer be free. It is equally true that the unionists—always concerned with their own patch—had no desire to welcome large numbers of newcomers looking for jobs. Political liberals were sympathetic to the Jews, but in post–World War II America conservatism was in the saddle. The Cold War against the Soviet Union, then in full swing, tended to move most Americans right of center. The churches and their national associations had been slow to respond to the Jewish appeal for help. In 1927–28 Jews, Catholics, and Protestants joined forces to establish the National Conference of Christians and Jews, primarily a lay organization whose leaders were eager to eliminate prejudice against all forms of religious expression and wished to further the ideals common to both Judaism and Christianity. Has this national conference—still active in the 1990s—made the world better for Jews and Christians? It is to be hoped that it has. But prejudices, ingrained for centuries, die hard.

Jewry's Attempt to Cope With Intolerance

In the 1940s Americans, plagued with many problems, could not be concerned directly with their Jewish fellow citizens, relatively so small a group. Each church, each ethnic group, each political party nursed its priorities, and the Jews were left to their own devices. For religiously minded Christians the rebirth of the Jewish state in 1948 was puzzling. In their eyes Judaism and Israel were anachronisms. The New Testament, they believed, had replaced the Old Testament. The Jews obviously paid no attention to this Christian theological postulate, but Christians had no wish to further Jewish infidelity. In many respects Christians found it difficult to aid Jews protesting disabilities imposed by a Christian nation. Often the best the Jews could hope for was indulgence. Jews—a tiny non-Christian entity—had to defend themselves, which they did.

Few Jews as individuals set out to remove disabilities. There is very little they could do. Most of them, when faced with survival problems, sought—and still seek—refuge in "flight," circumvention, evasion. Acculturation has its own positive value, but it is also a form of protective coloration. Jews who wanted to succeed in a Gentile world dressed like their fellow citizens, avoided Yiddishisms, forbore to observe the dietary laws, and chose non-Jewish names. One of the leaders of the Orthodox rabbinate called himself Theodore L. Adams. Jews today seem to have a penchant for Scottish first names: Bruce, Scott, Malcolm. In matters economic they sidle into the interstitial spaces (the cinema is a classic example). As pioneers they often lead where others fear to tread. They seek shelter—at times mistakenly—in the civil service; they favor the clothing business and are entrenched there. They merchandise themselves, hone their skills, exploit their personalities, build a better mousetrap. They emphasize education, seek graduate degrees, prefer self-employment, crowd into the free professions and the service industries. Nature favors them: Intramarriage among Jews tends to destroy distinct ethnicities; mixed marriages with Gentiles tend to produce progeny who are very much of an amalgam. In a famous study, *Changes in Bodily Form of Descendants of Immigrants*, the anthropologist Franz Boas proved that the American environment changed Jews physically. More and more the Jew has ceased to look like a Jew . . . if he ever did. The Jew looks like his Christian neighbor, the hooknosed Jew flourishing only in anti-Semitic cartoons.

Jews originally created four important national defense agencies: the American Jewish Committee, the Anti-Defamation League of B'nai B'rith (ADL), the American Jewish Congress, and the Jewish Labor Committee (JLC). In 1944 the AJC—an elite group—changed its oligarchic structure and established branch chapters in many cities. For years the committee prided itself on publishing (jointly with the Jewish Publication Society) the *American Jewish Year Book*, an indispensable reference work. In addition, the AJC sponsored a notable monthly periodical, *Commentary*. The committee was determined to reach this country's Jewish and Gentile intellectuals, men and women whose opinions were not without some influence. In the 1960s the AJC played an important part in inducing the Vatican to adopt guiding principles sympathetic to world Jewry. The Roman Catholic church had followers running into the hundreds of millions all over the world.

The ADL, established in 1913, devoted itself to the nuts-and-bolts task of confronting unending anti-Jewish assaults. Its followers were for the most part solidly bourgeois provincials. The members of the American Jewish Congress, lower-middle- and middle-middle-class metropolitans for the most part, were important because they initiated the strategy of securing favorable decrees and laws from legislatures, executives, and courts; the American Gentile masses respected constituted authority. Ultimately most disabilities imposed on Jews, blacks, and others were outlawed in the 1960s—at least on paper. The Jewish Labor Committee, working closely with Jewish and general unions both here and in Europe, was given a hearing by the AFL-CIO and by the Socialist parties in Europe.

When in 1934 the JLC was organized, the Nazis in Europe and their satellites in America had already begun to stir.

American Jewish leaders here realized what was at stake. Three years earlier, in 1931, the author of the annual Report on Contemporaneous History, speaking to the Central Conference of American Rabbis, wrote: "It is to be profoundly regretted that our Jewish organizations everywhere refuse to forget their differences and to unite for the sake of struggling Jews both here and abroad." Most Jewish leaders here in the United States were of the opinion that in unity there would be strength, and they attempted to achieve coordination among the national defense agencies, an effort in which they were unsuccessful.

Some communities established a Mayor's Friendly Relations Committee that included representatives of social, ethical, and racial groups. These seem to have been helpful. The national Jewish organizations, eager to help Jewry, published pamphlets, books, and scientific studies on the nature of prejudice. The anti-Semites certainly did not read this literature; the rational-minded Gentiles may have been influenced to read what Jews wrote . . . if they took the time to do so. What good did this expenditure of millions do? No one knows. The morale of Jewry may have been sustained by this avalanche of print, but in 1938 when Jews tuned in on Father Coughlin and listened to that mellifluous voice and its insinuations, their hearts sank. Still, Jewish defense agencies persisted in their appeals and—this must be emphasized—always fought for civil rights and immunities for *all* disadvantaged Americans. Equality was of one piece.

Jews and Black Civil Rights

American Jews have constantly been challenged by disabilities, prejudice, and historical events impinging on them. They have coped as best they could. Quite indirectly they became involved with white supremacist Klan groups. Though nominally anti-Jewish and anti-Catholic, the southern Klans of the post–World War II decades were primarily concerned with intimidating the blacks reaching out for equality. Seeking justice, individual rabbis—not all—made an effort to help them. These rabbis endangered their lives, and some synagogues were bombed. The southern Jews as a body, outnumbered sometimes a hundred to one, kept silent. Mississippi in the 1960s was home to about four thousand Jews, who constituted considerably less than 1 percent of the total population. Conditions were not so hopeless in New Orleans, where integrated meetings of blacks and whites were permitted in the civic auditorium—but not on the campus of Tulane University. In 1949 Rabbi Julian Feibelman of New Orleans invited the distinguished black diplomat Ralph Bunche to speak in his synagogue. His board gave its approval without violent reaction, yet this act required courage. In Atlanta, Rabbi Jacob M. Rothschild publicly supported his black fellow citizens as early as 1948; ten years later his synagogue was dynamited. The five men indicted for this crime were tried but released. In the 1960s a substantial number of Jews from the North—Freedom Riders—came South to help the blacks. They would come for a few days and then take the plane back North. Though occasionally arrested and beaten, they survived. In June 1964, three Northern Freedom Riders landed in Mississippi: Michael Schwerner and Andrew Goodman, Jews, and James Chaney, a black. They were murdered by the White Knights, a Klan group. Several of the Klansmen tracked down by the federal authorities were convicted and sent to the penitentiary. Rabbis Charles Mantinband of Hattiesberg and Perry Nussbaum of Jacksonville dared to raise their voices in defense of African Americans. In the late 1960s Nussbaum's synagogue and his home were bombed. The year 1967 was a bad one for Jews both in the North and the South; vandalism and bomb threats were common. Yet perspective must be maintained: Jews fulminated when their rights were abridged, but between 1882 and 1936, 3,383 blacks were lynched.

Relations Between Blacks and Jews

Jews in the second half of the twentieth century were disturbed by the rise of black anti-Semitic demagogues. These vituperative attacks found audiences in black studies courses and in some black Protestant churches and Black Muslim (Nation of Islam) conventicles. Individual blacks have in every recent decade expressed their contempt for Jews, whom they denounced as exploiters of black Americans. As one of them wrote: "Our contempt for the Jews makes us feel more completely American in sharing a national prejudice." This revelatory statement was made in a program published under the auspices of the Metropolitan Museum of Art in 1969. Several months earlier a fifteen-year-old had read a poem on a New York radio station:

> Hey Hey, Jew boy with that yarmulka on your head,
> You pale-faced Jew boy—I wish you were dead.

A Chicago African American said that Jewish doctors were injecting HIV into blacks. A noted Nation of Islam leader in that same city referred to Judaism as "a gutter religion." As early as 1669, John Locke, in a constitution he wrote for the Carolinas, said that anyone reviling a religion would be punished. Today the federal government and forty-seven states have hate-crime laws, but whether these laws of the 1990s will be enforced remains to be seen. American Black Muslims identifying with their Palestinian coreligionists are often anti-

Israel. Polls indicate a substantial number of black Jew-haters. Blacks as a body will not repudiate these anti-Semites; they close ranks and stand mute.

It is regrettable that the country's African Americans are no longer allies of the Jews as they were from 1910 to 1960. Emancipated by the 1964 Civil Rights Act, they have distanced themselves from the Jews in the hope of gaining a larger white support, which has turned out to be a misjudgment. American Jews, the labor unions, the liberals need black support. There are thirty million blacks in the United States who form an important or potentially important electorate. Jews number only five million, but they can help the blacks. Though Jews are only one-sixth as numerous as the blacks, there are almost as many Jews in the House of Representatives as there are blacks. Many blacks resent the rejection by most Jews of affirmative action. East European émigrés—perhaps one-quarter of them illiterate—began with nothing and pulled themselves up by their very bootstraps. They invite struggling blacks: Go thou and do likewise. Jews believe that blacks who are at the bottom of the social and economic ladder will rise only if they develop marketable skills. They do not realize how different the America of today is from the America the immigrants found at the beginning of the century. The Civil Rights Act of 1964 offers parity, not privilege.

The opportunities offered to blacks have helped Jews; the U.S. government is essentially egalitarian. Anti-Jewish blacks believe that they are upgrading themselves when they denigrate Jews, whom they deem inferior. This is a great comfort to those African Americans who struggle for survival. Believing they are oppressed by the "system," black Jew-bashers attack the whites

they deem most vulnerable. In this approach, the white su-
premacists and anti-Jewish blacks have much in common.

Is Anti-Jewish Prejudice in the United States a Real Threat?

American Jewry—never even 4 percent of the total population—took bigotry seriously. Was anti-Jewish bias such a threat?
Graced with hindsight, the historian can answer that anti-
Jewishness here was never a danger for a host of reasons. Social
security legislation pacified those who were fearful and less-
ened their need for a scapegoat. America is the richest land in
the world with enough for everyone. White Anglo-Saxon Protestants are more concerned with the multimillion blacks and
Catholics than with the five to six million Jews. Yes, but look at
the polls, which report consistently that one out of every five
Americans has no use for "Hebrews." That may be true, but
these Gentiles are not setting out to build concentration camps.
If Jews are doing well—and they are—then why fight intolerance? As a deterrent. Hatred of Jews has a dangerous potential.
In 315 Constantine the Great—a pro-Christian—enacted the
Roman Empire's first anti-Jewish law. Seventy-five years later
the Jew was well on the way to becoming a second-class citizen.
The children of Israel, Roman citizens, ultimately deprived of
political, social, economic, and religious rights, became the
ghettoized Jews of the Middle Ages.

In the 1930s, sensitive to Jew bashing, America's Jews
were determined to oppose all vestiges of ethnic prejudice.
They were successful in the next generation in removing most
of the disabilities that threatened their rights and opportunities.
By the 1960s they were protected by fair education laws.
Ultimately the numbers of Jews in the Ivy League colleges

increascd, and 12 percent of all college faculties were Jews—four times their demographic percentage. Sunday closing laws faded away. Employment agencies dared not openly discriminate against Jewish applicants. Housing and accommodation restrictions were outlawed. Christian church influences and practices in the public schools were radically reduced. When in 1957 the Soviet *Sputnik* was rocketed into orbit, America decided it was time to exploit Jewish talent, and many gates were opened. Equal rights legislation in 1964 forbade discrimination against any individual because of race, color, religion, or national origin. (The 1964 law included women among those entitled to equality). These acts had the blacks in mind particularly, yet the Jews benefited as well from the explicit wording of the laws.

Attacks on Jews have been constant here in North America since the seventeenth century. They continue, to a greater or lesser degree, at the end of the twentieth century. There are constant attacks on Jews as the embodiment of all evils. All attempts, however, to create an anti-Jewish political party have failed. The career of David Duke, a Louisiana Klansman, merits reflection. This politician ran for the Senate in Louisiana in 1990 and more than six hundred thousand voted for him (43.5 percent of the vote). In a gubernatorial race in 1991, which he lost, he secured some seven hundred thousand votes (55 percent of the whites cast their ballots for him). What does all this mean? No one can predict what the electorate will do. In the 1920s, as a graduate student in Berlin, I recorded the activities of the anti-Semites, the Nazis, in my diary. I brushed them aside as "kooks." Yet in 1932 millions voted for Hitler. Like David Duke, Hitler was a populist; the name of his party is important: The National Socialist German Workers Party.

WHAT ANTI-JEWISH PREJUDICE HAS DONE TO THE JEW

Here in the United States Jew hatred has always been a specter, never a threat to survival. Some Jews, conscious of their background, tend to lower their voices in public when discussing a Jewish theme. Some have changed their names: Cohen becomes Cole or Collier. Others, assimilationists determined to "pass" and disappear into the anonymous mass, avoid Jews, marry out, and deliberately rear non-Jewish families. If a few seek safety in low visibility, there are many who bristle and become more Jewish, if only by resentment. Some even become members of a synagogue and are "reborn" Jews. Most Jews are not cowed by Gentile disdain. Some become devoted Zionists. The impact of the State of Israel on American Jews is palpable; for myriads Israel is the sum total of their Jewishness. Most American Jews admire Israel, though the numbers who have settled there are inconsequential. The United States is home, their country, and they are determined to remain here.

14. The Jewish American

MAKING A LIVING

THE APPAREL INDUSTRY

Well into the 1930s there were many Jews employed in factories, primarily in the apparel and allied fields, and not only in New York City but in other large towns too. Moreover, it was not uncommon to find Jewish labor locals in the so-called non-Jewish unions. Thus there were organized bodies of Jews among the carpenters, meat cutters, butchers, and bookbinders, but Jews still felt more at home in the four "Jewish" unions: the International Ladies' Garment Workers; the Hat, Cap and Millinery; the Furriers; and the Amalgamated Clothing Workers of America. Though the largest ethnic group in these unions, the Jews were no longer the majority group. Under the New Deal these unions had come into their own and become powerful. Unfortunately, in the 1920s and 1930s, they were also riven by power struggles. The Communists tried to take over and often met with success until 1939, when Stalin, the Soviet leader, made a pact with the Germans. The four Jewish-led unions still constituted a "movement," making provision for the laborers after working hours. As internationalists, Marxists, the union leaders distanced themselves from Zionism. The unions had their own house organs, which were published in several different languages.

It was in the 1930s that Jewish unions began to turn to the right. Americanized, they accepted the country's mores and moved into the mainstream of American labor. The socialism of the leaders was fading. Roosevelt's New Deal had cut the ground from their feet by providing for the crippled, the aged, the poor, the unemployed. The New York Jewish workers voted with the Democrats but, shunning Tammany, in 1936 created the American Labor Party. America's refusal to admit many East European Jews after 1925 induced the socialist-led unions to look upon Palestine as a haven, and Zionism now became acceptable to many (Zion's Laborers, the Poale Zion, were already Zionists). Even Judaism was no longer brushed aside. Indeed many, if not most, of the non-Marxist needle-workers were religionists. These apparel unions were now becoming part of the Jewish body politic; they were certainly less schismatic.

What did the Jewish apparel unions do for their 260,000 members with locals in more than fifty cities? They embraced them. Over the decades the unions cut the weekly working hours from 70 to 32½; they insisted on a sanitary shop; the ILGWU maintained a union health center with many thousands of clients. The unions furthered collective bargaining and encouraged arbitration. The employer was not seen as an enemy—cooperation buttered more parsnips than strikes did! In pre-New Deal days the unions had made an effort to provide various forms of insurance, and there were labor banks, good housing for loyal members, athletics, scholarships for college-bound youths, educational challenges, and a vacation resort in the Pennsylvania mountains. Did any of these innovations inspire New Deal legislation? There is no question that individual Jews helped shape the New Deal programs.

WHITE-COLLAR WORKERS

Perspective is imperative. The garment workers were only a minor part of gainfully employed American Jewry. Most Jews in the land were part of an extended middle class that stretched from the petit bourgeois to the modestly affluent. (Even the humblest workers in the smaller towns or the big city suburbs owned their own homes.) The white-collar workers in the metropolises were frequently employees, while most Jews hoped to become self-employed (in the smaller towns many reached this goal). In general—even in the early decades of the twentieth century—Jews were moving up and out of ghetto homes and ghetto jobs. The native-born children of the Russians, Poles, Lithuanians, and Rumanians—the majority of America's Jewry—were white-collar men and women; the number of workers in the suit and garment factories was constantly diminishing. Jews were to remain in this industry permanently, but increasingly as owners, managers, clerical workers, and salesmen. This was one of the few industries where they had a chance to make a dollar. With exceptions, of course, the pre–World War II decades found them barred on the whole from banking, insurance, transportation, the utilities, and academe. Since many employment agencies would not place Jews, they had little choice but to become primarily retailers, "a nation of shopkeepers," jobbers, wholesalers, manufacturers. The phrase "Hart, Schaffner & Marx" was a synonym for a good suit; "Levis" was just another word for a durable pair of overalls. Jews were specialists in consumer goods and were always reaching out. During the 1930s, in Lynn, Massachusetts, forty-seven of the eighty-eight shoe factories were operated by Jews.

There were always a few individuals who created their own opportunities. More than one entrepreneur set out to build not only shopping centers and malls but whole cities. Levitt & Sons, Jews of Slavic origin, built Levittowns—three whole cities with many thousands of houses on Long Island and in New Jersey and Pennsylvania. East European wealth did not begin to take on significant proportions until the second half of the twentieth century, but decades earlier the Russian-born Samuel Rosoff (1882–1951) was already a wealthy man. After he landed here at the age of nine, one of his first jobs was to peddle magazines and newspapers on trains. He made money salvaging a steamship for the scrap iron and built an amusement park, canals, sewers, tunnels, and subways—$50 million worth. His hobby? Horseback riding.

It is literally true that in matters of business Jews are into everything. The Cones of North Carolina, textile manufacturers, employed fourteen thousand people. Was this an important enterprise? The cloth they shipped was only 1 percent of the total production in the South. Many Jews were still retailers, and as late as the second quarter of the twentieth century these relatively small stores accounted for 70 percent of the country's business. One can generalize: A few were rich, still fewer were richer. There was an extended middle class. Some of the German refugees of the 1930s also did well. Max Stern and his son built a pet supply business into a half-billion-dollar empire. On the whole Jews were successful.

In 1937 Jews constituted about one-fourth of the population of New York City but 55 to 65 percent of the town's lawyers, dentists, and physicians. They flocked to the professions because they believed in higher education. The professions were prestigious and lucrative, and they enabled Jews to be self-employed. As professionals, in descending order, American Jews were in law, commerce and finance, education, and medicine. Except for education, the percentage of Jews in these fields was much higher than that of the Gentiles. In the 1930s and 1940s, 77 percent of all American Jews were white-collar workers, while less than 14 percent were in manufacturing and industry. By 1950, 12 percent of America's Jews were relatively affluent. (All statistics cited, though vouched for by authorities, are necessarily approximate.) There was always wealth; there was always poverty. At least 20 percent of the country's Jews barely subsisted, and poverty breeds crime. The big-city ghettos had their share of bootleggers, labor racketeers, drug dealers, and professional assassins.

WRITERS, JOURNALISTS, AND THE PRESS

After the immigration acts of the 1920s closed American ports to all but a few Jewish newcomers, the Jews already here, overpowered by the environment, speedily became Jewish Americans or American Jews—or both. The Jewish American documented himself or herself in the printed word. There were many Jewish litterateurs, even among the East European newcomers, who produced nonfiction, fiction, and poetry. Some wrote best-selling novels, a few won Pulitzer Prizes. In later decades, three were Nobel laureates, the novelist Saul Bellow writing in English, his fellow novelist Isaac Bashevis Singer writing in Yiddish, and the poet Joseph Brodsky writing in Russian and English. Were these literary notables "Jewish" writers? Most of them were literary craftsmen who happened to be American Jews and mined their background, the life they knew best. A few exploited realism and emphasized the seamy side of Jewish life. One writer, German-born Ludwig Lewisohn (1882/83–1955), was the beau ideal of the younger American born of East European stock. At least four of his Jewish books, all written during the 1920s, are still well worth reading: *Up Stream, The Island Within, Mid-Channel,* and *Israel.* He became a passionate Jew: "As long as there is discrimination there is exile."

Important Jewish journalists abounded. Herbert Bayard Swope of the *New York World* popularized the phrases "New Deal" and "Cold War"; he spelled Negro respectfully with a capital *N.* The most influential twentieth-century American journalist was Walter Lippmann. The men who ruled America read him religiously. Lippmann began his career as a Marxist but moved over to the right. Jews and Judaism certainly annoyed him, and he ignored them both. Did his ancestral Jewishness haunt him? He had nothing to say about the Holocaust. Still, though he exorcised his Jewishness, he did not denigrate it in his columns—by contrast with Karl Marx, another journalist of Jewish ancestry who had savagely attacked Jewry a century earlier. Lionel Trilling finally made it at Columbia in the Department of English despite the fact that he was a Jew, a Marxist, and a Freudian.

There have been Jewish owners of newspapers all the way from New York to San Francisco. Some of these entrepreneurs have controlled chains. Moses Annenberg and his son Walter issued *TV Guide,* which at one time boasted a circulation of eighteen million. The Samuel Newhouse clan owned more than thirty papers, seven magazines, sixteen TV stations, five radio stations, and twenty cable TV stations. Adolph S. Ochs, a journalist bred in the bone, had built *The New York Times* into America's greatest daily well before World War II. A committed Reform Jew, Ochs was no Jewish nationalist but an American of the Jewish persuasion; he never forgot that *Times* read backward is *Semit.* Jews were active as major figures in almost every nationally important newspaper and newsmagazine. In the 1990s there were about seventeen hundred dailies, and Jews owned about 8 percent of the circulating news media.

Isaac Asimov (1920–92), the country's most successful writer of science fiction, wrote at least two hundred books and sold millions of copies. Among the women who received recognition even before World War II were novelists Fannie Hurst and Edna Ferber and playwright Lillian Hellman. Ann Landers's articles on "advice" were syndicated in twelve hundred postwar newspapers, and her voice was heard by millions.

Will the "serious" Jewish writers be read a century from today? No one knows. Perhaps a more important question pertains to Jews who today are leaders in the field of biblical and Talmudic studies. Is biblical research important? Of the more than five billion nominal religionists in the world, some three billion Christians, Moslems, and Jews have been influenced profoundly by the teachings of the Hebrew Bible.

Historians of American literature may choose to ignore Emanuel Haldeman-Julius, who published the "Little Blue Books" in the two decades before World War II. There were about two thousand titles, and some two hundred million copies were sold at 5 cents each.

STAGE AND SCREEN

Show business is Jewish business. Already in the nineteenth century there were few decades in which Jews were not active as writers, owners, managers, players, and patrons. Up to the 1920s, the Theatrical Syndicate—Marc Klaw, Abraham Lincoln Erlanger, and their associates—controlled over one thousand theaters, obviously a monopoly. The syndicate was succeeded by the Shuberts of Syracuse. Otto H. Kahn helped finance the

Theatre Guild. The Little Theatre movement brought the new and challenging in dramatic art to the cognoscenti. The number of dramatists of Jewish stock was legion. Some were award winners, and several were among Broadway's most successful writers. To be sure, Jewish issues were avoided, although many enjoyed *Abie's Irish Rose* where the intermarriage theme was played out sentimentally and unrealistically. Such a play enjoyed a long run, as if to spite the sensitive Jewish parent who dreaded a mixed marriage.

Unimpressed by Broadway guff, the theater was never eclipsed by the movie house, but for a time its very existence seemed threatened. Jews were among the cinema's pioneers as exhibitors, producers, directors, and distributors. By the late 1920s there were more than twenty thousand motion picture houses in the United States, and one hundred thousand people a week flocked to them. Paramount, Universal, Goldwyn, Metro-Goldwyn-Mayer, Columbia, United Artists, Warner Brothers, and Twentieth Century-Fox all had Jewish chief executives. David O. Selznick (1902–65) gave the world *Gone With the Wind* in 1939. Samuel Goldwyn's *The Best Years of Our Lives* won an Academy Award in 1947. The cinema has enriched the lives of men, women, and children on every continent. Jews as leaders in the industry have helped bring heaven down to earth.

As showmen it was the job of the Jews to entertain. This they did on the stage, in the cinema, and on radio and TV. Jewish comedians evoked the admiration of almost every American. Even today their names are on everyone's lips: Eddie Cantor, Al Jolson, Milton Berle, Jack Benny, Fannie Brice, Sophie Tucker, Sid Caesar, and the Marx brothers. Groucho (Julius Henry) Marx made millions laugh with his zany antics and his insults. It is no small thing to have brought pleasure into the lives of millions.

MUSIC

Al Jolson and Eddie Cantor were singers as well as comedians. Jolson, son of a cantor, starred in *The Jazz Singer*, the first picture where film and sound were synchronized. Jews had been interested in music ever since biblical days, when youthful King David played a stringed instrument. In twentieth-century America Jews were patrons, impresarios, composers, conductors, members of symphonies, opera stars, and virtuosi on various instruments, preeminent in particular as violinists, cellists, and pianists. Violinist Yehudi Menuhin made his debut in San Francisco with the symphony when he was eight. Vladimir Horowitz was a pianist with a worshipful following; at his height he traveled to concerts with his wife, his secretary, his own piano, his piano tuner, his recording engineer, and his cook—a far cry from the 1830s when the young Daniel Schlesinger, America's first piano virtuoso, had barely managed to secure a handful of students. The mining magnate Adolph Lewisohn (1849–1938) gave a stadium to City College in New York so thousands could attend musical concerts. Musical comedy and operetta appealed also to Jewish writers and composers, and a few were phenomenally successful. Bob Dylan (né Robert Zimmerman) entranced millions with his country music, the blues, folk rock, ballads. Johnny Marks's "Rudolph the Red-Nose Reindeer" sold millions of copies. Irving Berlin's "White Christmas" was more popular than many of the traditional yuletide carols. When in 1939 his "God Bless America" was sung on Memorial Day in Ebbets Field, the audience rose spontaneously, doffing hats.

ART

In the medieval and early modern centuries Jews achieved little distinction for their work in the graphic arts, although there were always many competent calligraphers and, on occasion, artists noted for their illuminated manuscripts. They produced haggadahs, ritual books for the Passover dinner ceremony. In the early nineteenth century Jewish portrait painters were not uncommon in this country. By the early 1900s, however, Jews had begun to stand out as sculptors, graphic artists, architects, art collectors, patrons, and critics. Louise Nevelson was one of the country's best-known sculptors, working primarily in wood. Alfred Stieglitz (1864–1946), the father of modern art photography, received more than 150 medals for his contributions to photography; he was also known for introducing modern European artists to the American art world. Edward M. Warburg, communal leader and philanthropist, furthered the ballet and helped establish New York City's Museum of Modern Art. In 1947 the Warburg home became the Jewish Museum of the Jewish Theological Seminary. A successful mining family made possible the John Simon Guggenheim Foundation for scholarship and the arts and the Solomon R. Guggenheim Museum. Benjamin Altman, the department store merchant, gave his $30 million collection of paintings to the Metropolitan Museum of Art (this did not deter a later director of that institution from publishing a brochure that included an attack on Jews). Joseph H. Hirshhorn (1899–1981), a Latvian immigrant who made a fortune in mining, gave the government about six thousand works of art, now on view at the Hirshhorn Museum and Sculpture Garden on the Mall in Washington, D.C. His mother, who brought him over as a boy, had worked twelve hours a day in a factory for $12 a week.

Rube (Reuben Lucius) Goldberg (1883–1970) was a beloved cartoonist. In the course of his long career he drew at
least fifty thousand cartoons, including the famous Boob McNutt
and Lolla Palooza. At the other end of the art spectrum was the
Russian-born Bernard Berenson (1865–1959). Reared and educated in Boston, he became a world-famous connoisseur and
historian of art. Louis Kahn (1901–74), an Estonian immigrant, was deemed one of the country's great architects. The
Detroit architect and builder Albert Kahn (no relative) designed and supervised the construction of the prestigious Detroit
Athletic Club, but he refused to attend the dedication because
Jews were denied membership.

Despite their lack of a tradition in painting and sculpture,
East European émigrés and their children turned quickly to
art. The Educational Alliance—the New York Jewish Settlement House—gave some of them their initial training. During
the 1930s, the decade of the Great Depression, a number of
these artists depicted the plight of the poor; others, in time
reacting against realism, turned to abstract expressionism in
painting and sculpture. Gifted individuals were invited to decorate federal buildings, to paint murals. A number of architects
and artists designed beautiful synagogues and ritual silver.

THE SOCIAL AND NATURAL SCIENCES

Jews had few opportunities to advance as members of university
faculties in the social sciences until the third quarter of the
twentieth century. The philosopher Morris R. Cohen was the
darling of the students in New York's City College, but then
City College was seen as a "Jewish" school. The editions of the
Jewish *Who's Who* disclose that slowly, very slowly, Jews were
beginning to make their way as college teachers of economics,

languages, and even English. Later they even became officers of scholarly organizations such as the American Historical Association. Abraham A. Brill was the prime organizer of the first psychoanalytical society in this country. Individual American Jews loomed large in chemistry, biology, physics, and medicine. Peter Goldmark, a Hungarian who came to these shores, invented the long-playing phonograph record and designed a color camera for television pictures. Jews could brag of their many Nobel laureates, far beyond their numerical proportions. Albert Einstein, a German Jewish exile, settled in the United States in 1933. The physicist Isidore Isaac Rabi (1898–1988), another immigrant and Nobel laureate, served on the Atomic Energy Commission. Austrian-born Karl Landsteiner (1868–1943) received world recognition and a Nobel Prize for his work in defining blood groups. A convert to Catholicism, he was indignant when included as a Jew in biographical lexica. Selman A. Waksman, another émigré who never lost his East European brogue, produced the first antibiotic. Jonas E. Salk and Albert B. Sabin immunized the world's children against polio. Gregory G. Pincus, who was born in predominantly Jewish Woodbine, New Jersey, in 1903, helped develop the birth control pill. During the course of the twentieth century the country has had many notable Jewish practitioners and researchers in pediatrics, preventive medicine, epidemiology, and psychiatry. It has been estimated that about 10 percent of America's physicians were of Jewish stock. "My son, the doctor!"

The World of Atomic Power

Jews were pioneers in the field of atomic power. Einstein had alerted President Franklin D. Roosevelt to the importance of the atomic bomb. Jewish physicists sensed its potential horror but were also aware that the German enemy was working in this field. America had no choice but to move forward. J. Robert Oppenheimer and Leo Szilard (1898–1964) were the fathers of the atom bomb. Edward Teller was the father of the infinitely more powerful hydrogen bomb. It is said that there were so many Jewish scientists in the Los Alamos laboratories that their Gentile confreres were facetiously given Hebrew or Yiddish names. Jews were also the administrators in this fearsome new science. David E. Lilienthal was the first chairman of the Atomic Energy Commission. When harassed by a U.S. senator who was a supporter of private utility interests, Lilienthal said: "All men are the children of God and their personalities are therefore sacred." Later Lewis L. Strauss chaired the commission. An autodidact who enjoyed reading the Latin classics, he went to synagogue on the Sabbath, occasionally conducted religious services, and became a rear admiral in the naval reserve. Hyman George Rickover, an immigrant who became a full admiral, was responsible for the first nuclear-powered submarine, the *Nautilus*. His enemies—they were legion—called him "that little Jew," though Rickover had distanced himself completely from Jews and Judaism.

ATHLETICS

Distinction in sports has virtually ensured instant Americanization and instant success. Fame and fortune came to many individuals in boxing, basketball, football, and baseball. In September 1934, on the Day of Atonement, the Detroit Tigers were fighting to win the pennant, but Hank Greenberg refused to play. Yom Kippur was sacred to him. The team lost:

> We shall miss him in the infield and
> Shall miss him at the bat
> But he's true to his religion—and I
> Honor him for that!

In 1938 Greenberg knocked out fifty-eight home runs. In metropolitan centers ethnic identity packed the bleachers. When a young Catholic baseball player joined the Yankees he was importuned to use his stepfather's name, Levy!

For decades prior to 1939 it was a rare year that saw no Jewish boxing champion in one of the weight classes. Benny Leonard (1896–1947), world lightweight champion, had sixty-eight knockouts and five losses; an observant Jew, he refused to fight on a Jewish holiday. At one time Barney Ross held three world champion divisional titles.

By the second half of the twentieth century beating out another man's brains was no longer a Jewish sport. The Jews had moved on to basketball. Nat Holman, the basketball coach for New York's City College, was reputed by some critics to be the most notable figure in this sport. After moving up and out to the suburbs, American Jewish athletes turned to golf and tennis, and not without some success: Dick Savitt distinguished himself on the courts at Wimbledon in 1951. In 1963 Sanford (Sandy) Koufax, pitching for the Los Angeles Dodgers, struck out over three hundred batters. Mark Spitz won an unprecedented number of Olympic gold medals in swimming.

POLITICS

As American citizens, Jews had no difficulty exercising their rights and immunities. As a minority group insistent on equality, they emphasized democracy. Some of these idealists in the

1920s and 1930s were devoted Communists until Stalin was exposed as a tyrant. Among them were Julius and Ethel Rosenberg, convicted of spying for the Soviets and executed in 1953. All the Communists in the United States—Jews and Gentiles—were never able to secure more than some ninety thousand votes in a presidential election. The Socialists were far more numerous, and always had many enthusiastic Jewish followers. The majority of Jewish Americans, however, voted the Republican or Democratic ticket. Most of them had been Jeffersonians ever since Woodrow Wilson's time. As voters Jews were concerned with survival in a polity where at least 97 percent of the citizens were nominal Christians.

Though a small group, the Jews were in no sense politically insignificant. The majority, living in the most populous states, had some capacity to swing elections. After 1948 they were dedicated to the challenge of keeping Israel alive with the aid of government grants and ordnance. In this task they were supported by AIPAC, the American Israel Public Affairs Committee, an effective lobby organized in 1954. The Jews were mindful in the 1960s that the Israeli state with its 1,880,000 Jews was surrounded by at least 25,000,000 Moslems, most of them hostile. They were also apprehensive—and justly so—about breaches of the wall between church and state. Fighting for equal rights for all, Jews served as a barometer of America's conscience.

Participation in the political system sometimes was simply a matter of exercising one's rights as a citizen by going to the polls. Other times it took the form of fighting to effectuate—or preserve—the meaning of the Constitution. Joel Elias Spingarn (1875–1939), a student of comparative literature, educator, poet, critic, and book publisher, was also president of the

National Association for the Advancement of Colored People (1930). Abraham Simon Wolf Rosenbach (1876–1952) was America's most distinguished rare book dealer. When in the early 1940s I first turned to the new field of American Jewish history, I visited "Dr. R." in his New York office and asked him if he had any important Jewish historical documents. "Yes," said Rosenbach, "I own the most valuable of all American Jewish documents. Look in the vault." On the floor, in a simple frame, was an eighteenth-century manuscript, one of the original copies of the First Amendment to the Constitution: "Congress shall make no law respecting an establishment of religion, or prohibiting the free exercise thereof."

Jews were active in politics on all levels, in towns large and small. They served as aldermen and mayors, state legislators and governors. It was not unusual for a Jewish governor on the Passover to invite his friends to the governor's house for the traditional seder (matzo ball soup was de rigueur). Governor James Thompson of Illinois, a Christian, also conducted a seder at the gubernatorial residence during the years he was in office. In Washington there were always Jews who served in important civil service posts, in the House, in the Senate, and in presidential cabinets. In 1993 there were at least ten Jews in the Senate and thirty-three in the House, most of them elected by Gentiles, not Jews. Barry Goldwater and Reuben O'Donovan Askew (born Goldberg) both of whom had a Jewish parent, were presidential candidates. Henry Kissinger (b. 1923) was an Orthodox German Jewish lad who came to this country as a refugee and ultimately graduated from Harvard, became a distinguished diplomat, and served in the Nixon and Ford administrations as secretary of state in 1973–1977. He was also the recipient of a

Nobel Peace Prize. For him, as for thousands of Jewish émigrés, America was truly a "land of unlimited opportunity."

Six Jewish men and one woman have served as associate justices of the United States Supreme Court during the twentieth century: Louis D. Brandeis, Benjamin N. Cardozo, Felix Frankfurter, Arthur Goldberg, Abe Fortas, Ruth Bader Ginsburg, and Stephen Breyer.

Henry Morgenthau Jr., secretary of the treasury under Franklin D. Roosevelt, made an effort to induce the president to consider the plight of the Jews under Nazi tyranny. Other Jews close to the president apparently did little if anything to help Europe's threatened Jews in central and eastern Europe. Sidney Hillman, like Rosenwald, Gompers, and Baruch in World War I, helped prepare his country for war as it faced the formidable German war machine. Herbert H. Lehman (1878–1963), who had learned his trade as food administrator on a vast scale salvaging East European Jews after World War I, served as governor of New York, as a United States senator, and as director of the United Nations Relief and Rehabilitation Administration during the World War II period when he fed millions all over wartorn Europe. In answer to a query from a Jewish youngster in 1960, Lehman wrote: "I am a Jew both by birth and conviction. It satisfies my spiritual needs, and I have strong faith in its teachings." Arthur F. Burns was a member of the president's Council of Economic Advisors in the 1960s; later in the 1980s he was appointed ambassador to the Federal Republic of Germany. In writing to a young bar mitzvah boy, Burns said: "God gave us the Torah [the Law] so that we may lead righteous lives, love our neighbors, and help the needy."

ACCULTURATING, ASSIMILATING, SURVIVING

It is interesting, but certainly not typical, that Strauss, Cardozo, Goldberg, Lehman, and Burns can be called "synagogue" Jews. Many eminent American Jews have not been synagoguegoers. As a rule, notables of Jewish birth have had but one goal in life, devotion to their careers. Accepted socially in the haut monde, they have had no need to look to their fellow Jews for psychic support. Some of America's distinguished Jewish virtuosi and symphony conductors were converts to Christianity. During World War II not a few Jews were annoyed that Richard Wagner's music was cultivated by Jewish-born conductors in a decade when millions of fellow Jews were being slaughtered by Wagner's spiritual disciples. Did Jews here in the United States turn their backs on these Jewish notables who, in a sense, had disdained them? In no sense. Jewry, always insecure and eager to shine in reflected glory, gladly embraced all Jews.

There were few Jews—this bears repetition—who could escape acculturation. Not even pious right-wing traditionalists were fully exempt. Acculturation, accommodation, is a device for survival. Americanization nearly always overpowered ethnicity's claims; the impulse to identify with one's Gentile American neighbors brooked few restraints. Melting, blending, is the history of American Jewry since the eighteenth century, when the Spanish-Portuguese, German, and Yiddish-speaking Jews in Shearith Israel began to intramarry. The later disparate German groups and East Europeans had all begun to disappear as such no later than the 1950s. In the United States, Jews, once a hodgepodge of warring ethnics, emerged from the crucible of that postwar decade as *American* Jews. "Thou shalt love thy neighbor as thyself" was interpreted by many—especially those in small towns—to mean: Live like your neighbors. Congregants in the little synagogue in Marion, Ohio, murmured a protest when the student rabbi raised his voice against Christmas trees. "I'm outraged," sputtered a member. "You mean I cannot hang up my stocking at home?" "We were just such a small group," said a local mother in Israel, "and we didn't want to make waves." Frequently—certainly not always—acculturation led to intermarriage. Intermarriage, however, posed no threat to Jewish survival before the second half of the twentieth century; prior to that time the highest intermarriage rate was about 7 percent. Individuals became members of Christian Science and Ethical Culture, but they most often still thought of themselves as Jews. There are no statistics for those who converted to Christianity, but there could not have been many. Conversion offered few if any advantages. Apostate Jews were despised by fellow Jews and referred to by the Christian clergymen as "our Jewish members." The convert was always in limbo.

It takes but one short generation to create a Jewish intellectual. Papa and Mama were Yiddish-speaking immigrants. The new generation took a hop, skip, and gigantic leap and landed in the abstruse world of intellectuality. Many children of the Jewish newcomers have gone to college, possibly as many as 80 percent in the post–World War II decades. A substantial percentage have earned graduate degrees, preferring the professions to the world of commerce. There is no question that by the second half of the twentieth century there were many Jews truly distinguished in the arts and sciences. In the first half of this century the Ivy League schools had set out to limit the number of Jewish entrants, and by the 1960s they were competing for Jewish presidents. One is tempted to pontificate: The newly emerging American Jew was a cultured citizen who in his own fashion was loyal to his ancient religious heritage. Since biblical days he has always been comfortably ensconced in two cultures, making his peace with Gentile values, as did the eighteenth-century philosopher Moses Mendelssohn, who was undeviatingly Orthodox yet truly modern. This qualification, however, is almost axiomatic: Jewish tradition has usually given way to the enveloping American culture. The more Americanized one became, the less Judaized one was. In general, Jews of the late twentieth century are either Jewish Americans, whose relationship to Jewry is tenuous, or American Jews, secularists and religionists who enjoy identifying themselves with their ancestral people.

AMERICA ACCEPTS THE JEWISH AMERICANS

During the long generation after World War II, a "revolution" in the United States had begun profoundly affecting American Jews. The Constitution of 1788 accorded them political equality on a national level, but it was not until the middle of the twentieth century that they were granted equality in academe and in the world of business. Jews now became presidents of Du Pont and Procter & Gamble. Restrictions were no longer imposed on them as students, faculty, and presidents even of America's Ivy League colleges. Most of the country's younger Jews were now college graduates, often superbly educated and thoroughly acculturated. But why were Jews now so well accepted in the world of the professions and the economy?

Once blacks were accepted as fellow citizens, Jews no longer looked too Jewish. The millions of Gentiles who abhor bigotry do not reject Jews; Christian religionists believe in the Fatherhood of God and its inevitable corollary, the brotherhood of all people. The millions of dollars Jews have sent abroad for philanthropic purposes were not earned from taking in one another's washing; the money came mostly from Gentile clients. Jews now marry with some frequency into presidential families. Dictionaries include dozens of Yiddish words. Hundreds if not thousands of Gentiles sign up for Jewish courses in the colleges. The U.S. government serves kosher meals to some summer school students. The House of Representatives holds no sessions on the High Holy Days. Jews serve frequently on the boards of Catholic institutions. The government has established a Holocaust Memorial Museum to document Nazi Germany's destruction of six million European Jews. There is a chapel for Jewish worship at the U.S. Military Academy. The Jewish worship pennant flies from the mast of navy ships when Jewish services are conducted. In March 1945—this was during World War II—Chaplain Roland E. Darrow, a Methodist, read the Friday night prayers for Jewish troops in the cathedral town of Rheims. He wore a Jewish prayer shawl and the traditional skullcap, and broke his teeth over the Hebrew, but he persisted gallantly.

Again, why in the middle decades of the twentieth century were Jews accepted almost everywhere they turned? *Brown v. Board of Education of Topeka* (1954), the Supreme Court decision that affirmed the legal equality and rights of all blacks, implied that Jews, too, were to be denied no immunities. Far more important for the co-optation of all Jews in all phases of American life and culture was the shock the American people sustained when they realized a few years after World War II that the Soviet Union had the atomic bomb, intercontinental nuclear missiles, and sputnik. Americans were obsessed with fear of the Soviet threat. Because Jews were needed by their fellow Americans, all roads were open to them, and they justified the confidence the citizenry had in them.

WHAT JEWS DID FOR AMERICA

Jews showed that they were Jewish *Americans* in many different ways, some easily approved of, some less easily applauded. Since colonial days Jews had given gifts that helped make the country that had accepted them a better place for all its inhabitants. The immigrant East Europeans and their children were necessarily slow to make multimillion-dollar gifts; they had come up from nothing and were tempted to hold on to what they had made by the sweat of their brow. Samuel Rosoff gave money to Christian churches, built a playground for blacks, and was generous to a Jewish hospital, a Catholic orphanage, and the Zionists. Two native-born philanthropists, Louis Bamberger and his sister, Caroline Fuld, endowed the Institute for Advanced Study at Princeton University. This center of learning, one of America's most distinguished nurseries of culture, was built on department store and radio station money. Wealthy Jewish philanthropists in the closing decades of the century donated immense sums. Walter H. Annenberg (b. 1908), a publisher of east European antecedents, has probably given close to a billion dollars to American institutions. Like most other generous entrepreneurs, most of his gifts have been to the community at large, not to Jewish organizations or causes. Interesting!

15. The American Jew

By the late 1920s a compact Jewish religioethnic community was in the making. At the end of the twentieth century, over 40 percent of all the Jews in the world live in the United States (no country has ever sheltered more Jews). Most are found in about thirty cities, and almost half of the country's children of Jewish origin live in New York and neighboring states. Jews in this one huge sprawling region dominate American Jewry, though there is a constant drift to the South, the new Southwest, and the West. (People are looking for sunshine and economic opportunity.) Many small Jewish communities in the Midwest and the South have faded away. Good roads and the automobile have induced people to move to the nearest larger Jewish community. The late twentieth-century compact Jewish community in the suburbs owes its being in the main to the closing of American ports to Jewish newcomers in the 1920s and, in consequence, the rapid Americanizing of the Jews already here and their increasing readiness to intramarry. Originally Jewry in this country was a variegated body of a dozen different ethnic groups. Here on the American scene they were thrown into a crucible and emerged in time as American Jews. What made for this alloy—the new Jew—was a common Jewish background, a sympathy for Zionism, a Jewish education, intramarriage, uniting to help distressed Jewish communities abroad, reacting to anti-Jewish prejudice—in short, a tacit acknowledgment that every Jew is responsible for every other Jew.

What are the components of a Jewish community? First there is a locale: a "ghetto," suburbia. A ghetto in the post–World War II decades means a voluntary physical and psychological haven; at six o'clock one is at home and can put one's feet up. This "ghetto" is a way of life that sustains Jews from the cradle to the grave. (Actually even longer—an expectant Jewish mother could go to a Jewish prenatal clinic; a synagogue will say kaddish for Jews a century after their bones have turned to dust!) America has two national ghettos: one on the East Coast—Baltimore to Portland, Maine; the other on the West Coast—San Diego to the new settlements north of the Golden Gate. There are at least five territorially smaller ghettos: greater New York, south Florida, Los Angeles, Chicago, and Philadelphia.

And who is a Jew? For the Jew, anyone is a Jew who says he or she is and who works closely with Jews. The Jews embrace all who call themselves Jews: religionists, secularists, the rootless, the ideological nothingarians. For the Gentiles anyone is a Jew for whom there is the slightest reminiscence of Jewish origin. And what does the Jew look like? The new Jew does not stand out: family names today are often neutral, and intramarriage with other Jewish ethnics and intermarriage with Gentiles have destroyed the Jewish type (if there ever was one).

The various "who's who" books demonstrate conclusively that ambience is all powerful. The East Europeans, fathers, sons, and daughters, went to college, became acculturated, and as Jewish Americans are ultimately no different from the "Germans" and the native-born who trace their forebears to the early 1700s. They all make their economic, political, and cultural contributions as Americans of Jewish descent. Thus by midcentury most Jews were both Jewish Americans and American Jews. (The degree of Americanicity and Jewishness varies with each individual; indeed a person may, at different periods of his or her life, modify attachment to American culture and to the Jewish heritage.) Ultimately, the aggregate, the body of Jewry, its Spanish-Portuguese, Germanic, and Slavic origins diminished or even entirely ignored, is simultaneously American and Jewish. Since the 1920s a totally new Jewish community has come to birth.

RELIGION

The Various Jewish Denominations

The basic components of a suburban Jewish community are synagogues, schools, a community center, a country club, a federation of welfare agencies, a community relations and defense committee, and some sort of Jewish community council. Although American Protestants have given birth to hundreds of sects, Jews can boast of only about a half dozen. The members of the American Council for Judaism, established in 1942, are classical Reformers who stand squarely on the 1885 Pittsburgh Platform. They want no Jewish state, though they have been willing to help Israelis as Jews. These individuals are American citizens of the Jewish persuasion. Their sense of Jewish peoplehood is not well developed, and today their numbers are few: The Nazis pushed many members of the council back into the Jewish ambit, and so did the anxious weeks of May and June 1967 when another holocaust seemed imminent, this time in the Middle East. Houston's Congregation Beth Israel was staunchly American Council in the 1940s. Today it is neo-Reform, traditionalist to a degree. The Holocaust convinced most American Jews that world Jewry must have a homeland where any Jew can go if persecuted. The State of Israel answers that need.

The Society for Humanistic Judaism (1969) rejects all forms of supernaturalism. Members have discarded the God concept but are practicing Jews in every other sense of the term. They are growing slowly. A related outlook, Reconstructionism, the brainchild of Rabbi Mordecai M. Kaplan, dates back to the 1920s. Judaism, according to Kaplan, is more than a religion; it is a civilization uniting an organic community, whereas religion by itself tends to be divisive. This movement is eclectic. It furthers tradition, yet is radically humanist in its theology; it is concerned with all Jews in the diaspora, yet accepts the centrality of the State of Israel. It has developed its own seminary, union of congregations, and rabbinical conference. The movement is a socioethnic religious complex that neglects no aspect of Jewish life. Reconstructionism has not become a large denomination because so many of its basic elements have long been accepted by the Reformers and the Conservatives. As a permissive group, it is also friendly to gays and lesbians.

THE ORTHODOX AND THE REFORMERS

Orthodoxy is Jewry's mother religion as Catholicism is Christianity's. As a religious system, Judaism is older than Christianity; indeed, it gave birth to that faith. Jesus lived and died as a Jew. For the Orthodox, biblical law is God's law and has been elaborated throughout the ages by the rabbis. Though making a gallant attempt to maintain itself, Orthodoxy has been virtually—and inevitably—overwhelmed by the American environment. Orthodox traditionalists are well organized with a full complement of supporting bodies and, like all American Jewish religious groups, have knowingly or not patterned themselves structurally on the Reformers. They have seminaries, Talmudic academies (yeshivot), all-day schools, and a university of their own, but they are a badly riven movement. Despite their loyalty to the past, nearly all the Orthodox are open to the impact of American culture. Most embrace the sciences and further the secular education of women. Orthodoxy's Yeshiva University is justly proud of its Stern College for Women. The Association of Orthodox Jewish Scientists set out to harmonize Orthodoxy and Science (1948). These Orthodox are entrenched happily in two separate worlds. In their Torah-true religion, however, the woman is still compelled to play a subordinate role. God has declared: "He [the husband] shall rule over her" (Genesis 3:16). The Orthodox emphasize kosher food, though many a Jew enjoys a green bagel on St. Patrick's Day. Kashrut is big business and the income from kosher certification is a prime source of revenue for Orthodox agencies. Over twenty thousand certified kosher products make kosher food a $30 billion industry (most of the people in America who turn to the kosher shelf in the grocery are non-Jews!).

Harry Fischel (1865–1948), a New York entrepreneur, built a fourteen-story apartment house and deliberately left a large space in the center from top to bottom. He was Orthodox and when he built a sukkah on the ground floor he wanted to envisage the very heavens as he ate and prayed during the fall harvest festival. The Young Israel group (1912) is completely American yet completely traditional. The Hassidic groups constitute the Orthodox extreme right wing. America's Orthodoxy is today the smallest of the mainstream denominations. The 1990 National Jewish Population Survey maintains that only 6.5 percent of all American Jews opt for Orthodoxy. The Orthodox are members of a national umbrella association, the

Synagogue Council of America (1925), but at best this alliance is an uneasy one. Because of its very nature Orthodoxy cannot make too many concessions to modernity.

The Reformers, who go back to 1824 in this country, are well organized. Their seminary has three campuses here and one in Israel. They are moving forward rapidly with almost nine hundred congregations and by the first decade of the twenty-first century may possibly exceed the Conservatives in numbers. Reform's classical phase lasted from 1885 to the middle of the twentieth century. It stood firmly on the Pittsburgh Platform, on Judaism as an all-embracing universalist faith convinced that its mission was to usher in a Messianic age: "Mine house shall be called a house of prayer for all people" (Isaiah 56:7). Rabbinic law, the halakah—though not the tradition's ethical system—was formally rejected by the Reformers in 1885. They would have rejected much of biblical law, too, but feared the Old Man, their spiritual and organization leader Isaac M. Wise, no radical as a Reformer but one who insisted that God himself had given the Ten Commandments to Moses.

It was during the decades of the mid-twentieth century that classical Reform experienced the full onset of a revolution and ultimately was bypassed by the neo-Reform movement. After the 1919 Versailles Treaty the European and American worlds began to turn to the right, and liberalism languished. In 1922 Rabbi Stephen S. Wise, a Reformer, established the fervently Zionist Jewish Institute of Religion in New York as an alternative to classical Reform's Hebrew Union College. The Holocaust and the U.S. government's indifference to its horrors convinced many that the universalistic mission concept was visionary. In 1937, when the Reform rabbis reacted to Nazism and adopted a pro-Zionist religious program, Jewish nationalism was finally in the Reform saddle. Two basic influences induced the Reformers to move to the right: Europe and America had rejected the Jews, but opportunism, too, was never absent—the leaders, competing with a rapidly growing Conservatism, were eager to recruit the American-born youth of East European stock who had traditional roots.

The espousal of Zionism was not the only radical change in Reform. Ritual and ceremony were also altered. The skullcap was donned by many and the prayer shawl too. New prayer books were patterned in part more directly on the traditional siddur. Hebrew was cultivated. Bar and bat mitzvah became de rigueur. Bowing and swaying in prayer became more accepted, and much talk of an optional code of Jewish law was heard. At the same time, the movement embraced some radical departures from tradition: Gay and lesbian congregations were admitted into the Union of American Hebrew Congregations. The Sabbath service was often shifted to Friday night, and individuals who had a Jewish father and a Gentile mother were declared fully legitimate Jews if they evinced Jewish loyalties. A woman wrote Rabbi S. B. Freehof asking if she could say kaddish for her pet dog. His answer was no, but she could memorialize him through gifts to charity.

Cantors helped lead the neo-Reform service; day schools were encouraged; public dinners were kosher. The Union of American Hebrew Congregations and the Central Conference of American Rabbis were moved at midcentury from Cincinnati to New York City where Conservatism was strong and Orthodoxy still had a tenacious toehold. Spirituality was not dominant; religion was now primarily a form of Jewish ethnic identification. Reform remained a liberal religious movement, indeed the largest in the world. Reform synagogues grace every town of size in the United States. The movement still struggles to retain a rational creed, works for social and economic justice, preaches a broad biblical universalism, and, through its rabbis, has made its way into the general community. Classical Reform, barely alive today, had wanted to embrace the world and found it was only hugging itself. It had wanted to save the world; neo-Reform wants to save Jews. Neo-Reform will probably grow because so many Jews appear to be moving theologically to the left, but how many moving to the left will resist full assimilation?

CONSERVATISM

Solomon Schechter after 1902 revamped the Conservative movement of the 1880s that originally had been very close in spirit to Orthodoxy. The new denomination speedily became a new movement, one Americanistic and Jewishly traditional. It modified the Law through tacit salutary neglect, though in theory the Law was never disavowed. Many Reform and Christian religious mores like family pews and modern music in synagogues were adopted. The Conservatives were nurtured by a great seminary with a fine museum and a magnificent library. The findings of modern research were accepted. A hundred years later relatively few Conservatives keep strictly kosher homes, and women serve as rabbis and cantors, hold office in synagogues, and insist on equality in all matters of marriage and divorce. In their prayers most Conservative Jews reject the traditions of resurrection, animal sacrifices, and belief in the coming of a Messiah.

Conservatism, which has grown very rapidly, was sympathetic to the religiosocial "fellowships," *havurot*, which were in many respects an echo of the counterculture of the 1960s. Dozens or more of such fellowships have since made their appearance, most though not all of them educational and inspirational in intent. They have developed their own literature and manuals. Some fellowships were linked to the synagogues; others were autonomous.

THE TREND TOWARD A COMMON JUDAISM

The *havurot*, whether Conservative, Reform, Reconstructionist, or autonomous, offer a striking example of diversity, yet all American Jewish religious denominations have much in common. Jews take pride in their religious traditions going back for more than three millennia. Many Jews who settled in suburbia in the post–World War II decades joined synagogues—in response quite likely to American Christianity's belief that a respectable person must belong to a church. But joining a synagogue is not only a bow to established American mores, it is a prime form of identification as a Jew. Other indices to Jewish identity in suburbia abound: It is a common tendency in American Jewish religious life to make the Friday night service the important one, since Saturday has retained its American priority as a business day. Because of the Orthodox insistence on the dietary laws, a communal "peace of God" has assured everyone that at all Jewish citywide functions "the dietary laws will be observed." Decorum rules everywhere. The sermon of course and commonly an increasing portion of the ritual are in English. The music tends to be modern or Israeli. Even many modern Orthodox have begun insisting that men and women sit together. The organ has long since made inroads even among the Conservatives. There has often been a choir that included women. Bar and bat mitzvot are virtually universal. By the last quarter of the century, indeed, the bar and bat mitzvah observances had become so numerous that they even dominated the Sabbath, and to a degree they helped revitalize the Sabbath morning service. Almost everywhere many men—and not a few women, too—began wearing skullcaps even though covering one's head in prayer is only a custom, not a mandated Jewish law. The voice of the people is the voice of God. Wearing a yarmulke (or *kippah*, as Israeli Hebrew has it) has become important, proving that one is a Jew. In the smaller communities where ritual compromises are inevitable if the single congregation in town is to survive, one and the same officiant would occasionally conduct services for Reformers and Orthodox. (Imagine a Catholic priest presiding at a Unitarian religious service!) But there is a lesson here: Theology is finally unimportant; kinship and sociability are paramount.

There are estimated to be between two thousand and three thousand synagogues in the United States. At any one time about 40 percent of America's Jews are affiliated with a religious institution (many more may be sympathetic, but membership is expensive). A somewhat American common Judaism is emerging with a left wing and a right wing. The rightists, adhering strictly to the traditional Law, are comparatively few in number. Most of the country's Jews, from the modern Orthodox to the humanists, are moving to the left. Common to all the modernists are insistence on decorum, the use of English as well as Hebrew, good music, a choir, family pews, bar and bat mitzvah observances, and an English sermon. Many of the affiliated worshipers light candles on Friday night, Hanukkah, and the holidays; some observe dietary laws, tack a mezuzah on the doorpost, attend or even make a seder, contribute to Israel, and now and again read a Jewish book. A minority decorate their Christmas trees!

Most religionists believe that the Judaism they practice is a superior faith—which pleases historians, who are equally convinced that no Jewish community can survive without a commitment to Judaism. And the Israelis? They tend not to be theists so much as civil religionists, but their Judaism has much in common with that of the American Jewish masses.

JEWISH EDUCATION

There has been a great change in the community attitude toward education. Originally Judaism expected the family to assume responsibility for the education of the children, though the community would step in when there was no family or where poverty prevailed. As early as the first decade of the twentieth century, American Jewish communities began to realize that they must move to educate their youth. This was the American way; the civic community had assumed responsibility by establishing public schools in antebellum days. The shortlived kehillah of New York City in 1910 had cherished the hope that the Jewish community would accept the burden of educating its young and encouraged the formation of bureaus of Jewish education, which ultimately failed to compete with the synagogues, still determined to monopolize religious education. By the end of the twentieth century, the federations, reaching out for unity and power, had begun subsidizing some all-day schools. The social work executives realized that if there were no Jews there would be no federations. Religious education came to be seen as a federation imperative, a radical move that is likely sooner or later to put the federations on a collision course with the Jewish religious denominations.

Most Jews believe that there can be no survival of Jewry without formal instruction in Jewish learning and religious tradition—this even though Jewish education is no guarantee of permanent loyalty. One thing *is* certain: Education is a positive constructive force; the more schooling, the more basis for loyalty. (Education is thus something of a contrast with philanthropy to the poor, with Zionism, and with efforts to combat anti-Semitism, all responses to pathological conditions, to poverty, oppression, and hatred.) Jewish education casts a wide net, informal and formal. Informal education is continuous and significant. Jews read books and newspapers; some are members of the Jewish Publication Society; they listen to sermons, to Jewish radio and television programs; they are taught in community centers, in summer camps, and in other venues. Many go to the university Hillels; others join Zionist groups, Hadassah in particular.

Jewish Secular Schools

Formal Jewish education may be religious or secular. In the early and middle decades of the twentieth century, East European secularists, Zionists and laborites, maintained afternoon Yiddish schools and camps where some Hebrew, ethics, history, literature, and music were cultivated, but these efforts rarely survived the decline of their beloved Yiddish. Secularist social work schools were established in 1925 and 1947. It is worthy of note that the school established in 1947 called itself the Training Bureau for Jewish Communal Service. The concept of local Jewry as a unified community was burgeoning, and Jewry was no longer a mélange of autonomous groups. Most Jewish religious groups have by now organized communal social work training schools of their own. Yeshiva University and Brandeis

University were established by Jews with Judaic goals in mind. Both schools are sympathetic to Judaism the religion, as well as to more secular expressions of Jewish outlook.

RELIGIOUS SCHOOLS

In general Jewish elementary religious schools are of three types: late-afternoon schools, weekend Sunday schools, and all-day (parochial) institutions. The Orthodox and the Conservatives favor the afternoon schools and emphasize Hebraic education; the Reformers for the most part favor weekend schools, though many of them require their students to attend some afternoon classes. The curricula of the afternoon schools have much in common: Hebrew reading, history, religious practices, music, Israeli songs. Bar mitzvah and bat mitzvah training ends at thirteen, but many congregations continue with confirmation classes for adolescents, and in some areas communal high schools are making an appearance. On a higher level, the Jewish Chautauqua Society of the National Federation of Temple Brotherhoods has long sponsored college courses and one-day lectures in more than a thousand American colleges and universities.

JEWISH ALL-DAY SCHOOLS

The *novum* in American Jewish history is the startling increase in all-day schools. Approximately every fourth Jewish child goes to an all-day school where both Jewish and secular subjects are taught. There may be as many as one hundred thousand boys and girls in these elementary and high schools. Why should there be all-day tuition schools in America where public education is free and universally available? All-day schools were first opened by Jews in British North America and continued well into the nineteenth century. By the Civil War period America's growing public school system had destroyed the basis for Jewish all-day schools. East Europeans opened an all-day school in New York City in 1886, but they were interested in the religious not the secular subjects. As pious traditionalists, they were trying to save the Jewish souls of their youngsters in this assimilatory Godless land where integration constantly threatened. Only a handful of these miniyeshivas, as they were called, came into being before World War II. After the war, Europe's Polish and Russian Jews—immigrant survivors of the Nazi massacres—developed the all-day schools here. Their goals were religious; they feared that acculturation would lead to assimilation. American freedoms are indeed a threat to most fixed traditions. The rigidly traditional National Society for Hebrew Day Schools, Torah Umesorah (Learning and Tradition, 1944), has helped bring to birth a movement that now numbers some four hundred elementary and high schools where Bible and Talmud are curricular priorities. These tradition-true day schools nurse an uncompromisingly Orthodox cultural world of their own. The curricula and instruction in the Jewish and secular studies meet teaching and informational standards. The Orthodox all-day school protagonists, eager for government funding, are willing to break down the wall between church and state; they live in a tight little environment of their own.

Even so, the all-powerful American ambience is always present. In the course of the late twentieth century the Conservatives and Reformers have opened schools of this type. In part at least, these two large denominations wanted to inculcate loyalty to their doctrines, but they were also aware that the standards and discipline in the public schools they had abandoned now left much to be desired. The Holocaust and Israeli nationalism have also left their impress.

The Jewish secondary religious educational institutions have done well. There are training schools for teachers in almost every metropolitan center, and a number of these are now colleges, authorized to grant degrees. The major Jewish denominations all have seminaries where almost every facet of Jewish learning is cultivated. The Reformers, the Conservatives, and the Reconstructionists ordain women as well as men.

Most striking in a way is the work of the Orthodox in furthering Talmudic studies. There are well-entrenched Talmudic academies in Baltimore, New York, Brooklyn, Lakewood, New Jersey, Cleveland, Chicago, and other cities. Very impressive is the fact that hundreds if not thousands of individual Jews, laymen, aspire to read a page of Talmud daily. This is a remarkable achievement.

In brief, the advocates of all-day schools offer the rationale that these parochial schools will raise a generation of leaders. (This has yet to be demonstrated.) The congregational and all-day schools now prevail; the rebbe—the private teacher—the Talmud Torah, and the communal bureau of education are all languishing. What is important is that most American Jewish boys and girls are probably getting some Jewish education at some time in their lives. The Orthodox make sure that their girls are all given Jewish schooling, although the sexes are not mixed. Youngsters of today are usually better educated Jewishly than their parents.

JEWISH CULTURE

What is American Jewish culture? One may define it as the beliefs, arts, institutions, and writings of Jews in these United

349

States, but can we ignore the writings of Gentiles on Jewish thought? Cannot Christians make a contribution to Jewish culture? Though dozens of Jews have written on early rabbinic thought, nothing on the subject is superior to the three volumes of the Gentile scholar George Foote Moore, *Judaism In the First Centuries of the Christian Era*. There are numerous novels, short stories, poems, plays, librettos, and musical comedies written by Jews, some on Jewish themes. It is immaterial whether these artists want to be known as American or as Jewish writers. Many of these men and women—all of them born Jews—were in their day or are today household names: Saul Bellow, Bernard Malamud, Clifford Odets, Arthur Miller, Ludwig Lewisohn, Elmer Rice, Irwin Shaw, George S. Kaufman, J. D. Salinger, Henry Roth, Philip Roth, Norman Mailer, Lillian Hellman, Neil Simon, the Gershwins, Edna Ferber, Sidney Kingsley, Isaac Bashevis Singer, Tillie Olsen, Moss Hart, Richard Rodgers, Oscar Hammerstein II, and Cynthia Ozick. As much can be said for Abraham Cahan and his *Rise of David Levinsky*, Mary Antin and her *Promised Land*, and Betty Friedan and her *Feminine Mystique*. Louis Harap, in his three-volume *The Jewish Presence in Twentieth-Century American Literature*, analyzes the works of many notable litterateurs—all "good names," though in another generation they will have been shunted aside to make room for new luminaries. American Jewish "culture" is an ongoing process.

THE WORLD OF YIDDISH

American Yiddish literature flourished and became a force in this country's cultural life, but obviously it had no real future after 1925 when East Europeans were no longer deemed desirable immigrants. Yiddish speakers and language lovers in this country were doomed to die off, and they have not been replaced. The Yiddish theater, a precious part of their very existence, was a great comfort to the immigrant masses thirsting for a familiar word and the chance to shed a tear. The intelligentsia among them, discerning and critical, moved up Broadway to the English-language theater. On the way north in the 1920s, they created a Yiddish art theater, a good theater by any standard. Yiddish literature continued to flourish after the 1920s. Millions still read the language and loved its poetry, its stories, its humor, its earthiness. New schools of thought arose, influenced by American themes and traditions. They ignored the travail of their proletarian fathers and no longer tried to save the world. They sought instead to express themselves, to bare their inmost thoughts and emotions.

The press was always the heart and soul of the American Yiddish world. It is sad, but one by one the newspapers perished. The Orthodox *Tageblatt* was the first to depart. The old world could not compete with the new. The traditionalist press, the bourgeois journals, the liberal, socialist, and communist newspapers have all vanished. The *Forward* lasted into the 1980s as a Yiddish paper and moved into the 1990s as an English-language weekly. Other newspapers, too, tried to save themselves with an English page or column. What is their epitaph? What did they accomplish? For nearly a century they educated, Judaized, entertained, and Americanized a host of newcomers and supported the Jewish trade unions fighting for a living wage. The Yiddish press helped these human beings survive and helped readers make the difficult transition from backward Russia to enlightened America. The press brought knowledge of the arts and sciences to a people who had lived in darkness, and put a brake on dejudaization, on assimilation. As late as

351

the 1990s Yiddish refused to give up the ghost. At that time there were still seven Yiddish national organizations, including the YIVO Institute for Jewish Research with its millions of pages of archival material. On the eve of the twenty-first century, New York could still brag that it was publishing fourteen Yiddish periodicals.

THE PERSISTENCE OF HEBREW

Though Yiddish was a demotic tongue, the vernacular of the masses, it could not survive in English-speaking America. Hebrew, so long a religious tongue, will never die while there is a single Jew who reads the Hebrew prayer book. Even Christians in North America's British colonies cultivated the holy tongue, the language of their beloved Old Testament, but their proficiency was pitifully meager. The Jews, who have had a permanent community here since the late seventeenth century, have always read and studied the language of the Bible. East European Hebraists, poets, writers, and enlighteners (Maskilim) began arriving in America in the 1860s, though they never gained a substantial following. English brooks no rivals. Zionism has stimulated Hebraic studies, but there has never been a viable, self-supporting Hebrew press in this country. Overseas editions of Israeli papers have also precluded the rise of a significant Hebrew press in the United States. The subsidized biweekly *Hadoar* (The Post, 1921) and *Bitzaron* still appear, but their readers are relatively few.

The gifted Hebrew poets and essayists who made their homes here in the first half of the twentieth century have mostly moved on to the new State of Israel where they had a rosier future. There has been a permanent Hebrew-speaking federation in the United States ever since 1922; its members speak of the "primacy of Hebrew in Jewish life, culture and education," but their goal is clearly unrealistic. It is true, however, that the language and its literature remain very much alive today in this country. Hebrew is even taught in some American public schools, though students are now more likely to go to Jerusalem to perfect their knowledge of the Sacred Tongue or its secular Israeli heir. Dozens of seminaries and secular colleges in the United States offer courses in classical and modern Hebrew. Some rabbinic seminaries require a year of study in the Holy Land. Zionist "emissaries," dispatched by the Israelis, encourage Americans to cultivate Hebrew. In the 1990s nine Hebrew periodicals were still published in New York City. The Los Angeles Israeli immigrants have a Hebrew paper of their own, which may assuage their guilt at having left their Mediterranean homeland.

THE SCIENCE OF JUDAISM AND ITS PRESS

No aspect of Jewish culture is more important than the so called science of Judaism. This critical study of the Jewish past and its literature came to birth in the early nineteenth century in Germany and found a home in America as early as the 1830s. The twentieth century has seen popular and technical works pour forth constantly from university presses, commercial publishers, and theological seminaries. The Jewish Community Centers Association of North America—the former Jewish Welfare Board—today sponsors the Jewish Book and Music Councils, which over the years have issued more than fifty annuals listing practically all English, Yiddish, and Hebrew works published in this country. The Jewish Publication Society, with its thousands of subscribers, began to distribute its books in 1890, but several years earlier the B'nai B'rith published *The Menorah* (1886–1907), an excellent periodical with contributions from notables. In 1915 the country's young Jewish intellectuals founded the *Menorah Journal*, distinguished for its artistry and intellectuality. For a generation it made a strong impression on aspiring American Jewish college youth and possibly crossed the seas and induced German Jews to publish *Der Morgen* (The Dawn, 1924). In 1938 the American Jewish Committee came out with the *Contemporary Jewish Record*, an excellent popular scientific magazine, but in 1945 the committee, eager to extend its reach, abandoned the *Record* in order to publish its monthly *Commentary*, meant to influence America's white collar intellectuals, both Gentiles and Jews. Thousands read this journal, which has become something of an icon for late twentieth-century political neoconservatives.

Seminaries, the Annenberg Institute (né Dropsie College), the YIVO Institute, the Association for Jewish Studies, the American Jewish Historical Society, the Leo Baeck Institute, and the American Jewish Archives all have periodicals and publications. Early in the twentieth century the Jewish Publication Society published Louis Ginzberg's monumental seven-volume *Legends of the Jews* and in 1985 issued a brand-new English translation of the Hebrew Bible, the most accurate English rendition of Holy Scriptures (though unfortunately it lacks the beautiful lilt of the original King James version). Researchers here lean heavily on three multivolume English-language Jewish encyclopedias. American Jewish scholarship can bear comparison with that of any other cultural center.

NEWSPAPERS

Most Americans Jews are reached by the local Jewish weeklies. At the end of the twentieth century there are at least two hundred, and New York alone has about ninety. The American Jewish Periodical Center, established in 1957 on the campus of the Hebrew Union College in Cincinnati, has rescued dozens of Jewish periodicals from the ash can. Every Jewish denomination, every American Jewish cultural group, every large labor union has had its own paper. It is a tribute to America that even the Hassidic women of Brooklyn publish a very readable periodical, while *Hadassah Magazine* reputedly enjoys a circulation of about three hundred thousand. Even Ladino-speakers had their own Judeo-Spanish paper until the middle of the twentieth century. Originally about twenty-five thousand Levantines came to these shores and struggled to survive. Today, one hundred thousand strong, they are well integrated into the American Jewish community and have seen their numbers augmented by Israeli and North African arrivals. There is no one outstanding American Jewish paper, unless we assume that *The New York Times*, because of the huge number of Jews in New York City and neighboring states, publishes all the Jewish news fit to print.

The newspapers and the national magazines bring their readers news, enlightenment, and pride in the achievements of fellow Jews. These loyalties have been heightened by apprehensions, the specter of the Holocaust, the impact of Zionism and Jewish education, the magic wrought by almost instantaneous communication, and always the concern for Israel. Today's Anglo-Jewish newspapers are generally superior to those published in the 1920s. Their editors are sophisticated and knowledgeable, sometimes even brilliant. The big metropolitan weeklies are multimillion-dollar enterprises and important vehicles of opinion. Every group has its paper; German newcomers can still read *Aufbau* (Building Up), which first appeared in 1934. Many turned to Trude Weiss-Rosmarin's scholarly, perceptive, and courageous *Jewish Spectator* (1935). Though different in many respects, the best of the American Jewish serials compare favorably today with England's *Jewish Chronicle* (1841).

But America's Jewish press is faced with a problem. A number of the papers are controlled by the local welfare federations, and others are often heavily subsidized by them. Eager to meet their huge budgets, the federations expect these papers to emphasize the constant crises in Israel and elsewhere. Crises produce cash, so federations, which get about half the money raised, hammer away at Israel's problems, and American news— except for evidences of anti-Semitism—must frequently take second place. No subsidized press can be completely free.

SUMMARY

Where is Jewish culture as a formal discipline being cultivated in the United States? Primarily in the Midwest on the mother campus of the Hebrew Union College and in the New England and New York areas. Millions of Jews live at least on the fringe of Jewish culture. During the second half of the twentieth century, academic and commercial presses have published or republished about twenty-five thousand books in English, Yiddish, and Hebrew. There are numerous large Jewish libraries, and Israel excepted, no other country has produced as many Jewish books as America and its five million Jews.

Cultural agencies? There are camps, the press, the pulpit, elementary religious and all-day schools, community centers, Hillels, seminaries, Talmudic academies, and at least fifty national Jewish cultural organizations. No Jew associating with other Jews can finally escape the impact of Jewish culture.

SOCIAL AND PHILANTHROPIC ORGANIZATIONS

THE JEWISH COMMUNITY CENTER

No religious organization is without its element of sociability. There have always been societies and agencies dedicated to leisure and recreation: fraternal orders, country and city clubs, synagogue-centers, and Jewish community centers. The synagogue-center set out to offer its members a host of religious and nonreligious benefits, and in small towns this all-inclusive organization may well be the community's basic institution. Activities for adolescents are an integral and important part of the programming sponsored by B'nai B'rith, Hadassah, Hillel, Zionist organizations, Young Israel, and all the Jewish religious denominations. The Jewish community center grew out of the older YM-YWHA and the settlement house, both of which were dedicated to the Americanization of newcomers. The community center movement now copes with a new challenge, rejudaization, especially with hundreds of thousands of Israelis and émigrés from the former Soviet Union settling here. The Americanization process begins anew.

In the closing decades of the twentieth century, the locale of the Jewish community centers generally shifted to suburbia (though New York City has a Y that is an important cultural and social agency well beyond Jewish communal boundaries). The Jewish community center, uniquely Jewish and American, furthers identification without demanding religious affiliation. Basically the center is a community recreational and cultural institution. It offers everyone in town recreation, health programs, drama, lectures, arts and crafts, day and residential camps, and often a swimming pool. The many centers in this country have hundreds of thousands of members. If the secular-minded sponsors of the first centers hoped to eclipse the synagogue, they erred. Centers cannot compete with synagogue offerings of religion and a Jewish education. The center is one of the few American Jewish institutions that has made the transatlantic crossing eastward to Israel and some twenty other foreign lands.

A basic problem: Centers have never found it easy to come to terms with the rock-ribbed Orthodox. The traditionalists tolerate no "work" on the Sabbath. Saturday is a free day for most youth and adults, and observant Orthodox Jews curtail Saturday programs when in truth they might be well advised to enlarge them. One notable rabbi laid down the law: "You can swim but you cannot wring out your wet swimming suits. That is work and as such is forbidden on the seventh day of the week."

THE FEDERATIONS AND JEWISH WELFARE FUNDS

It is really in America's early national period that the roots of the welfare federation lie, in the attempt of American Jewry's first communal charities to emancipate themselves from synagogueal control. By the 1820s charities were beginning to cooperate. The multiple drives and solicitation of individual donors had became a headache. In the years after the Civil War the words "United Hebrew" or "United Jewish" documented the drive toward institutional mergers. By the 1890s federations had become a reality. At first they merely collected funds at one fell swoop. Then they moved to allocate monies and thus became the dominant communal agency. On the eve of World War I the concept of a general community chest (now the United Way) making provision for joint distribution of charities for the larger society, including the Jewish charitable efforts, was adopted in Cleveland at the suggestion of Martin A. Marks, a Jew. As early as the 1940s practically every large city in the United States had adopted the concept of the community chest, and each had its Jewish component. Even so, America's Jews were never happy with the concept of a community chest that collected and doled out funds to both Jews and Gentiles. Jews thought of themselves as having a higher standard of living and giving. They knew, too, that they could not expect Gentiles to support Jewish schools, finance agencies fighting anti-Semitism, rehabilitate a devastated Jewry in Russia, Poland, and the Balkans, and help Jewish Palestine.

By the 1990s there were at least two hundred Jewish federations in the country, embracing a total of eight hundred communities with budgets made up by government grants, United Way allocations, and the United Jewish Appeal–Jewish Welfare giving running into the millions. The beneficiaries are local, national, and international Jewish agencies. Federations are staffed by college graduates educated at social work institutions. Their national organization called itself the Jewish Communal Service Association of North America (1899); the federation outreach is continental. The professional workers, often secular-minded individuals of East European stock, are "Jewish" in their approach. The basic agencies of the federations concern themselves with children, orphans, the family, the aged, and the sheltered work shop for the disadvantaged. The needs of senior citizens have made it imperative to fashion new institutions to supply their wants, special apartments and recreational facilities. Psychiatric aid is emphasized. The budgets of the huge Jewish hospitals are met largely by fees and government payments, not by the federations. Though the federations give Jewish hospitals relatively little support, and despite the fact that most patients are Gentile, Jews still insist on maintaining Jewish hospitals and even their own medical schools; the ambience is comforting. Even in smaller communities, there were—and still are—one or two nonprofessionals who concern themselves with the federation. The *American Jewish Archives* in 1951 wrote that Jewish social workers had pioneered in twenty-nine different areas.

Jewish giving has created a community that in effect includes all Jews wherever they are.

Why do Jews give? If they are religious the answer is simple: Giving is a mitzvah, charity is prescribed by God. If they are not religious they give because of crises and the conviction that any Jew in need must be helped. That feeling led in the 1920s to the creation of a supplementary Jewish Welfare Fund to provide for local, national, and international Jewish needs, since once again multiple campaigns for charities were becoming a nuisance. The funds needed were now raised annually by the United Jewish Appeal and divided among the local Jewish federations, national Jewish organizations, and transatlantic institutions. Since 1948, a very substantial percentage, hundreds of millions, has gone to the State of Israel. The funds raised have served to tie all Jews together. The UJA has great prestige and power, and is important as evidence of an elemental Jewish unity.

The federation tends to control the community because it funds practically all agencies except the synagogues. The Council of Jewish Federations, the national overall organization—originally a planning and advisory institution—seems to be moving to become an administrative agency. If it succeeds in exercising influence over the United Jewish Appeal—and the hundreds of millions of dollars at its disposal—it may well rival in importance the Conference of Presidents of Major Jewish

Organizations, although the latter's goals have been primarily political, pro-Israel. The national and local religious groups, always wary, are not happy that some federations are subsidizing the all-day religious schools. As federations increase in power, the synagogues and rabbinate almost inevitably will diminish in prestige. But Jewish religious forces will never tolerate encroachments. On the eve of the twenty-first century, there is no evidence that the federation is seriously threatening the reach of the forces of religion.

THE JEWISH COMMUNITY ASSERTS ITSELF

A destructive worldwide depression started in 1929. The 1930s saw Nazism, fascism, and an autocratic Communism ruling much of Europe. Reactionaries in the United States could not escape European influences: German Nazi groups and home-grown fascist organizations sprang up here in the United States. The typical Jew looked to the four national defense groups for help, but there was little they appeared able to offer in these very bad times. Angry and disappointed with the New York agencies that could perform no miracles, local communities spontaneously created community relations committees. Each committee hired an administrator to thwart the anti-Semites; learning on the job, many of these administrators soon became professionals. It was important that these new organizations include all the Jewish forces in town, among them groups hitherto largely ignored: the East European immigrants, the new money, the synagogueal groups. In this crisis situation everyone was now made welcome. The federation soon began financing this new agency. In effect, the new community relations committee helped further the forces working to create an all-inclusive Jewish community. Sixty years later, by the 1990s, there were in the United States approximately one hundred such committees working closely with the National Jewish Community Relations Advisory Council (1944).

Obviously, if there was to be a thriving integrated community instead of a welter of autonomous societies and institutions, an overall plan was needed, and in America that plan would have a democratic makeup. Every city in which Jews lived had a non-Jewish or general council and an elected head. The Jewish council secured no real authority; at best it was a sounding board, at worst a sort of Polish parliament. The 10 percent who gave 80 percent of the money never lost power. Even so, the community as such was not powerless: Whoever did not oppose the anti-Semites, give to the federation, help Israel, and work to free the Soviet Jews was—is—"outside the camp." Give and you are a good Jew; refuse to give and you are disdained.

The Place of Women and Their Organizations

The vote granted women in 1920 opened new vistas for Jewish women: They would sooner or later become federal administrators, judges, members of the House and the Senate, and finally even justices of the United States Supreme Court (1993). They were writers, poets, authors, and college presidents. For women, too, America had finally become "the land of unlimited opportunity." Of course distinguished women have been esteemed in Jewish life ever since biblical times, sometimes among non-Jews, too. London-born Bilhah Abigail Levy Franks (1696–1756/65), a voracious reader of good literature, was a frequent visitor to the governor's mansion in colonial New York. Rebecca Gratz (1781–1869), an Orthodox Jew, played a role in Philadelphia's Gentile social and philanthropic circles. Rachel Mordecai

(1789–1838), of Warrenton and Wilmington, North Carolina, was an intellectual. Ernestine Rose (1810–92), a native Pole, was one of America's leading feminists and egalitarians.

In the 1840s when the feminists were stirring, a group of German-speaking Jewish women established the Independent Order of True Sisters. They may not themselves have been feminists, but they were obviously possessed of a female consciousness. Sometime after the Civil War Anna Rich Marks, a Polish Jew, was stopped at a tollhouse in the Utah Territory. When she was not allowed to move forward with her load of goods, she summoned her bodyguards and with drawn guns they continued. When her right to a building lot was disputed, she again pointed her weapons, and when the Denver and Rio Grande Railroad attempted to cross her lands, she and her men held it off till they paid her price. (And Mr. Wolff Marks, her husband? He gave sticks of candy to the children who came to their store.) At the Pittsburgh Conference in 1885, Kaufmann Kohler, the author of the Reform Platform, demanded absolute equality for women. His colleagues ignored him and nearly ninety years passed before a woman was ordained.

Women were not daunted. The National Council of Jewish Women was organized in 1893. By 1927 almost two thousand Jewish women's organizations had arisen in this country. By the 1950s, at least two women in tiny communities are known to have volunteered to conduct religious services. In the 1960s and 1970s Bella Abzug, Gloria Steinem, and Betty Friedan were recognized as leading feminists. Gerda Lerner, a refugee, was elected president of the American Historical Association with its many thousands of members. In 1971, a handful of New York women started fighting for women's rights in the Conservative movement; two decades later they had reached most of their goals. When the *World Almanac and Book of Facts* listed the country's twenty-five most notable women for the year 1984, nine were of Jewish descent. No later than the 1980s, women were accorded practically all rights and privileges in Reform and Conservative synagogues. Only the Orthodox, on the whole, were immovable in denying their women equality and maintaining them religiously as second-class citizens. But in the 1990s the women's struggle was far from won. In many fields and in all American Jewish institutions women were subject to lesser pay and fewer opportunities. Proverbs Chapter 31 tells us that a woman of valor is one who makes sure that her husband "hath no lack of gain." The Jewish woman of valor as the twenty-first century begins is fighting to secure rights for herself and all other females.

Philanthropic work—often volunteer—has long been an accepted field of endeavor for American Jewish women. Hadassah has been an important and popular women's organization since 1913. Another excellent example of philanthropy supported by America's Jewish women is the Organization for Rehabilitation through Training (Women's ORT, 1927), which funds technical training for Jews in Israel, Europe, South America, the United States, and other lands. ORT has more than one hundred thousand members in this country.

A NATIONAL JEWISH UMBRELLA ORGANIZATION?

American Jews have always been slow to organize on a nation-wide basis. They failed to do so in 1789 when George Washington's secretariat suggested it (the president's office did not want to cope with individual congregations). The Board of Delegates of American Israelites, the country's first national Jewish agency, came into existence in 1859, more than two hundred years after the first Jews settled in New Amsterdam. This unity was not religiously motivated, but rather Jews joined together to bring relief to threatened and oppressed Jews abroad. The first national Jewish religious organization, the Union of American Hebrew Congregations, was organized in 1873. The Anti-Defamation League of the B'nai B'rith rose in 1913 to stop Jew-baiting. Two years later America's Jews joined together in the Joint Distribution Committee to aid war-stricken fellow Jews in Europe. World War I also gave birth to the Jewish Welfare Board, which provided for men and women in the armed forces (1917). By the 1920s the Jewish Telegraphic Agency was purveying world news to America's Jewish newspapers. When American ports of entry were closed to most Jewish newcomers (as well as to non-Jews from eastern and southern Europe) in 1924, it was inevitable that America's Jews would meld and seek to structure themselves nationally. In 1926 Reform, Conservative, and Orthodox religionists came together in an alliance of sorts, the Synagogue Council of America. In 1932 the nationwide Council of Jewish Federations and Welfare Funds made its bow. At the dawn of the twenty-first century the council represents two hundred Jewish federations, which include hundreds of communities. Because of its access to the huge United Jewish Appeal monies, the council may one day become the dominant American Jewish national agency.

In the 1930s Jews were called upon to defend themselves, thus bringing a large degree of unity to the local emerging Jewish communities. Distraught town and city leaders looked in vain for leadership—or results—to the disparate defense agencies: the American Jewish Committee, the American Jewish Congress, the Anti-Defamation League, and the Jewish Labor Committee. Actually, there was little that American

Jewry—even almost five million strong—could do during a period of widespread xenophobia and economic despair. Only after the Nazi regime had already destroyed Germany's Jewish citizenry financially and socially did Jews in the United States finally forge an overall national defense group, the General Jewish Council (1938), which proved an egregious failure. In 1939, however, American Jews did succeed in establishing the United Jewish Appeal, which devoted itself to relieving the needs of Jews in Europe and in Palestine/Israel. The Joint Distribution Committee, a partner to UJA, brought aid to Jews in some thirty different lands. Patterning itself on the American Jewish Congress of 1916–20, representatives of American Jewry met together in 1943 as the American Jewish Conference. Many hoped that this new national congress would give American Jewry an effective umbrella organization, but this hope, too, proved illusory. The leaders who had convened the conference demanded that a sovereign Jewish state be created in Britain's Palestine Mandate; the delegates assented gladly. The handful who had hoped for a permanent Jewish "legislature" were grievously disappointed. In 1949, after the State of Israel was proclaimed, the American Jewish Conference adjourned, never to reassemble. The different national Jewish organizations, present through their representatives, had no desire to create an American national assembly that would threaten their autonomy.

The federations were fully aware that the American Jewish Conference had no interest in creating a strong American organization to deal with the problems of Judeophobia in this country. Annoyed with the waste of money and the overlapping activity, the large metropolitan communities that had been financing the four different defense agencies insisted in

1944 on establishing the all-inclusive National Community Relations Advisory Council. All the defense organizations were expected to work harmoniously together, which they did not do. Baffled, the federations brought in a distinguished non-Jewish sociologist to remedy this situation. His recommendations were rejected by the American Jewish Committee and the Anti-Defamation League, both of which had too much to lose. When the dust finally settled there were still three national defense agencies operative in the 1950s: the Anti-Defamation League, the American Jewish Committee, and the National (Jewish) Relations Advisory Council (NJCRAC), which included all of America's local Jewish relations agencies as well as the Jewish Labor Committee and the American Jewish Congress. The role of the NJCRAC was merely advisory, however—it had no substantial budget. The Anti-Defamation League and the American Jewish Committee may yet find it advisable to unite, especially if they run into financial trouble. The American Jewish Congress suggestion that Jews fight to outlaw disabilities by executive, court, and congressional action has been adopted by the defense agencies.

Always in need of help and political influence, the State of Israel was supported by the American Israel Public Affairs Committee (AIPAC, 1954), which has demonstrated great competence and become very influential. A year later, another pro-Israel group made its appearance, the Conference of Presidents of Major American Jewish Organizations (COP). In the course of time COP has expanded its program to serve as a quasi-American Jewish overall agency. The delegates of the fifty-some agencies have no authority, but they have given American Jewry the semblance of leadership. Their efforts and activities have been reenforced by other national groups that have helped Soviet and Ethiopian Jews to reach Israel. During the 1990s American Jews could proudly boast that they were supporting more than 350 national organizations. Most had limited objectives, but all had some loyal followers.

There is no indication that American Jewry is moving toward the creation of a representative umbrella agency comparable to the Canadian Jewish Congress or the Board of Deputies of British Jews. The vested interests of the important national Jewish agencies remain an effective bar to the creation of a permanent American Jewish assembly. Since Jews will always help Jews abroad if they have the means to do so, the present philanthropic agencies pose no threat to the current American national Jewish defense organizations.

KLAL YISRAEL: REACHING OUT TO WORLD JEWRIES

Jews in the United States were drawing together during the 1990s on several different levels. National and international needs were driving the various Jewish ethnic and social groups to forge a unified local community. The many millions they sent abroad documented their devotion. Worldwide anti-Semitism evoked a sense of common Jewish brotherhood; the determination to keep the State of Israel alive became a passion. Instant communication through radio, television, and computer linkages put virtually every Jew in the world in every other Jew's home.

The U.S. government set out after World War II through its Pax Americana to dominate the globe. American Jewry, following the flag, set out to embrace world Jewry. Jews in the

United States aspire to help all foreign Jewries politically, religiously, and philanthropically. For decades the American Jewish Committee, the B'nai B'rith, and the American Jewish Congress have worked closely with allied foreign Jewish agencies, while the Jewish Labor Committee has maintained close ties to Europe's socialist governments and labor unions. In matters religious, the Orthodox—especially the Agudath Israel and the Lubavitcher Hassidim—have maintained close relations with Torah-true Jews in Europe and Israel. Conservatism has its World Council of Synagogues. The Reformers through their World Union for Progressive Judaism have developed a following in Britain, France, Holland, Israel, Australia, and New Zealand. American Jewry worked with the papacy from 1965 on to secure an authoritative statement denouncing anti-Semitism and acknowledging the Judaic origins of Christianity and also to bolster Israeli efforts to establish diplomatic relations with the Vatican State. Roman Catholics have come a long way since the 1860s when the Jews in papal Rome were, at best, second-class citizens.

These political and religious involvements with Europe's Jewries were of modest proportions, but the philanthropic impact on Jewish life in Europe, North Africa, and Asia was vital. Ever since 1915 the Joint Distribution Committee has poured billions into Europe and Israel to sustain their Jewries. This giving of their means on the part of three to six million American Jews is, relatively speaking, the greatest nongovernmental philanthropic feat in all history. The Jews in the United States have labored to save the beleaguered Jews of Eastern Europe, and just a few years and another war later they worked heroically to save the pitifully few survivors, the *shearit ha-peletah*. Between 1933 and the 1960s, an estimated 150,000–200,000 Jews, quota immigrants, refugees, and displaced persons, came to the United States. America's Jews also did what they could to help France when it offered refuge to North African and Middle Eastern Jews who had no future in their Moslem homelands.

America's immigration policies have been more generous in the post–World War II decades than in the years after World War I. Among the many different Jewish ethnic groups that found a home here are Iraqis and Persians, some of whom came with means and soon made a place for themselves. They have not been assimilated into the Jewish communities in whose midst they have settled, but they and their children do identify as Jews, most often as religionists. Large numbers of Israelis and Soviet émigrés have also found a home here. In the 1960s several Jewish organizations began trying to induce the Soviets to allow their Jews to emigrate, and when the Soviet empire began to collapse in the late 1980s American Jews turned energetically to the task of salvaging and rebuilding Eastern Europe's Jewish communities. Millions were spent to encourage Jewries in the Soviet Union's successor Commonwealth of Independent States. The U.S. government has also worked to this end.

The Israelis—secularists for the most part—are slow to become a part of the Jewish communities where they have found homes and have tended to live off by themselves. Whether these Israeli nationalists will identify with their Jewish neighbors remains to be seen. The Soviet immigrants are a different problem. Many of them, indoctrinated by the Soviet system for two generations, have little to induce them to become Jews religiously, though there is always the possibility that in decades to come these émigrés will turn to American Jewry for psychic support. Whether their children will be exposed to Jewish religious schools is moot.

Thus, in the final decade of the twentieth century, Jews in America are faced with the challenge of rehabilitating German, Baltic, Polish, Russian, Austrian, Hungarian, and Balkan Jewish communities. It will not be easy. Populous North African and Asian Jewries have not been annihilated. Six hundred thousand Jews stretching all the way from Morocco to Iran, some in communities two thousand years old, were exiled or compelled to leave by the Moslem authorities. By 1993 there were only ten thousand Jews remaining in all of North Africa. From the 1290s to the 1490s England, France, Spain, and Portugal mercilessly exiled their Jews or forced them to convert; today these four lands offer Jews freedom and opportunity. This should be borne in mind: There is always the hope that the oppressor of yesterday may become the savior of tomorrow. As of today new Jewish communities are rising in all the lands east of the Rhine deep into Siberia. If the United States of Europe comes into being as a viable federation, it may one day very well foster a powerful new Jewish community that will rival America's.

Constant challenges will face American Jewry. Affluent South African Jewry, for example, may face a severe crisis as the postapartheid government assumes control of the economy. Israel's relations with her neighbors, even though improving, will long continue problematic. Its need for American support, both governmental and private, will also continue. Jews in Russia cannot expect to breathe free so long as the post-Soviet economy remains unstable. On the other hand, if the North American Free Trade Agreement is really effective, Mexican and Canadian Jewry will become part of an expanded continental complex of world Jewish significance.

AMERICAN JEWS AND ISRAEL

The New State of Israel: A Messianic Dawn

After World War II an asylum was still desperately needed for the refugee remnant in Europe and the threatened Jewries who lived in Moslem lands. The world was not without a sense of guilt for the millions of Jews who perished because they had been denied a haven in Europe and in the United States. From 1945 to 1948, thousands of Jews, many in displaced persons camps, illegally infiltrated Palestine. The British left Palestine on May 15, 1948. The previous day the Jews of Palestine had published a Declaration of Independence guaranteeing equality to all in social, political, and religious matters—a promise that has not been and perhaps cannot be fulfilled. Given the rights and immunities granted Jews, Arab citizens might ultimately take over the country and even be able to deny Jews parity. Present-day Israel is like the preconstitutional United States. An established church—the Orthodox rabbinate in this case— enjoys privileges denied non-Orthodox Jewish religionists.

President Truman recognized the new State of Israel immediately, though it was not easy for him to take this action. The State Department, with Arab oil in mind, was not sympathetic to Jews. The president had been harassed by the Zionists and the dogged Rabbi Silver. Palestine, Truman knew, was essentially an Arab land, but if the Zionists were denied American recognition, they could always turn to the Soviet Union for aid, and the latter was the great American obsession. Like his fellow Americans, Truman wanted no dealings with the Soviets but understood that xenophobic Americans would object strenuously to the admission of large numbers of refugees. On the other hand, Truman was willing to admit some Jews in distress into the United States but hoped that many more would be permitted to enter their ancient homeland. Truman had a number of Jewish aides who were pro-Zionist; his cardplaying buddies were Jews. Eddie Jacobson, once Truman's partner in a haberdashery, was no Zionist, but he was eager to help his people and did so by intervening with the president. Was Truman a philosemite? He was a decent human being but also a typical country boy from Barton County, Missouri. It is not surprising, therefore, that he occasionally spoke of "smart Hebrews" and "kikes." Truman, like General Grant, could not jump out of his skin. But he was not inveterately anti-Jew.

What Zionism Has Done for American Jewry

It was Zionism that drove the American Jewish community to push for the sanctuary that is now Israel. Many, possibly most, American Jews rejoice in the rebirth of the ancient homeland after almost two thousand years. Jews are proud of being just like all other ethnics. They now have a tangible rock whence they were hewn, a land that they can visit, see, touch. As romantics, Jews glow when they envision the Israelis as latter-day Maccabeans who have sacrificed their lives to build a modern-day Jewish homeland. American Jews exult in Israel's successes. These newcomers in the Middle East have made great industrial strides; in less than half a century they have turned Israel into an impressive industrial commonwealth. In what was once a neglected malarial Ottoman outpost, Israel is today a cultural center with colleges and universities, an excellent technical school, a large press, museums, hosts of scholars and litterateurs, artists, and composers of a new music with a lilt all its own. Israeli Hebrew songs are sung in almost all American synagogues, replacing the classical German Jewish melodies of

Louis Lewandowski and Solomon Sulzer. Zionism has rejudaized American Jewry and restored the balance between acculturation and tradition. The once Protestantized Union of American Hebrew Congregations, the B'nai B'rith, the American Jewish Committee, the Jewish Labor Committee, the Joint Distribution Committee, America's formerly anti-Zionist press—all these institutions and organizations and media are back in the traditional folkish fold. Zionism, concern for Israel, and the German Holocaust have effected a modern Judaic miracle.

The restorationist ideal, the love of Israel, has made American Jewry generous. Hadassah, the United Jewish Appeal, the State of Israel Bonds Organization, and almost every Israeli institution of size depend on American largesse. American Jews in 1939, angry at the British for threatening to close Palestine to imperiled Jews, opened their pocketbooks. From 1939 to the late 1970s, Jews in the United States gave Israel over $8 billion in cash or in purchase of bonds. Who supplied these immense sums? The fabulous rich? Yes, in large part. Everyday folk in 3,750 cities, towns, and hamlets also gave what they could. In almost all American Jewish periodicals, Israeli news commands the most space (which may or may not be a blessing). For some American Jews, Zionist-sponsored Israel is a religion; for others an icon; for all an imperative responsibility. Jewish nationalism has become a form of identification with the capacity to embrace all Jews.

On May 16, 1948, two days after Israel proclaimed its independence, a mass meeting was held in New York City. One hundred thousand men and women crowded into Madison Square Garden to hear Herbert H. Lehman and Henry Morgenthau Jr. speak. Symbolically these two men represented the native elite, but all who were present that day—down to the humblest garment worker—had a sense of community that encompassed all Jews everywhere. Zionism was largely responsible for this feeling. Israel, the flesh and blood of Zion, can be all things to all Jews: The Socialists in 1948 were about to build a Marxist state; the romantics were glad to welcome a nation of farmers; the Orthodox were eager to support a state where Jewish ritual and Law—Torah—would be honored; the intelligentsia exulted in a renascent Jewish culture; secularists were encouraged to believe that secularism could become an acceptable substitute for a religion that could only be divisive; political liberals hoped for an exemplary democracy.

The rebirth of a Jewish state after twenty centuries confronts the American Jew with a problem. Can the United States—and will United States Jewry—continue to support the Promised Land? Israel has thus far been financially and politically dependent on American Jewry and its ability to win the support of the American government and people. The Jewish state has few natural resources. The land is minuscule in size; water is scarce; its Jews are surrounded by Moslems who outnumber them ten to one. Faced with enemies who if victorious would literally drive them into the sea, Israeli Jews will always remain a people under arms even as they strive to patch up a peace with their neighbors. And if this new state goes down the drain, what will the Gentiles think of us? This fear haunts American Jewry.

There are some who say that Zionism is the greatest movement in all American Jewish history. This is debatable. Reform and Conservatism with their two million members have revolted (in one form or another) against two thousand years of hierarchical authority and have effected the most radical change in Jewish history since the eighth-century Karaites broke with

Pharisaic (rabbinic) Orthodoxy. Zionism and Israel are powerful but cannot solve the Jewish problem. The world still looks askance at the Jew in all lands. Even so, as long as there is an Israel there will be pride and a home for every Jew in distress.

What American Jews Have Done—and Do—for Zion

American Jewry was concerned about the new state. Jewry here worked closely with the United States government, the world's most powerful empire, to make sure that tiny Israel did not get the short end of the stick. How tiny was Israel? The United States landmass was more than four hundred times larger than the Jewish republic.

American Jews as a whole did much for Zion: They provided leaders, money, political influence, medical care, a prophetic voice. Beginning in 1897, when the Zionists first met in Basel, American Zionists enlisted several notables who guided the destiny of this restorationist movement in the United States: Richard J. H. Gottheil, Henrietta Szold, Louis Brandeis, Julian Mack, Stephen S. Wise, Abba Hillel Silver, Louis Lipsky, Emanuel Neumann, and Judah Leon Magnes, the founder-president of the Hebrew University and Israel's outstanding protagonist of equal rights for the Arab natives (only too often Magnes was a voice crying in the wilderness).

American Jews also provided much of the funding that helped to create the new state. No national or international movement can prosper without large amounts of cash. Collections by the United Jewish Appeal and later the sale of Israeli bonds ran into the billions. Through political activity the Zionists, the American Israel Public Affairs Committee, and the Conference of Presidents of Major American Jewish Organizations induced the U.S. president and Congress to make huge sums available to the new Israeli commonwealth and to supply it with arms and planes when it was threatened with disaster at the hands of its Soviet-supported Moslem neighbors.

Above all, American Jewry made it possible for the new state to provide a home for distressed millions. Without the help and the intervention of the American Jewish community one may well question if there would ever have been a new Land of Promise. The fall of Germany's Weimar Republic in 1933, one of Europe's great democratic states, had taught Jewry—if not the whole world—that no free land has a guarantee of survival. American Jews are happy that insecure coreligionists in South Africa, in the South American lands, and in the former Soviet territories can always find in Israel a fallback, an escape hatch. The United Jewish Appeal brought money; the Zionists and their friends brought hope and vision.

By the time that the State of Israel was established, most non-Zionists and even many anti-Zionists had made their peace with Zionist goals and with the new Jewish republic. As early as 1945, a poll disclosed that only 10.5 percent of America's Jews were opposed to a Jewish state. The following year Reform Judaism's Union of American Hebrew Congregations refused to withdraw from the Zionist-controlled American Jewish Conference (1943–49). All Jews here knew that it was imperative for world Jewry to have a home in which refugees, displaced persons, and future exiles were welcome.

In 1950, when Jacob Blaustein, the head of the American Jewish Committee, met with David Ben-Gurion, Israel's prime minister, and made it clear that—despite Israel's Law of Return, which gave most Jews automatic citizenship—American Jews owed no allegiance to the State of Israel, the prime minister agreed with Blaustein. American Jews were very happy to welcome the new Jewish state but had no intention of settling in Israel themselves; America was their home. It is worth noting that the Israeli leader dealt in this crucial instance with the American Jewish Committee and not with American Zionists. The American Zionists had led the struggle here to establish the new state, but once the republic of Israel was called into being, the Israelis preferred not to deal with them but with more powerful forces in the American Jewish community. Israel's leaders, at the time all Europeans, would tolerate no interference from the American Zionists; there could be but one captain on the ship of state. In consequence, there was little need for American Zionist organizations, and they declined in numbers. (Hadassah, primarily a philanthropic society, may well have been an exception.) Zionism will always be weak when Israel is strong; the converse is also true. Zionism, standing in the wings, is not moribund, only temporarily quiescent, its leaders well aware that America's powerful pro-Israel organizations are not controlled by official Zionists.

It is questionable if Israel could have preserved its independence without the political and financial aid of the U.S. government and American Jews. This third Jewish commonwealth in 1948 promised the world that it would become a fully democratic polity. It falls short of fulfilling that promise. A completely democratic policy would grant the country's large Arab minority actual equality, which the Israelis fear as still too hazardous an approach. In the long run, Israelis fear that Jewish sovereignty might be threatened. But it is not only vis-à-vis its Arab citizens that Israel is less than fully democratic: As of today Israel supports an established Orthodox "church" that insists on disabling all non-Orthodox Jewish religionists—all Conservative and Reform Jews—though Moslems and Christians enjoy virtually complete religious freedom. Nearly 80 percent of all Israelis are secularists or civil religionists, without pronounced sympathy for the Orthodox establishment. American Jewry has poured millions into a country to support a rabbinate that has no tolerance for the religious views and practices of the American Jewish masses!

Despite the fact that 85 percent of all American Jews resent Israel's established Orthodoxy, practically all Jews in the United States are very proud of the achievements of the Jewish state. Its individual level of efficiency is unique in the Levant. Its scientific achievements bear comparison with those in the United States and Europe. The Hadassah Medical Center in Jerusalem has a notable record. Israel's willingness to absorb more than five hundred thousand Russians, Ethiopians, and Asians is a remarkable act of faith and courage. And the country's way of coping with Palestinian restiveness and international Arab boycott policies has won much admiration in America. Israel's armies have been generally victorious; four wars were fought between 1948 and 1973 before the Arabs realized that Israel was not going to disappear. Since 1974 discretion has generally prevailed over valor in Israeli policy (though the interlude of the Lebanese War in 1982–83 was an exception). In 1979 the Egyptians and the Israelis signed a formal peace. In 1993 and 1994 agreements were concluded with the Palestinians and the Jordanians, and an accord seemed thinkable even with the Syrians—all this thanks to American efforts. American Jews will never forget that Israel is the only country in the world where they can go as of right; Israel's emotional impact on all Jews is exhilarating. American Jews, however, have not made aliyah. America is their home; Israel is for those Jews who need refuge or seek to improve themselves.

By the 1960s, to be sure, Israel had become in reality a client state of the Americans. The United States indicated a strong readiness to support Israel with armaments and with billions of dollars in grants. The basis for this relationship is complex: The politicians in Washington have hoped that American Jewish voters would never forget the source of all these benefits, but it is at least equally true that a sturdy democratic Israel is America's most reliable friend in the unstable, authoritarian, and oil-rich Middle East. The huge sums given Israel by America's Jews were dispatched via the Zionist-dominated Jewish Agency, though American Jewish leaders have not always found the agency's use of the funds to accord with American standards of strict accountability. If Israel ever stops aspiring to become or to be seen as an ideal polity, the love affair between the two major Jewries will cool (but it is unlikely ever to fade completely).

American Jews will always help Israel and, when necessary, send it billions, but will never owe allegiance to its government. Israel may claim world Jewish leadership, but American Jewry exercises it. As the twenty-first century dawns, the American Jewish community effectively asserts: The Law does *not* come forth from Zion, the word of the Lord does *not* go forth from Jerusalem.

WILL THE AMERICAN JEWISH COMMUNITY SURVIVE?

The twentieth century, in a way the greatest if also the most tragic in diaspora history, witnessed the rebirth of a Jewish state and the achievements of American Jewry. Will American Jewry survive? As early as the 1820s, an eminent American politician maintained that Jews could not survive unless persecuted, but he has been proven wrong. Jewry here has prospered without persecution. Intermarriage is obviously a major threat, and it is uncontestable that hundreds of thousands of "Jews," children of at least one Jewish parent, have assimilated completely and are no longer members of the Jewish community. Thus far "outreach," salvaging a few, has succeeded; it remains to be seen how many will be saved in the future. In appealing to Americans of Jewish descent, men, women, and children who have turned away from their ancestral people, the Reformers have been the boldest and most innovative.

What keeps Jews Jewish? Ethnicity is a principal factor. The Holocaust has moved many. The Israeli wars have enkindled them. Jewish nationalism has provided a haven for many secularists. Then there is the *davka* Jew: determined to remain Jewish, come what may; anti-Jewish rejection serves only to fire this individual's Jewish loyalties. Many Jews are proud of Jewish progress in the arts and sciences, admire Israel, and exult in the prophetic exhortations, the last and best hope of humankind. They are an organic body with the will to survive. After all, despite innumerable obstacles they have persisted for the last twenty-five hundred years. Possibly the most successful factor making for survival has been adaptation. Jews have learned to live comfortably in two cultures, the American and the Judaic. They have learned to balance acculturation and survival. Adaptation of course varies with the individual: The more one is an American, the less in all probability one is a Jew. But experience teaches that one may be only 5 percent Jewish yet that 5 percent will be precious and potent.

Synthesis is the essence of Jewish history. The Jews may worship the Golden Calf and yet reach out for the Ten Commandments. The core Jew elects to stay in the Jewish community and does not want to be lost among the faceless and amorphous millions. Every child of Abraham has his or her own niche, whether a Brooklyn Hassid or a justice of the U.S. Supreme Court. Being Jewish is a kind of "insurance" guaranteeing psychic support. And if one can read Hebrew, one can walk into any synagogue in the whole wide world, pick up a prayer book, and be at home. Folkways and folk foods tie Jews to their people. Consider these few lines describing the experience of a Jewish soldier in the Pacific Solomon Islands in March 1943, during World War II:

> The noise [of the bombardment] was indescribable and I never knew whether that particular breath I drew was going to be my last one. But honest, Chaplain—and you will think I was crazy—all I could think of in the midst of that confusion and thunder, all I could think of was a hot pastrami sandwich. If I only had a hot pastrami sandwich! And right there in that foxhole on Guadalcanal, I vowed that if I ever came away from the Solomons alive, the first thing I was going to do when I hit the good old U.S.A. was to buy myself the biggest hot pastrami sandwich in the country.

How can we talk of survival after the reality of the Holocaust? Jews realize that their only salvation lies in their omniterritoriality. Jews must live everywhere, for there are few great countries that over the centuries have spared their Jews. The eleventh-century Jewish commentator, Rashi, told his people—and all succeeding generations—that God had shown

His goodness to the Jews in scattering them among the nations: "If they are scattered they cannot all be annihilated at one fell stroke."

Jews glory in their survival. They refuse to disappear.

Estimates of Jewish Population in the United States, 1654–1992

1654:	25	1870:	200,000
1700:	200–300	1880:	230,000–280,000
1776:	1,000–2,500	1890:	400,000–475,000
1790:	1,243–3,000	1900:	937,800–1,058,135
1800:	2,000–2,500	1910:	1,508,000–2,349,754
1818:	3,000	1920:	3,300,000–3,604,580
1820:	2,650–5,000	1927:	4,228,029
1824:	6,000	1937:	4,641,000–4,831,180
1826:	6,000	1940:	4,770,000–4,975,000
1830:	4,000–6,000	1950:	4,500,000–5,000,000
1840:	15,000	1960:	5,367,000–5,531,500
1848:	50,000	1970:	5,370,000–6,000,000
1850:	50,000–150,000	1980:	5,500,000–5,920,890
1860:	150,000–200,000	1992:	5,828,000

Chronology of American Jewry, 1585–1993

1585   Joachim Gaunse (Ganz) lands on Roanoke Island.

1649   Solomon Franco remains in Boston for a brief period until "warned out."

1654   Twenty-three refugees land in New Amsterdam in August or September. They probably came from Brazil.

1655–64   New Amsterdam has an organized Jewish community.

1664   The English conquer New Amsterdam and rename it New York.

1678   Newport Jews buy a cemetery but there is no permanent community.

1730   New York Jews build their first synagogue, Shearith Israel.

1733   Savannah has an organized Jewish community. It does not become a permanent community until the 1790s.

1740   The British Plantation Act offers Jews a limited form of citizenship.

1740s   Philadelphia Jewry has a cemetery and conducts services.

1745   The last time Portuguese is used in the official records of Shearith Israel, New York.

1750s   Newport has an organized Jewish community.

1750	Charleston, South Carolina, has an organized Jewish community.
1755	New York Jewry has an all-day school.
1760s	Philadelphia Jewry has an organized Jewish community. Montreal has an organized Jewish community.
1763	Newport builds its first synagogue.
1776	The British colonies in North America emerge as the United States of America.
1777	New York State emancipates its Jews.
1780s	Richmond has an organized Jewish community.
1783	Philadelphia Jewry establishes the first immigrant aid society in the United States.
1784	Charleston, South Carolina, Jewry establishes its first social welfare organization.
1787	The Northwest Territory Act offers Jews equality in all future territories and states.
1788	The United States Constitution is adopted by a majority of the states. Under federal laws—but not state laws—Jews are given full rights.
1791	The Bill of Rights becomes part of the Constitution. The First Amendment guarantees freedom of religion.
1796	Dr. Levi Myers of Georgetown, South Carolina, is the first Jew to serve in a state legislature.
1801	Charleston, South Carolina, establishes the first American Jewish orphan care society.
1802	The first United States Ashkenazic synagogue, Rodeph Shalom, is established in Philadelphia.

1819	Rebecca Gratz helps organize the Female Hebrew Benevolent Society.
1824	Charleston, South Carolina, Jewry organizes the first Reform Jewish religious group in the United States, the Reformed Society of Israelites.
1825	Mordecai Manuel Noah proposes the founding of a Jewish colony on Grand Island, New York.
1829	Isaac Leeser, the father of American modern Orthodoxy, becomes the hazzan-minister-rabbi of Congregation Mikveh Israel in Philadelphia.
1830s	Substantial numbers of German Jews begin immigrating to the United States.
1837	The first Passover Haggadah is printed in America and published by S. H. Jackson.
1838	Rebecca Gratz establishes the first Jewish Sunday school in the United States in Philadelphia. It is Orthodox.
1840	Abraham Rice, the first diplomate rabbi to officiate in America, takes office in Baltimore.
	American Jews protest the persecution of Jews in Damascus.
1840s–50s	Leo Merzbacher, Max Lilienthal, Isaac Mayer Wise, Bernhard Felsenthal, David Einhorn, Samuel Adler, and other German rabbis come to America to serve the new German congregations and are active in promoting reforms in Judaism.
1841	Charleston's Beth Elohim becomes the first permanent Reform Jewish synagogue in the United States.
	David Levy Yulee is the first Jew to serve in Congress and also to become a United States senator.

389

1843 Isaac Leeser, hazzan of the Sephardic synagogue of Philadelphia, publishes the *Occident*, a strong advocate of Orthodoxy.

B'nai B'rith, a mutual aid and fraternal order, is established.

1846 Isaac Mayer Wise, the organizer of the American Jewish Reform movement, comes to the United States from Bohemia.

1852 The first East European congregation in New York City is organized.

1853 Isaac Leeser publishes an English translation of the Bible.

1854 Isaac Mayer Wise becomes rabbi of Congregation B'nai Yeshurun in Cincinnati, where he remains until his death. He begins to publish the *Israelite*, later the *American Israelite*.

1855 David Einhorn, a theological liberal, arrives in the United States.

Rabbi Isaac M. Wise calls a meeting in Cleveland, Ohio, to organize American Jewry religiously on a national scale. It is unsuccessful.

1859 In November the Board of Delegates of American Israelites is organized, the first attempt by American Jews to create an overall national Jewish organization.

The Jews of the United States meet in several towns, protesting the action of the papal authorities who seized Edgar Mortara, a Jewish child, and reared him as a Catholic.

1860 Morris Raphall becomes the first rabbi to open a session of the United States Congress with prayer.

1861–65 At least three Union officers of Jewish origin are brevetted generals during the Civil War.

1862 The United States government appoints army chaplains to serve Jews.

Judah P. Benjamin, formerly a United States senator, is appointed secretary of state of the Confederacy.

1862 On December 17 General U. S. Grant expels some Jews from the area occupied by the Army of the Tennessee on the charge that they engaged in commercial traffic with the South. The expulsion decree, General Orders Number 11, is speedily revoked by Lincoln.

1863 Samuel Gompers, the founder of the American Federation of Labor, lands in New York.

1865 Jacob H. Schiff, later a national Jewish leader, arrives in New York from Germany.

1867 Isaac Leeser establishes Maimonides College, a short-lived rabbinical school.

1869 A group of Reform rabbis under the leadership of Samuel Hirsch and David Einhorn meets in Philadelphia to publish the first statement on the Jewish Reform position in America.

1871 *Hazofeh B'eretz Hahadashah*, the first Hebrew weekly in America, is published.

1873 The Union of American Hebrew Congregations is established in Cincinnati. Its founders hope it will embrace all American synagogues.

1875 The Hebrew Union College is established in Cincinnati, Ohio, to prepare rabbis for all types of American Jewish synagogues.

1876 Felix Adler creates the Ethical Culture movement.

1877 New Hampshire is the last state to offer Jews political equality.

Joseph Seligman is refused admission to the Grand Union Hotel in Saratoga Springs, New York.

1880   The Union of American Hebrew Congregations publishes the first census of American Jewry. Estimate: 250,000.

1881   The pogroms in Russia impel East European Jews to immigrate to the United States in large numbers.

1882   A Yiddish play is performed in New York City.

1885   The Pittsburgh Platform is adopted by a number of left-wing Reform rabbis.

Kasriel H. Sarasohn launches the *Tageblatt*, the first Yiddish daily paper, in New York City.

1886   The Jewish Theological Seminary Association is formed.

The Conservative movement is established in New York City.

1887   The Jewish Theological Seminary, the nursery of Conservative Judaism, opens in New York City.

1888   The Jewish Publication Society of America is founded.

Several anti-Semitic works are published in New York City.

Socialists establish the United Hebrew Trades in New York City.

Rabbi Jacob Joseph is elected chief rabbi of New York's Orthodox. He accomplishes little, if anything.

1889   The Central Conference of American Rabbis—basically a Reform institution—is established by Isaac M. Wise.

1891   Baron Maurice de Hirsch, European philanthropist, establishes the Baron de Hirsch Fund to further American Jewry, especially the East European émigrés.

1892	The American Jewish Historical Society starts its work.
1893	The Educational Alliance, a settlement house, opens on New York City's Lower East Side.
	The National Council of Jewish Women is founded.
	The Jewish Chautauqua Society is organized.
1895	The Central Conference of American Jewish Rabbis rejects the authority of halakah, Jewish traditional oral law.
1897	The first American yeshiva of a European type (Rabbi Isaac Elchanan Theological Seminary) is founded in New York City.
	At a meeting of the Central Conference of American Rabbis, Rabbi Isaac M. Wise denounces the new Zionism of Theodor Herzl.
	The socialist *Jewish Daily Forward* publishes its first issue in New York City.
1898	The Union of Orthodox Jewish Congregations of America is established.
	The Federation of American Zionists is established in New York City.
1899	The National Conference of Jewish Charities is organized.
	American Jewish Yearbook begins publication.
1900	The Arbeter Ring (Workmen's Circle), dedicated to educational, social, and recreational purposes, commences its activities.
	The Rabbinical Assembly, the organization of Conservative rabbis, is established.
	East European labor groups organize the International Ladies' Garment Workers Union.

1902 The Union of Orthodox Rabbis of the United States and Canada is founded.

   Solomon Schechter is elected head of the Jewish Theological Seminary. He furthers Conservatism as a separate Jewish denomination.

1903 Reacting to the murder of Jews in Kishinev, Russia, American Jewry moves to become a more tightly knit community.

   Kaufmann Kohler is elected president of the Hebrew Union College.

1906 The twelve-volume *Jewish Encyclopedia* is completed.

   The American Jewish Committee, a secular defense organization, is established by the American Jewish elite.

   Jewish students at Harvard establish the Menorah Society, a cultural organization.

   During this year 153,748 Jewish immigrants arrive in the United States; most are East Europeans.

1907 Rabbi Stephen S. Wise establishes the Free Synagogue.

   Sidney Hillman arrives in the United States. Later he becomes a famous labor leader and a prominent New Deal politician.

   Dropsie College for Hebrew and Cognate Learning is chartered in Philadelphia as a graduate school awarding the Ph.D. degree.

1909 Gifts from Jacob H. Schiff lead to the establishment of Jewish teachers' training programs at the Jewish Theological Seminary and the Hebrew Union College.

   The Kehillah (Jewish community) of New York City is established. This is an (unsuccessful) attempt to organize New York City's East European Jews. Judah L. Magnes is its head.

The Hebrew Sheltering and Immigrant Aid Society (HIAS) is formed.

1910   The first Yiddish secular school system is established by the socialist Zionists, Poale Zion.

1911   American Jewry succeeds in inducing Congress to abrogate the 1832 treaty with Russia because the czarist regime would not honor an American passport carried by an American Jew.

A fire in the Triangle Shirtwaist Factory costs the lives of some 140 women. Most were Jews.

1912   Louis Marshall, one of America's most distinguished Jewish layman, becomes president of the American Jewish Committee.

Young Israel is organized on the Lower East Side in New York.

Hadassah, the Women's Zionist Organization of America, is established by Henrietta Szold.

1913   The B'nai B'rith Anti-Defamation League sets out to limit anti-Jewish agitation in the United States.

Labor Zionist Alliance (formerly Farband Labor Zionist Order) is established.

The Intercollegiate Menorah Association is organized.

The United Synagogue of Conservative Judaism is organized.

The Promised Land by Mary Antin is published. It is an immigrant's evaluation of the United States.

1914–15   The American Jewish Joint Distribution Committee unites various American Jewish ethnic groups to salvage East European Jewry.

1915   Leo Frank is lynched in Marietta, Georgia.

Rabbi Isaac Elchanan Theological Seminary and Yeshiva Etz Chaim (an Orthodox elementary school) are united under Bernard Revel.

Moses Alexander, a German Jewish immigrant, is elected governor of Idaho.

Henry Hurwitz edits the *Menorah Journal*.

1916   Louis D. Brandeis is appointed to the United States Supreme Court.

1917   An English translation of the Hebrew Bible is published by the Jewish Publication Society of America.

United States enters World War I. About 200,000 Jews served in the armed forces.

The National Jewish Welfare Board is created to serve the religious needs of American Jews in the army and navy.

The British government issues the Balfour Declaration favoring the establishment of a homeland for Jews in Palestine.

On November 7 the Bolsheviks gain control of Russia.

Jewish Telegraphic Agency, serving the Jewish and general press, is established.

1918   The first American Jewish Congress meets in Philadelphia and sets out to induce the great powers meeting in Paris to establish a Jewish homeland in Palestine and to protect East European Jewry through the granting of minority rights.

Yiddish Art Theater is initiated by Maurice Schwartz.

The Women's League for Conservative Judaism is formed.

1920s   These years are a time of much anti-Jewish sentiment in the United States. Most notable is the anti-Jewish activity of Henry Ford, 1920–27.

1920   Henry Ford's *Dearborn Independent* begins publishing anti-Semitic propaganda, including the *Protocols of the Elders of Zion.*

1921   *Hadoar* (Hebrew periodical of Histadruth Ivrith) begins publication. It emphasizes the primacy of Hebrew in Jewish culture.

1921, 1924 The Immigrant Acts of 1921 and 1924 close America to East European Jews and others. This legislation is motivated, in part, by pseudo-scientific racial concepts.

1922   Reconstructionism, created by Mordecai M. Kaplan, creates its first organized manifestation, the Society for the Advancement of Judaism.

            Agudath Israel of America, an Orthodox organization, is established.

            A permanent American Jewish Congress representing the Zionist-minded East European element is founded.

            Hebrew Theological College opens in Chicago.

            Stephen S. Wise founds the Jewish Institute of Religion, training rabbis (mostly for the Reform group) with a more national orientation than that given by Hebrew Union College.

1923   The first B'nai B'rith Hillel Foundation is established at the University of Illinois at Champaign-Urbana.

1925   The Synagogue Council of America is organized.

1926   The World Union for Progressive Judaism is founded.

1927   A survey shows that there are Jews in 9,712 towns and rural districts. There are 4,228,000 Jews, 17,500 Jewish organizations, and 3,118 congregations in the United States.

1928 The National Conference of Christians and Jews is established to further interfaith activities in the United States.

The Rabbi Isaac Elchanan Yeshiva grows into Yeshiva College, the first general institution of higher education under Jewish auspices.

1929 The Union of Sephardic Congregations is organized.

The American Academy for Jewish Research is established.

The Jewish Agency is enlarged to embrace Zionists and non-Zionists to further the Jewish community in Palestine.

1930s In the late 1930s German Jewish refugees start arriving in the United States.

1932 The Council of Jewish Federations is established. It advises two hundred Jewish federations in the United States and Canada.

1933 Nazis gain strength in Germany and anti-Semitic groups appear in this country.

1934 The Jewish Labor Committee is established.

Judaism as a Civilization by Mordecai Kaplan is published, and the *Reconstructionist* magazine appears.

1935 The Central Conference of American Rabbis is taken over by Zionists in a political coup, one of the first steps toward the founding of neo-Reform.

The Rabbinical Council of America, an organization of the English-speaking Orthodox rabbis, is formed.

1937 A survey shows 4,771,000 Jews in the United States and 3,728 congregations.

The Central Conference of American Rabbis adopts a somewhat pro-Zionist program.

1938   Father Charles E. Coughlin, a Catholic priest, denounces the Jews on the radio. His audience numbers in the millions.

In July an international conference meets at Évian to help refugee Jews. Very little is accomplished.

1939   The British White Paper on Palestine is issued and immigration to that country is reduced to a trickle. World War II begins in Europe and the first news of the slaughter of the Polish Jews reaches America.

Felix Frankfurter becomes an associate justice of the United States Supreme Court.

The United Jewish Appeal is founded to support Jewish humanitarian programs in the United States and abroad.

1940   The YIVO Institute for Jewish Research moves from Vilna, Lithuania, to New York City.

The Jewish Reconstructionist Foundation is formed by Mordecai Kaplan.

1941–45   Over five hundred thousand Jews serve in the American armed forces during World War II. There are numerous Jewish generals and several Jewish admirals.

1942   American Zionists adopt the Biltmore Program, demanding the creation of a Jewish Palestine.

Jews in the United States become aware of the massacre of Jews in Eastern Europe by the invading Germans.

Some anti-Zionist Reform rabbis and anti-Zionist laymen organize the American Council for Judaism, the one organization in American life that upholds the position that the Jews are only a religious group and in no way a nationalist group.

1943   The American Jewish Conference recommends that Palestine become a Jewish commonwealth.

Jews become aware of the Holocaust. The American authorities, including high-ranking Jewish leaders, do little to induce Roosevelt to admit European Jewish refugees in substantial numbers to the United States. Secretary of the Treasury Henry Morgenthau Jr. is an exception.

The Central Conference of American Rabbis adopts a resolution agreeing that both the Zionist and anti-Zionist positions are compatible with Reform Judaism.

Samuel Belkin becomes president of Yeshiva College.

Maurice N. Eisendrath becomes president of the Union of American Hebrew Congregations.

1944   President Roosevelt establishes the War Refugee Board.

The National Society for Hebrew Day Schools (Torah Umesorah) is founded.

1945   Yeshiva College becomes Yeshiva University.

The United States unleashes the atom bomb on the Japanese. Jews are among the nuclear scientists who perfect the atom, hydrogen, and neutron bombs.

1945–52   Under directives of President Truman, hundreds of thousand of displaced persons are admitted to the United States; many are Jews.

1947   The Jewish Museum of the Jewish Theological Seminary of America moves into the former Warburg mansion in New York City.

On November 29 the United Nations General Assembly votes to divide Palestine into two sovereign states, one Jewish and one Arab.

The American Jewish Archives is established on the campus of Hebrew Union College in Cincinnati.

1948   Brandeis University is established in Waltham, Massachusetts, as the first secular university in the United States under Jewish auspices.

On May 14 Israel declares its independence. The United States government immediately recognizes the new state.

On May 15 the British leave Palestine; the Arab armies soon attack Israel.

1950   The Hebrew Union College and Jewish Institute of Religion merge.

Rabbi Menachem Mendel Schneersohn succeeds his father-in-law as rebbe of the Lubavitch Hassidim.

1951   The major Reform organization, the Union of American Hebrew Congregations, is moved from Cincinnati to New York City.

1952   The Federal Republic of Germany signs an agreement to pay Holocaust survivors and Jewish institutions outside Israel $822 million as reparations for the Holocaust.

1954   Stern College for Women, first liberal arts women's college under Jewish auspices, is opened.

1955   The Leo Baeck Institute is established in New York City.

The Conference of Presidents of Major American Jewish Organizations, one of American Jewry's most powerful organizations, is formed.

1956   Statistics in the *American Jewish Year Book* show a great increase in Jewish synagogue membership in the previous fifteen years, particularly in the Reform and Conservative groups, and a great increase in Jewish religious school attendance.

Israel, provoked by Arab marauders, invades Egyptian territory and is joined by England and France, but all withdraw their forces under United States and Soviet pressure.

1964   Congress passes the Civil Rights Act that, on paper at least, fully guarantees all rights to blacks and Jews.

1965   An Immigration and Nationality Act is passed. The quota system is revised, but the admission of immigrants is still rigorously limited.

1967   Israel emerges victorious in the Six-Day War against Arab enemies.

1968   The Reconstructionist Rabbinical College is established.

1969   The Association for Jewish Studies is formed.

1971   Touro College is founded in New York City.

1972   The Hebrew Union College ordains the first woman rabbi.

1973   The Yom Kippur War begins when Egypt and Syria attack Israel. Israel again emerges victorious.

1975   The United Nations General Assembly declares Zionism "a form of racism and racial discrimination." This resolution is repealed years later.

1979   Israel and Egypt sign a peace treaty.

1983   The Jewish Theological Seminary faculty votes to ordain women as rabbis.

1984   The Central Conference of American Rabbis adopts a resolution accepting the principle of patrilineal identity.

1985–90 The U.S.S.R. falls apart. Numerous Russian Jews immigrate to the United States.

1993   The Israelis and Palestinian Arabs seek to reconcile their political differences.

Bibliography

Abelow. Samuel P. *History of Brooklyn Jewry*. Brooklyn, 1937

Adler, Cyrus. *I Have Considered the Years*. Philadelphia, 1941.

———, ed. *Jacob Schiff: His Life and Letters*. 2 vols. Garden City, N.Y., 1928.

———, ed. *The Jewish Theological Seminary of America: Semi-Centennial Volume*. New York, 1939.

———, and Aaron M. Margalith. *With Firmness in the Right: American Diplomatic Action Affecting Jews, 1840–1945*. New York, 1946.

Adler, Frank. *Roots in a Moving Stream: The Centennial History of Congregation B'nai Jehudah of Kansas City, 1870–1970*. Kansas City, 1972.

Adler, Selig, and Thomas E. Connolly. *From Ararat to Suburbia: The History of the Jewish Community of Buffalo*. Philadelphia, 1960.

American Jewish Archives. *Manuscript Catalog of the American Jewish Archives, Cincinnati*. Boston, 1971. First supplement, 1977.

American Jewish Year Book, 1899 to date.

American Jews in World War II: The Story of 550,000 Fighters for Freedom. 2 vols. New York, 1947.

Antin, Mary. *The Promised Land*. Boston, 1912.

Bauer, Yehuda. *My Brother's Keeper: A History of the American Jewish Joint Distribution Committee 1929–1939*. Philadelphia, 1974.

Benjamin, Israel Joseph. *Three Years in America, 1859–1862*. 2 vols. Philadelphia, 1956.

Bentwich, N. *For Zion's Sake: A Biography of Judah Magnes.* Philadelphia, 1954.

———. *Solomon Schechter: A Biography.* Philadelphia, 1938.

Berger, Graenum. *Black Jews in America: A Documentary With Commentary.* New York, 1978.

Berman, Myron. *Richmond's Jewry, 1769–1976.* Charlottesville, 1979.

Bernheimer, Charles S., ed. *The Russian Jew in the United States: Studies of Social Conditions in New York, Philadelphia, and Chicago, with a Description of Rural Settlements.* Philadelphia, 1905.

Bernstein, Herman. *The Truth About the Protocols of Zion: A Complete Exposure.* New York, 1935.

Blau, Joseph L., and Salo W. Baron. *The Jews of the United States, 1790–1840: A Documentary History.* 3 vols. New York, 1963.

Blum, Isidor. *The Jews of Baltimore.* Baltimore, 1910.

Bogen, Boris D. *Jewish Philanthropy: An Exposition of Principles and Methods of Jewish Social Service in the United States.* New York, 1917.

Brandes, Joseph. *Immigrants to Freedom: Jewish Communities in Rural New Jersey Since 1882.* Philadelphia, 1971.

Breck, Allen D. *A Centennial History of the Jews of Colorado, 1859–1959.* Denver, 1960.

Bregstone, Philip P. *Chicago and Its Jews: A Cultural History.* Chicago, 1933.

Cahan, Abraham. *The Education of Abraham Cahan.* Philadelphia, 1969.

Chyet, Stanley F. *Lopez of Newport: Colonial American Merchant Prince.* Detroit, 1970.

———, ed. *Lives and Voices: A Collection of American Jewish Memoirs.* Philadelphia, 1972.

Cohen, Naomi W. *A Dual Heritage: The Public Career of Oscar S. Straus.* Philadelphia, 1969.

————. *Encounter with Emancipation: German Jews in the United States, 1830–1914.* Philadelphia, 1984.

————. *Not Free to Desist: The American Jewish Committee, 1906–1966.* Philadelphia, 1972.

Campbell, Monroe. *The First Fifty Years: The History of the National Council of Jewish Women.* New York, 1943.

Critical Studies in American Jewish History; Selected Articles from American Jewish Archives. 3 vols. Cincinnati, 1971.

Davidson, Gabriel. *Our Jewish Farmers and the Story of the Jewish Agricultural Society.* New York, 1943.

Dawidowicz, Lucy S. *On Equal Terms: Jews in America 1881–1891.* New York, 1982.

Davis, Moshe. *The Emergence of Conservative Judaism: The Historical School in 19th Century America.* Philadelphia, 1963.

Dinnerstein, Leonard. *The Leo Frank Case.* New York, 1968.

Dobkowski, Michael N., ed. *Jewish-American Voluntary Organizations.* Westport, Conn., 1986.

Editors of Fortune. *Jews in America.* New York, 1936.

Elazar, Daniel. *Community and Polity: The Organizational Dynamics of American Jewry.* Philadelphia, 1976.

Elbogen, Ismar. *A Century of Jewish Life.* Philadelphia, 1944.

Elzas, Barnett A. *The Jews of South Carolina, from the Earliest Times to the Present Day.* Philadelphia, 1905.

Encyclopaedia Judaica. 16 vols. New York, 1971-72.

Endelman, Judith. *The Jewish Community of Indianapolis, 1849 to the Present.* Bloomington, 1984.

Epstein, Melech. *The Jew and Communism: The Story of Early Communist Victories and Ultimate Defeats in the Jewish Community, USA, 1919–1941.* New York, 1959.

———. *Jewish Labor in U.S.A. 1914–1952: An Industrial, Political, and Cultural History of the Jewish Labor Movement.* New York, 1953.

Ezekiel, Herbert T., and Gaston Lichtenstein. *The History of the Jews of Richmond, from 1769 to 1917.* Richmond, 1917.

Feibelman, Julian B. *A Social and Economic Study of the New Orleans Jewish Community.* Philadelphia, 1941.

Fein, Isaac. *The Making of an American Jewish Community: The History of Baltimore Jewry from 1773 to 1920.* Philadelphia, 1971.

Feingold, Henry. *The Politics of Rescue: The Roosevelt Administration and the Holocaust, 1938–1945.* New Brunswick, N.J., 1970.

———. *Zion in America.* New York, 1974.

Finkelstein, Louis, ed. *The Jews: Their History, Culture and Religion.* 2 vols. New York, 1960.

Fish, Sidney M. *Aaron Levy: Founder of Aaronsburg.* New York, 1951.

Friedman, Lee M. *Early American Jews.* Cambridge, 1934.

———. *Jewish Pioneers and Patriots.* Philadelphia, 1942.

———. *Pilgrims in a New Land.* Philadelphia, 1948.

Friedman, Theodore, and Robert Gordis. *Jewish Life in America.* New York, 1955.

Gal, Allon. *Brandeis of Boston.* Cambridge, 1980.

Gale, Joseph, ed. *Eastern Union: The Development of a Jewish Community.* Elizabeth, N.J., 1958.

Gartner, Lloyd P. *The History of the Jews of Cleveland.* Cleveland, 1978.

———. *Jewish Education in the United States: A Documentary History.* New York, 1969.

Glazer, Nathan. *American Judaism*. Chicago, 1972.

Glazer, Simon. *The Jews of Iowa: A Complete History and Accurate Account of Their Religious, Social, Economical and Educational Progress in This State; a History of the Jews of Europe, North and South America in Modern Times; and a Brief History of Iowa*. Des Moines, 1904.

Goldstein, Israel. *A Century of Judaism in New York: B'nai Jeshurun 1825–1925*. New York, 1930.

Goldstein, Sidney, and Calvin Goldschneider. *Three Generations in a Jewish Community*. Englewood Cliffs, N.J., 1968.

Goren, Arthur A. *The American Jews*. Cambridge, 1982.

———. *Dissenter in Zion: From the Writings of Judah L. Magnes*. Cambridge, 1982.

———. *New York Jews and the Quest for Community: The Kehillah Experiment, 1908–1922*. New York, 1970.

Grinstein, Hyman B. *The Rise of the Jewish Community of New York, 1654–1860*. Philadelphia, 1945.

Grusd, Edward. *B'nai B'rith: The Story of a Covenant*. New York, 1966.

Gurock, Jeffrey S. *American Jewish History: A Bibliographical Guide*. New York, 1983.

———. *When Harlem Was Jewish, 1870–1930*. New York, 1979.

Gutstein, Morris A. *Priceless Heritage: The Epic Growth of Nineteenth Century Chicago Jewry*. New York, 1953.

———. *The Story of the Jews of Newport: Two and a Half Centuries of Judaism, 1658–1908*. New York, 1936.

Halpern, Ben. *The American Jew: A Zionist Analysis*. New York, 1956.

Handlin, Oscar. *Adventure in Freedom: Three Hundred Years of Jewish Life in America*. New York, 1954.

Hapgood, Hutchins. *The Spirit of the Ghetto: Studies of the Jewish Quarter of New York*. Cambridge, 1967.

Harap, Louis. *Creative Awakening: The Jewish Presence in Twentieth-Century American Literature, 1900–1940s.* New York, 1987.

————. *Dramatic Encounters: The Jewish Presence in Twentieth-Century American Drama, Poetry, and Humor and the Black-Jewish Literary Relationship.* New York, 1987.

————. *The Image of the Jew in American Literature: From Early Republic to Mass Immigration.* Philadelphia, 1974.

————. *In the Mainstream: The Jewish Presence in Twentieth-Century American Literature, 1950s–1980s.* New York, 1987.

Harris, Leon. *Merchant Princes: An Intimate History of Jewish Families Who Built Great Department Stores.* New York, 1979.

Hebrew Union College-Jewish Institute of Religion. *Dictionary Catalog of the Klau Library Cincinnati.* 32 vols. Boston, 1964.

Helmreich, William B. *The World of the Yeshiva: An Intimate Portrait of Orthodox Jewry.* New York, 1982.

Herscher, Uri D. *Jewish Agricultural Utopias in America, 1880–1910.* Detroit, 1981.

————, and Stanley F. Chyet, eds. *A Socialist Perspective on Jews, America and Immigration.* Cincinnati, 1980.

Hershkowitz, Leo, ed. *Wills of Early New York Jews (1704–1799).* New York, 1967.

————, and Isidore S. Meyer, eds. *The Lee Max Friedman Collection of American Jewish Colonial Correspondence: Letters of the Franks Family (1733–1748).* Waltham, Mass., 1968.

Hertzberg, Arthur. *The Jews in America: Four Centuries of an Uneasy Encounter: A History.* New York, 1989.

Hertzberg, Steven. *Strangers Within the Gate City: The Jews of Atlanta 1845–1915.* Philadelphia, 1978.

Higham, John. *Strangers in the Land: Patterns of American Nativism.* New York, 1970.

Hourwich, Isaac A. *Immigration and Labor: The Economic Aspects of European Immigration to the United States.* New York, 1922.

Howe, Irving. *World of Our Fathers.* New York, 1976.

Janowsky, Oscar I., ed. *The American Jew: A Composite Portrait.* New York, 1942.

———, ed. *The American Jew: A Reappraisal.* Philadelphia, 1964.

———. *The Jews and Minority Rights, 1898–1919.* New York, 1933.

Jewish Communal Register of New York City, 1917–1918, The. New York, 1918.

Jewish Encyclopedia, The: A Descriptive Record of the History, Religion, Literature, and Customs of the Jewish People from the Earliest Times to the Present Day. 12 vols. New York, 1901–06.

Jewish People, The: Past and Present. 4 vols. New York, 1946–55.

Jick, Leon A. *The Americanization of the Synagogue, 1820–1870.* Hanover, N.H., 1976.

Joselit, Jena. *Our Gang: Jewish Crime and the New York Jewish Community, 1900–1940.* Bloomington, 1983.

Joseph, Samuel. *History of the Baron de Hirsch Fund: The Americanization of the Jewish Immigrant.* 1935.

———. *Jewish Immigration to the United States from 1881 to 1910.* New York, 1914.

Kagan, Solomon R. *Jewish Contributions to Medicine in America from Colonial Times to the Present.* Boston, 1939.

Kallen, Horace P. *Cultural Pluralism and the American Idea: An Essay in Social Philosophy.* Philadelphia, 1956.

Kanter, Kenneth Aaron. *The Jews of Tin Pan Alley: The Jewish Contribution to American Popular Music, 1830–1940.* New York, 1982.

Kaplan, Mordecai. *Judaism as a Civilization: Toward a Reconstruction of American Jewish Life.* New York, 1967.

Karff, Samuel E., ed. *Hebrew Union College-Jewish Institute of Religion at One Hundred Years*. Cincinnati, 1976.

Karp, Abraham. *A History of the United Synagogue of America, 1913–1963*. New York, 1964.

————, ed. *The Jewish Experience in America: Selected Studies from the Publications of the American Jewish Historical Society*. 5 vols. Waltham, Mass., 1969.

Karpf, Maurice J. *Jewish Community Organization in the United States: An Outline of Types of Organizations, Activities, and Problems*. New York, 1938.

Katsh, Abraham I. *Hebraic Contributions to American Life*. New York, 1941.

————. *Hebrew in American Higher Education: And an Analysis of Hebrew Influence on American Life*. New York, 1941.

————. *Hebrew Language, Literature, and Culture in American Institutions of Higher Learning*. New York, 1950.

Katz, Irving I. *The Beth El Story, with a History of the Jews in Michigan before 1850 and Three Hundred Years in America by Dr. Jacob R. Marcus*. Detroit, 1955.

Kayserling, Mayer. *Christopher Columbus and the Participation of the Jews in the Spanish and Portuguese Discoveries*. New York, 1894.

Klaperman, Gilbert. *The Story of Yeshiva University, The First Jewish University in America*. New York, 1969.

Kohn, S. Joshua. *The Jewish Community of Utica, New York, 1847–1954*. New York, 1959.

Korn, Bertram Wallace. *American Jewry and the Civil War*. Philadelphia, 1951.

————. *The American Reaction to the Mortara Case: 1858–1859*. Cincinnati, 1957.

————. *The Early Jews of New Orleans*. Waltham, Mass., 1969.

————. *Eventful Years and Experiences*. Cincinnati, 1954.

————. *Jews and Negro Slavery in the Old South*. Elkins Park, Pa., 1961.

Landesman, Alter F. *Brownsville: The Birth, Development and Passing of a Jewish Community in New York*. New York, 1969.

Landman, Isaac, ed. *The Universal Jewish Encyclopedia: An Authoritative and Popular Presentation of Jews and Judaism since the Earliest Times*. New York, 1939–43.

Lang, Harry, and Morris C. Feinstone, eds. *Gewerkschaften: Issued by the United Hebrew Trades on the Occasion of Its Fiftieth Anniversary as a Trade Union Central Body in Greater New York*. New York, 1938.

Learsi, Rufus. *The Jews in America: A History*. Cleveland, 1954.

Lebeson, Anita Libman. *Jewish Pioneers in America, 1492–1848*. New York, 1931.

————. *Pilgrim People*. New York, 1950.

LeMaster, Carolyn Gray. *A Corner of the Tapestry: A History of the Jewish Experience in Arkansas, 1820s–1990s*. Fayetteville, 1994.

Levine, Allan E. *An American Jewish Bibliography: A List of Books and Pamphlets by Jews or Relating to Them Printed in the United States from 1851 to 1875, Which Are in the Possession of the Hebrew Union College-Jewish Institute of Religion Library in Cincinnati*. Cincinnati, 1959.

Lifson, David. *The Yiddish Theater in America*. New York, 1965.

Linfield, Harry S. *The Jews in the United States, 1927: A Study of Their Number and Distribution*. New York, 1929.

————. *Statistics of Jews and Jewish Organizations: Historical Review of Ten Censuses, 1850–1937*. New York, 1939.

London, Hannah R. *Portraits of Jews by Gilbert Stuart and Other Early American Artists*. New York, 1927.

Lubove, Roy. *The Progressives and the Slums: Tenement House Reform in New York City, 1890–1917*. Pittsburgh, 1962.

411

Lurie, Harry L. *A Heritage Affirmed: The Jewish Federation Movement in America*. Philadelphia, 1961.

Marcus, Jacob Rader. *The American Jewish Woman: A Documentary History*. New York, 1981.

―――. *The American Jewish Woman, 1654–1980*. New York, 1980.

―――. *American Jewry, Documents, Eighteenth Century: Primarily Hitherto Unpublished Manuscripts*. Cincinnati, 1959.

―――. *The Colonial American Jew, 1492–1776*. 3 vols. Detroit, 1970.

―――. *Early American Jewry*. 2 vols. Philadelphia, 1951–53.

―――. *Memoirs of American Jews, 1775–1865*. 3 vols. Philadelphia, 1955–56.

―――. *United States Jewry, 1776–1985*. 4 vols. Detroit, 1989–93.

―――, and Judith M. Daniels, eds. *The Concise Dictionary of American Jewish Biography*. 2 vols. Brooklyn, 1994.

Margalith, Aaron. *With Firmness in the Right: American Diplomatic Action Affecting Jews, 1840–1945*. New York, 1977.

Markens, Isaac. *The Hebrew in America: A Series of Historical and Biographical Sketches*. New York, 1888.

Mason, Philip P., ed. *Directory of Jewish Archival Institutions*. Detroit, 1975.

Meites, Hyman L. *History of the Jews of Chicago*. Chicago, 1924.

Metzger, Isaac. *A Bintel Brief: Sixty Years of Letters from the Lower East Side to the* Jewish Daily Forward. Garden City, N.Y., 1971.

―――. *A Bintel Brief: Letters to the* Jewish Daily Forward, *1950–1980, Volume II*. New York, 1981.

Meyer, Isidore S., ed. *Early History of Zionism in America*. New York, 1958.

Meyer, Michael A. *Response to Modernity: A History of the Reform Movement in Judaism*. New York, 1988.

Moise, L. C. *Biography of Isaac Harby with an Account of The Reformed Society of Israelites of Charleston, S.C., 1824–1833.* 1931.

Morais, Henry Samuel. *The Jews of Philadelphia: Their History from the Earliest Settlement to the Present Time.* Philadelphia, 1894.

Morris, Robert, and Michael Freund, eds. *Trends and Issues in Jewish Social Welfare in the United States 1899–1952.* Philadelphia, 1966.

Morse, Arthur D. *While Six Million Died: A Chronicle of American Apathy.* New York, 1967.

Nadell, Pamela S., ed. *Conservative Judaism in America.* Westport, Conn., 1988.

Nodel, Julius J., and Alfred Apsler. *The Ties Between: A Century of Judaism on America's Last Frontier.* Portland, Ore., 1959.

Oren, Dan A. *Joining the Club: A History of Jews and Yale.* New Haven, 1985.

Parzen, Herbert. *Architects of Conservative Judaism.* New York, 1964.

Philipson, David, ed. *The Letters of Rebecca Gratz.* Philadelphia, 1929.

———. *My Life as an American Jew.* Cincinnati, 1941.

———. *The Reform Movement in Judaism.* New York, 1931.

Plaut, W. Gunther, ed. *The Growth of Reform Judaism: American and European Sources until 1948.* New York, 1965.

———. *The Jews in Minnesota: The First Seventy-five Years.* New York, 1959.

Pool, David de Sola. *Portraits Etched in Stone: Early Jewish Settlers, 1682–1831.* New York, 1952.

———, and Tamar de Sola Pool. *An Old Faith in the New World: Portraits of Shearith Israel, 1654–1954.* New York, 1955.

Postal, Bernard, and Lionel Koppman. *A Jewish Tourist's Guide to the U.S.* Philadelphia, 1954.

413

Publications of the American Jewish Historical Society. Philadelphia, 1893 to date.

Rabinowitz, Benjamin. *The Young Men's Hebrew Association (1854–1913).* New York, 1948.

Rakeffet-Rothkoff, Aaron. *The Silver Era in American Jewish Orthodoxy: Rabbi Eliezer Silver and His Generation.* New York, 1981.

Raphael, Marc L. *Abba Hillel Silver: A Profile in American Judaism.* New York, 1989.

———. *Jews and Judaism in a Midwestern Community: Columbus, Ohio 1840–1975.* Columbus, 1979.

———. *Profiles in American Judaism: The Reform, Conservative, Orthodox, and Reconstructionist Traditions in Historical Perspective.* New York, 1985.

Reznikoff, Charles, ed. *Louis Marshall: Champion of Liberty, Selected Papers and Addresses.* 2 vols. Philadelphia, 1957.

———, and Uriah Z. Engelman. *The Jews of Charleston: A History of an American Jewish Community.* Philadelphia, 1950.

Rischin, Moses. *An Inventory of American Jewish History.* Cambridge, 1954.

———. *The Promised City: New York Jews, 1870–1918.* Cambridge, 1962.

Robinson, Ira, ed. *Cyrus Adler: Selected Letters.* 2 vols. Philadelphia, 1985.

Robison, Sophia M., ed. *Jewish Population Studies.* New York, 1943.

Rockaway, Robert. *The Jews of Detroit: From the Beginning, 1762–1914.* Detroit, 1986.

Rogoff, Harry. *An East Side Epic: The Life and Work of Meyer London.* New York, 1930.

Rosenbach, A. S. W. *An American Jewish Bibliography: Being a List of Books and Pamphlets by Jews or Relating to Them Printed in the United*

States from the Establishment of the Press in the Colonies until 1850. New York, 1926.

Rosenberg, Stuart E. *The Jewish Community in Rochester, 1843–1925.* New York, 1954.

Rosenbloom, Joseph R. *A Biographical Dictionary of Early American Jews: Colonial Times through 1800.* Lexington, Ky., 1960.

Rosenstock, Morton. *Louis Marshall, Defender of Jewish Rights.* Detroit, 1965.

Rosenthal, Frank. *The Jews of Des Moines: The First Century.* Des Moines, 1957.

Rothkoff, Aaron. *Bernard Revel: Builder of American Jewish Orthodoxy.* Philadelphia, 1972.

Rubin, Saul J. *Third to None: The Saga of Savannah Jewry, 1733–1983.* Savannah, 1983.

Sanders, Ronald. *The Downtown Jews: Portrait of an Immigrant Generation.* New York, 1969.

Sarna, Jonathan D. *JPS: The Americanization of Jewish Culture, 1888–1988: A Centennial History of the Jewish Publication Society.* Philadelphia, 1989.

———. *Jacksonian Jew: The Two Worlds of Mordecai Noah.* New York, 1981.

———, and Nancy Klein. *The Jews of Cincinnati.* Cincinnati, 1989.

Schachner, Nathan. *The Price of Liberty: A History of the American Jewish Committee.* New York, 1948.

Schappes, Morris U. *A Documentary History of the Jews in the United States, 1654–1875.* New York, 1950.

———. *The Jews in the United States: A Pictorial History, 1654 to the Present.* New York, 1958.

Schechter, Solomon. *Seminary Addresses and Other Papers.* Cincinnati, 1915.

Schiff, Alvin I. *The Jewish Day School in America*. New York, 1966.

Schoener, Allon, ed. *Portal to America: The Lower East Side, 1870–1925*. New York, 1967.

Shapiro, Yonathan. *Leadership of the American Zionist Organization, 1897–1930*. Urbana, Ill., 1971.

Sherman, C. Bezalel. *The Jew within American Society: A Study in Ethnic Individuality*. Detroit, 1961.

Shinedling, Abraham I. *West Virginia Jewry, Origins and History, 1850–1958*. 3 vols. Philadelphia, 1961.

Singerman, Robert, ed. *Judaica Americana: A Bibliography of Publications to 1900*. 2 vols. New York, 1990

Sklare, Marshall. *America's Jews*. New York, 1971.

———. *Conservative Judaism: An American Religious Movement*. New York, 1972.

———. *The Jewish Community in America*. New York, 1974.

Soltes, Mordecai. *The Yiddish Press: An Americanizing Agency*. New York, 1925.

Stern, Malcolm, comp. *First American Jewish Families: 600 Genealogies, 1654–1977*. Waltham, Mass., 1977.

Straus, Oscar S. *Under Four Administrations from Cleveland to Taft: Recollections of Oscar S. Straus*. Boston, 1917.

Sutton, Joseph A. D. *Magic Carpet: Aleppo-in-Flatbush: The Story of a Unique Ethnic Jewish Community*. 1979.

Swarsensky, Manfred. *From Generation to Generation: The Story of the Madison Jewish Community, 1851–1955*. Madison, Wisc., 1955.

Swichkow, Louis J., and Lloyd P. Gartner. *The History of the Jews of Milwaukee*. Philadelphia, 1963.

Synott, Marcia G. *The Half-Opened Door: Discrimination and Admissions at Harvard, Yale, and Princeton, 1900–1970.* Westport, Conn., 1979.

Tcherikower, Elias, ed. *The Early Jewish Labor Movement in the United States.* New York, 1961.

Toll, William. *The Making of an Ethnic Middle Class: Portland Jewry over Four Generations.* Albany, 1982.

Trachtenberg, Joshua. *Consider the Years: The Story of the Jewish Community of Easton, 1752–1942.* Easton, Pa., 1944.

Uchill, Ida Libert. *Pioneers, Peddlers, and Tsadikim.* Denver, 1957.

Urofsky, Melvin I. *American Zionism from Herzl to the Holocaust.* Garden City, N.Y., 1975.

———. *A Voice That Spoke for Justice: The Life and Times of Stephen S. Wise.* Albany, 1982.

Wald, Lillian. *The House on Henry Street.* New York, 1915.

Watters, Leon L. *The Pioneer Jews of Utah.* New York, 1952.

Waxman, Meyer. *A History of Jewish Literature.* Vols. IV and V. New York, 1960.

Waxman, Mordecai, ed. *Tradition and Change: The Development of Conservative Judaism.* New York, 1958.

Weinberger, Moses. *People Walk on Their Heads: Jews and Judaism in New York.* New York, 1982.

Whiteman, Maxwell. *Copper for America: The Hendricks Family and a National Industry, 1755–1939.* New Brunswick, N.J., 1971.

Wiernik, Peter. *History of the Jews in America from the Period of the Discovery of the New World to the Present Time, With a Survey of Forty Years of Jewish Life in America, 1932–1972 by Irving J. Sloan.* New York, 1972.

Wischnitzer, Mark. *To Dwell in Safety: The Story of Jewish Migration Since 1800.* Philadelphia, 1948.

———. *Visas to Freedom: The History of HIAS.* Cleveland, 1956.

Wischnitzer, Rachel. *Synagogue Architecture in the United States: History and Interpretation.* Philadelphia, 1955.

Wise, Isaac Mayer. *Reminiscences.* Cincinnati, 1901.

Wolf, Edwin 2nd., and Maxwell Whiteman. *The History of the Jews of Philadelphia: From Colonial Times to the Age of Jackson.* Philadelphia, 1957.

Wolf, Simon. *The American Jew as Patriot, Soldier and Citizen.* Philadelphia, 1895.

———. *The Presidents I have known from 1860 to 1918.* Washington, D.C., 1918.

Wyman, David S. *The Abandonment of the Jews: America and the Holocaust, 1941–1945.* New York, 1984.

Index